Children's Literature and Culture
(Vol. 4)
Garland Reference Library of Social Science
(Vol. 1043)

Children's Literature and Culture

Jack Zipes, Series Editor

White Supremacy in Children's Literature

Characterizations of African Americans, 1830–1900

Donnarae MacCann

Garland Publishing, Inc.
A member of the Taylor & Francis Group
New York & London
1998

Library of Congress Cataloging-in-Publication Data

MacCann, Donnarae.
    White supremacy in children's literature : characterizations of
African Americans, 1830–1900 / Donnarae MacCann.
        p.   cm. — (Children's literature and culture ; vol. 4. Gar-
land reference library of social science ; vol. 1043.)
    Includes bibliographical references (p.   ) and indexes.
    ISBN 0-8153-2056-6 (acid-free paper)
    1. American literature—19th century—History and criticism.
2. Afro-Americans in literature. 3. White supremacy movements—
United States—History—19th century. 4. American literature—White
authors—History and criticism. 5. Children's literature, American—
History and criticism. 6. Characters and characteristics in literature.
7. Racism in literature. I. Title. II. Series: Garland reference library of
social science ; v. 1043. III. Series: Garland reference library of social
science. Children's literature and culture series ; v. 4.
PS173.N4M33 1998
810.9'3520396073'09034—dc21   97–37620

Cover illustration: Jessie C. Glasier, "Ole Mammy Prissy," *St. Nicholas Magazine,* October 1887, p. 920.

Printed on acid-free, 250-year-life paper
Manufactured in the United States of America

In fond memory of
Jonathan W. Walton Jr.

Contents

Preface

Assembling materials from different fields is an effort to deepen understanding of complex subjects. It is the method of American studies, the discipline that shaped the present project. Specifically, I have tried to keep nineteenth-century portrayals of Blacks and pertinent facets of social history in the same range of vision. I have looked at the white supremacist civilization that produced a white supremacist children's literature, and documented the ideology of white racism as formulated for young reading audiences.

My work on this subject was compelled by the conviction that social history is knowable and that social understanding is malleable and potentially progressive. But the record must be laid bare in clear and specific terms. In endeavoring to achieve this clarity, I have been aided by members of the University of Iowa academic community.

In particular I want to extend thanks to those who helped with the dissertation on which this book is based. I owe an endless debt to the late Jonathan W. Walton Jr.—my primary teacher in the field of African American history and the chairperson of my dissertation committee until his sudden passing just months before the work's completion. Dr. Walton was a person of extraordinary character and spirit, a dedicated scholar, an inspiration to his students. He renewed in me an enthusiasm for historical research and continually revitalized my faith in the interdisciplinary American studies process.

Professors Kathleen Tessmer, Albert Stone, and the late Darwin Turner were invaluable as editorial advisers, content experts, and teachers. Dr. Robert Weems was kind enough to join my committee after Dr. Walton's passing, and I much appreciated his participation and advice. Dr. Fredrick Woodard, the current director of the African American World Studies Program at the University of Iowa, took Dr. Walton's place and steered me through the dissertation's completion. He was standing by at that time of crisis and mourning, and I must add that he has been standing by as a supportive friend for over a decade. We are engaged in an ongoing conversation about literature and culture, a conversation that helped lay the groundwork for this study.

Finally I am grateful to my husband, Dick, who assisted me in large and small ways and offered support when I felt swamped by real or imagined difficulties.

A Note on Usage

In this study the term "Black" is used to mean all peoples of African descent. People of mixed African and European descent come under this heading since they generally face the same problem as other Blacks in the United States and other Western nations. The term is capitalized because it refers to a specific population, the peoples historically connected by the Black diaspora.

In recent years the term "White" has taken on a similar meaning, referring to people of European descent. We now find "White" used in books, conferences, and college courses that specifically focus on a field called White studies. I capitalize the term when it designates or implies an ethnic population, but not in instances where the "color line" is the primary connotation (as in "white supremacy," "white racism," "white hegemony" and so on). In such value-oriented fields as history, sociology, and art, labels become quickly outmoded; the usages in this book reflect current self-definition within groups as well as my own preferences.

Introduction

Cultural and social historians have a useful tool in the record created by children's books. The simple, transparent images contrived for the young are often an unselfconscious distillation of a national consensus or a national debate. They reveal, for example, the degree to which postbellum society retained features of the slavery era; they illustrate how the white supremacy myth infected the mainstream collective consciousness in both epochs. And that myth was perceptible in literature for the young whether the narrative was essentially an antislavery or proslavery tract. The extraordinary predictive power of children's books is evident in this nineteenth-century drama. Given the ambivalent and/or biased messages directed toward the young, there was little reason to expect a de facto egalitarianism in the postbellum years. This book tells the story of this paradox. The defeated slavocracy was in many respects a cultural winner.

Literary, political, biographical, and institutional history are combined in these pages as a way to reveal the scope of the white supremacist ideology. The antislavery cause accelerated the momentum toward war, but then vanished in the regressive milieu of peace—in the romanticized plantation stories, ambivalent protest novels, and prejudiced adventure fiction. Legal emancipation was neutralized in public consciousness by racist tale-telling. And the other institutions that impinged upon children's lives—schools, churches, libraries, the press—joined in promoting the notion of race hierarchies. Black identity was presented as of less value than European American identity. Blacks were expected to accept a restricted status and role in the American civil community. European American children were expected to keep African Americans in check, in a subservient position.

To understand such a philosophy, we need to consider several variables.[1] We need to look at the texts of children's books and periodicals, the biographical history of writers, the social/political and institutional contexts, the aesthetic conventions of the times, and any special characteristics of audience response. Intellectual history is illumined by means of this interdisciplinary approach, and children's literature practices are seen as belonging to a historical/cultural continuum. Americanist Gene Wise has noted that "historical reality as experienced by people is multiple, with many faces on a variety of different planes . . ."; subsequently, "we must assume . . . a plurality of angles on our materials."[2] These "angles" are described here in relation to children's literature and its intersection with other social forces.[3]

A Social/Political Focus

Literature is an art form riddled with socially imbued uncertainties. It can be argued that children's literature makes even latent social tensions transparent because books for the young are a means of socialization—a means for handling those stresses and uncertainties. Malcolm Cowley has noted how literature is less abstract than other art forms and more socially relativistic. He writes:

Literature is not a pure art like music, or a relatively pure art like painting and sculpture. . . . Instead it uses language, which is a social creation. . . . The study of any author's language carries us straight into history, institutions, moral questions, personal stratagems, and all the other aesthetic impurities or fallacies that many new critics are trying to expunge.[4]

The kind of "impurities" Cowley refers to are compounded in children's literature because cross-generational activities tend to be purposeful—purposeful in directions beyond an interest in artistic form. A move into youth culture on the part of creative artists is, among other things, a move in the direction of culture maintenance or culture change. This point is but a logical extension of the findings of such sociologists as Peter L. Berger and Thomas Luckmann, especially their analyses of the formation and durability of social institutions.

In describing the emergence of stable social structures in *The Social Construction of Reality*, Berger and Luckmann note the way individual actions become shared and routinized, and then passed down to the next generation. Put differently, individual behaviors gain historicity and acquire the feel of objective realities. The comment "There we go again" is changed to "This is how things are done."[5] To deny the passing down process that occurs in children's books is practically to deny the process by which societies are developed and maintained. The social component in objects created for the young is therefore one of the most basic concepts that a children's literature historian has to work with.

R. Gordon Kelly has given Berger and Luckmann some of the credit for the method he used in researching late-nineteenth-century children's periodicals. In *Mother Was a Lady*, Kelly enables us to see that it was not only nineteenth-century children who were being socialized through the literature; this literature was, for the socializers, a means of stabilizing social assumptions that were under some strain. As a literary historian, he found a book-centered approach incomplete because the literature of the nineteenth century had both an institutional and an ideological base. It was among society's methods of legitimizing itself. Through literature for the young, particular groups reveal their values and preoccupations. Kelly explains the process as follows:

> We may properly regard a group's children's literature, then, as constituting a series of reaffirmations over time of that body of knowledge and belief regarded as essential to the continued existence of the group, for not only must children be convinced of the validity of the truths being presented to them, "but so must be their teachers. . . ." By creating fictional order, children's authors . . . may also renew their own commitment to certain principles of social order—for example, shaping their fictional response, in part, to meet threats posed by alternative belief systems.[6]

The sensitive approach suggested here has enabled Kelly and others to answer important questions about the literature of the past and about those who produced and circulated it. But this method has not corrected some misreadings of books about Blacks because historiography and sociology have themselves been rationalizations of the existing establishment. For example, historians have often oversimplified the messages in children's antislavery stories by inferring that they were also antiracist (which many were not). And one of the highly Eurocentric interpretations of post–Civil War books is that they represent a golden age in children's literature.[7] On the contrary, it was "the Nadir" (as historian Rayford W. Logan has defined the period following Reconstruction). Unless book historians unreasonably separate the interests of European American and Black children, it is hard to see how the classics that featured Blacks can be viewed as distinguished works. A society's classics, however, are rarely challenged. Except in the publications of the Council on Interracial Books for Children (a nonprofit organization established in 1966),[8] opposition has seldom been directed against white supremacist classics.

For a more pluralistic historiography, the concepts of mainstream sociologists must be amended with the insights included in Joyce Ladner's anthology, *The Death of White Sociology*.[9] In this work essayists examine the historical development and the limitations of white sociology to reveal how sociological studies have been skewed by a Eurocentric perspective about family life, government, education, and so on. Children's literature is not one of the case studies in that volume, but writers offer generalizations that are pertinent to the work of the children's book critic and historian. With the exception of a few abolitionist narratives, children's books have generally treated Black characters stereotypically, or they have excluded them entirely. The latter tactic—exclusion—provided a means in the twentieth century of escaping the embarrassing connection that could be drawn between American racism and the racism of the Nazis. Black characters in children's books make this literature an important area of Black studies, and there is considerable agreement among Ladner's group of contributors as to underlying elements in Black studies. For example, self-definition is seen as a prerequisite of self-determination. Historically, Blacks in the United States have had a marginal status because the Black community has been infused with white cultural symbols through the educational system, while at the same time this community has been subjected to isolation and social restrictions.

To understand this outside status, it is necessary, says sociologist E. Franklin Frazier, to comprehend the slavery experience.[10] In other words, it is important in Black studies to recognize the historically unique situation of American Blacks rather than try to conceptualize their history within the framework of worldwide political and economic oppression. This does not rule out the study of institutions within a multinational power structure. Such studies are seen by many theorists as a necessary part of Black sociology. The kind of "systems" scrutiny often suggested simply changes the focus from the less fortunate groups to the powerful, and especially to the analysis of those domineering forces that require an underclass in order to function.[11]

A further conceptual issue addressed in Black studies is the problem of media control. A shift to Black participation (and in some cases control) is essential to correct distorted cultural imagery.

In addition to these substantive concerns, Black studies specialists point to a variety of methodological needs. For example, there is need for an end-use methodology that links theory and practice, that does not lose sight of quality-of-life issues.[12] There is need for the candor that describes value-free sociology as a myth. There is an advantage seen in multifaceted, contextual approaches to research.[13] The latter point is a given for those who consider the sociology of knowledge to be one of the more fruitful paradigms. If what one knows is intrinsically connected with the society to which one belongs, then self-definition (and self-determination) is dependent upon an apprehension of the social structure.

Mainstream attitudes that are passed down to children cannot be revised in a pluralistic direction until such substantive and methodological issues are incorporated into the critic's frame of reference. They impact upon authors and upon the network of workers who disseminate children's books. The latter group in particular, the "gatekeepers," need to be studied. While creative writers have a range of private and public motivations, gatekeepers are usually either commercial or public agents. A close look at this layer of book people is indispensable.

Institutional "Gatekeepers"

There is a growing realization that authoring, publishing, and marketing are an interlocking system. This perception is especially pertinent to the historian of children's literature because the socialization role of the author makes it desirable that institutional barriers be kept to a minimum. Unless the diverse segments of the publishing and educational systems harmonize, the purposeful move from adult to youth culture on the part of authors becomes fruitless. Put simply, cultural arbiters within institutions are a potential barrier as well as a potential facilitator of the author/audience connection. Moreover, the gatekeepers reflect more of the cultural consensus than a single author can reflect, and their activities foster trends within the communication system. Part of the historian's job, therefore, is to discover how these gatekeeping forces are either setting the stage for specific literary canons or muffling dissident voices.

In dealing with works from the nineteenth century, historians can examine the change from simple to more complex institutional structures. They can trace the way new organizations such as children's libraries and special youth divisions in the American Library Association influenced the socialization process because people throughout the children's book field often played multiple parts. The same individuals wrote the books, invented new genres, set up schools, wrote child-rearing manuals, and participated in Sunday school unions. Others established juvenile periodicals, served as publishing company executives, reviewed books, produced literary anthologies, and contrived stories for children simultaneously. New professionals moved throughout the system from one post to another and carried out diverse functions (e.g., administered libraries, served on book prize juries, established professional committees).

Donald Dunlap describes gatekeepers as unobtrusive but highly active:

Middlemen [sic] are often faceless. They are also powerful, for they exert control over the popular artist and the artifact. Their success depends in no small way on their ability to read the pulse of mass society . . . to enlarge the audience, or to create a new audience that previously did not exist.[14]

Because gatekeepers give such single-minded attention to "the pulse of mass society," they can cause problems for American minorities. As a group primarily recruited from the European American mainstream, these professional gatekeepers tend to limit communication. Black author and librarian Arna Bontemps has explained the potential miscarriage of justice in this system. He makes his point by alluding to an old tale. He describes how Ole Sis Goose is sailing on the lake and is captured by a fox who threatens to pick her bones. "You got your nerve, telling me I can't sail on the lake. This is a free country. We are going to tell this to the judge . . . [But inside the courthouse] She noticed that the judge, he was a fox, and the attorneys, they were foxes, and all the jurymen, they were foxes, too. So they tried Ole Sis Goose, and they convicted her, and they executed her, and they picked her bones." Bontemps makes his point clear about the communication network:

The editor is apt to be a fox. The publisher, like as not, could turn out to be a fox. The critics who review the book, the editors and publishers of the publications that carry the reviews, they're foxes. The salesmen who put the book on the market, the booksellers, the selection committees— even most of the readers—are all foxes, too.[15]

The blurring of distinctions between "foxes" has an added dimension in the field of children's literature where there is a blurring of distinctions between commerce-oriented and education-oriented institutions. In such cases, a conflict of interest can easily arise, and the child then loses the youth advocates that the community believes it has provided in its educators.

Evidence of such difficulties can be found in professional journals and academic studies. Joseph Turow has examined the portion of the publishing industry that concerns children in his study, *Getting Books to Children: An Exploration of Publisher-Market Relations.*[16] A broader inside view of the publishing world is available in *Books: The Culture and Commerce of Publishing* by Lewis A. Coser, Charles Kadushin, and Walter W. Powell.[17] In the field of Black studies, Nancy Larrick checked on the quantity of children's books about Blacks and reported on her findings in "The All-White World of Children's Books."[18] The Council on Interracial Books for Children did periodic studies of publishing activities vis-à-vis minority children in its publication, *Interracial Books for Children Bulletin* (a journal published between 1966 and the mid-1980s). There are also useful biographies and autobiographies, as for example, John Townsend Trowbridge's *My Own Story*, an invaluable portrait of the mid-nineteenth-century publishing scene.[19]

To the cultural historian, an interesting aspect of these gatekeeper groups is their apparent unawareness that they are serving specific institutional goals. They tend to be mediators with a purist position about art. However, despite the tension that can exist between their institutional roles and their artistic ideals, the gatekeeper's articulation of an art-for-art's-sake thesis has had an important function. By creating aesthetically powerful analyses, gatekeepers have induced more stringent artistic standards.

The Aesthetic Focus

The formal features in a text either empower or enfeeble it. Eloquence, clarity, textural richness, strength of characterization, plausibility of plot—these are among the elements that can give a text an almost autonomous sense of strength. On the other hand, circumstances surrounding the reading experience, as well as reading readiness, have a lot to do with what makes a text compelling in a child's eyes. Children seem able to make something out of nothing, or conversely, remain oblivious to the most manifest literary delights. Peter Hunt sees this problem as inherent in the art form:

Unlike other forms of literature, which assume a peer-audience and a shared concept of reading (and which can therefore acknowledge, but play down, the problem of how the audience received the text) children's literature is centered on what is in effect a cross-cultural transmission. The reader, inside or outside the book, has to be a constant concern, partly because of the adult's intermediary role, and partly because whatever is implied by the text, there is even less guarantee than usual that the reader will choose (or be able) to read in the way suggested.[20]

But irrespective of this unpredictability in the young reader, the generalization still holds that formal qualities need to be treated as a significant cultural variable. In earlier eras, this variable was discussed by literature specialists in terms of high art or high culture. Now theorists treat high art (more inventive art) and low art (more formulaic art) as two points on a continuum. They see the reader as able to make use of both. From this perspective (developed by John Cawelti in "Notes Toward an Aesthetic of Popular Culture"),[21] a historian can examine a range of cultural uses and meanings in a work. The high art dimension—formal elements that impact on meaning—will not be neglected. The critic will engage in the close reading that uncovers patterns, ironies, resonances, and the kinds of spontaneity and inventiveness that often make a work memorable over time.

The case for aesthetic sensitivity and analysis in children's literature has been made by Lois R. Kuznets. She advocates cultural pluralism combined with the approach of the New Critics—that is, the scrutiny of the structure created by an author out of plot, characterization, theme, imagery, symbolism, point of view, and time and space projections.[22] The historian needs this perspective because it is a way to discover a certain kind of wholeness in a literary object, and that wholeness affects the synthesizing that is the historian's job.

However, the very elements that loom large in a New Critic's dissection are highly culture-bound. The formalistic elements that Kuznets sees as a prerequisite to discussion of a book's political (i.e., rhetorical) level changes somewhat if one is referring to a Black aesthetic, a Hispanic aesthetic, and so on. The cultural specificity of the work is not its political content alone; it is also part of its stylistic content.

In "Towards a Black Aesthetic," Hoyt Fuller writes about nuances of style and speech in the works of Black writers—distinct qualities that come directly out of the Black world.[23] Summarizing his sense of a Black aesthetic, Julian Mayfield writes: "[It is] our racial memory and the unshakable knowledge of who we are, where we have been, and springing from this, where we are going."[24] Addison Gayle Jr. has noted that "a critical methodology has no relevance to the Black community unless it aids men [sic] in becoming better than they are."[25] The Council on Interracial Books for Children makes a related point when it argues that when books cause children harm and pain, "one can hardly talk about their 'beauty'; the inner ugliness of their racism . . . corrupts the very word itself."[26]

Literary criticism, then, is not a purely descriptive exercise. Yet even at a descriptive level, the uniqueness of Black experience is the basis for defining new critical tools. Gayle presents the case:

[T]here are few [Black artists] . . . who would disagree with the idea that unique experiences produce unique cultural artifacts, and that art is a product of such cultural experiences. To push this thesis to its logical conclusion, unique art derived from unique cultural experiences mandates unique critical tools for evaluation.[27]

A pluralistic perception of art (as defined in Black studies) includes formal, pragmatic, and culture-specific features. The power and authenticity of a work are influenced by these intermingling dimensions.

But there remains the theoretical argument that the power in a work is a negotiated power—that the audience is in command. Reading is a learned phenomenon that is influenced by a range of personal experiences. As noted above in the Peter Hunt quotation, children have not completely learned the system and constitute a particularly volatile group of respondents.

A student of multicultural art works may, therefore, find little reason to explore the artistic subtleties of a narrative for children if the work has a white supremacist outlook to begin with. The evaluation becomes an academic exercise when it is clear that the child will not be able to handle the inferences of inferiority or superiority that a white supremacist book conveys. When a status is imposed on youngsters—a status that isolates them from their peers—this cruel barrier calls for critical response. In short, critics are obliged to subordinate, to some degree, a conventional theory of art to a theory of effects.

Young People and Audience Response Theory

Reader response theory springs from a new level of solicitude for the reader. It involves an exploration of how a reader makes meaning from a text, and the intent underlying such exploration includes the idea that meaning should be beneficial. This welcome human focus is combined with a generalization from gestalt psychology: that the mind handles holistic configurations better than fragmented ones.

A person's history as a reader, therefore, has impact upon how meaning will be created from that otherwise static entity: a text. This is not to say that the text does not invite a response. The arrangement of techniques, norms, and worldviews enables a critic to look for the implied reader, to search out whatever predisposes readers of a given background to find meanings that the text suggests.

This focus shifts literary criticism in the direction of a basic truism—that communication is a two-way affair including speaker and listener. But at the same time it does not lose sight of the definable techniques that book-centered critics have tried to pinpoint. According to Aidan Chambers in "The Reader in the Book," the techniques used by writers for children help to create a tone of intimacy or solidarity that draws the child into the reading experience.[28] Chief among these devices is the use of a narrative point of view that captures a child's perspective, whether the specific voice is first person or third person. The child's nonliterary approach (stemming from meager literary experience) is thereby overcome without downplaying the child's potential for apprehending complex issues.

Another kind of author-child connection that helps young readers negotiate meaning is the set of cultural assumptions and references that writers use as common ground between themselves and implied readers. Readers go along with such unexplained references unless they are so alienating that they seem designed to exclude them. Put another way, writers have room to appeal to childhood curiosity by extending the frame of reference, but they do not have the option of degrading a child's sense of self.

A reader-directed theory emphasizes fluidity in the reading experience, and at the same time harmonizes with other critical methods. It takes account of cultural components in a narrative, thus reinforcing the work of the sociologist-critic. It takes account of the mediation role that adults typically assume in relation to the young. It incorporates in its methods close attention to formal literary devices. It supports child development issues, but does not lock a critic into a set of concepts that lack rules of evidence (for example, concepts that are as ontological as those attributed to Freud, Jung, Piaget, Erikson, and others.)

Such an eclectic approach accommodates the diverse agenda of the cultural historian. But it is not a method that can be easily used in studies removed in time from the researcher's own era. It is difficult for a present-day scholar to determine the cultural gaps a writer might leave for a nineteenth-century child to fill in. The supply of clues will be limited.

Also a problem arises if a monocultural perspective is retained. Just as concepts from Black aesthetics and sociology need to be incorporated into children's literature theory, so the reader response theorist needs to be acquainted with Black-child-care studies and manuals (e.g., *Black Child Care*,[29] by Black psychiatrists James P. Comer and Alvin F. Poussaint; *Black Children: Their Roots, Culture, and Learning Styles* by Janice E. Hale-Benson).[30] With this background, it should not be difficult for the reader-response critic to discern the white supremacist myth in children's books. From wide acquaintance with problems of alienation, Comer and Poussaint advise Black parents in ways that are equally pertinent to literature professionals. Some survival strategies relate to books:

> *We believe that as long as a book presents Blacks with dignity—be it set in the suburbs, inner city, or Africa—it is satisfactory reading. . . . Books about African ceremonies and customs can prevent your child from developing the negative attitudes about Africa with which our generation is still struggling. . . . Books depicting black, brown, yellow, red, and white children are one way of preparing your child for tomorrow. Books that present different cultures provide you with an opportunity to help your child understand that people are different. . . . You don't want to let some adult "humorist" take care of his own anger and hate feelings at your child's expense.[31]*

One job for historians is to discover why such specific protective strategies are necessary—why classic publications denied Blacks dignity, distorted the quality of the African heritage, and provided a convenient channel for hate feelings. These issues have been insufficiently analyzed by theorists; however, historian Samuel Pickering Jr. points critics in a direction that could lead to a more pluralistic practice. He notes that many children's books (being structurally simple) do not warrant multiple close readings. He says that "close readings are often less valuable than broad readings which examine both the text and the world beyond."[32] This perspective is seen as advantageous for all types of critics:

Because many of society's concerns are reflected in children's literature
more rapidly than in other literary studies, except in higher journalism,
critics of children's literature are uniquely able to reach out from their
studies and embrace other critical and social concerns. With the poten-
tial for, almost necessity of, drawing heavily upon other studies, good
criticism of children's literature could in the future become a model for
much literary study.[33]

Pickering sees cultural trends as among the other studies that
should have a place on the agenda of children's book specialists. Similarly, I would say that the white supremacy myth warrants the close
attention of both social historians and children's book historians.

"White Supremacy" and Related Terms

An examination of the white supremacy myth brings two concepts
into the foreground: race prejudice and institutional racism. These
phenomena are continuously interacting. When institutional forms
of racism were weakened, as in the overthrow of legal slavery, they
were often reconstituted in different configurations. People are the
cogs in institutional machines, and if prejudice is a permanent fix-
ture in the mind, progressive change will be tenuous at best. But an
overemphasis on individual prejudice results in an exercise in futility. Abolitionists spent years urging slave masters to repent by manu-
mitting their slaves, but Southern politicians responded with congressional action that often penalized the North. It was an unequal
fight.

As indicated by these generalizations, prejudice is the psychological level of the race-discrimination problem. Institutional racism is the public-policy level, and implies that the people behind the
policies have power to both reward and penalize. Sometimes the
policies are "up front," as when schools are segregated; sometimes
they are more subtle, as when opportunities for education are se-
verely limited, housing arrangements are covertly discriminatory, and
so on. Individual prejudice is dangerous because action usually follows thought. Institutional racism is dangerous in a more chronic
manner—that is, unjust practices become so fixed that the unfair
social structure is both rigid and inequitable; it is, as they say, an

establishment. Stokely Carmichael and Charles V. Hamilton have described the two levels of racism:

When white terrorists bomb a black church and kill five black children, that is an act of individual racism, widely deplored by most segments of society. But when in the same city—Birmingham, Alabama—five hundred black babies die each year because of the lack of proper food, clothing, shelter and proper medical facilities, . . . that is a function of institutional racism.[34]

The term "racism" has become such a code word in recent years that it sets off emotional reactions, whether the word is used narrowly (i.e., when it alludes to differences related to so-called biological makeup), or is used broadly to represent every discriminatory action. George M. Fredrickson avoids this problem by using the term "white supremacy" in his comparative study of American and South African history. He views the latter term as more descriptive of the processes he studies. "White supremacy," he says, "refers to the attitudes, ideologies, and policies associated with the rise of blatant forms of white or European dominance over 'nonwhite' populations."[35] At the public level, this myth of superiority entails restrictions of meaningful citizenship rights. It is more than prejudice because, as Fredrickson explains: "It suggests systematic and self-conscious efforts to make race or color a qualification for membership in the civil community."[36]

This systematic process in literature changes with shifts in political circumstances. Cultural racism seems to have been a given in the minds of White abolitionist writers. That is, the imposition of their cultural heritage upon others was a foregone conclusion. The bigotry of the postbellum period in the South was perhaps the result of postwar self-justification. This intolerance took the form of both political and cultural repression. The latter term refers to the use of institutional force to impose cultural valuables (perspective, language, art, music, religion, and so on) on a group deemed innately inferior.

Ethnocentrism—the "tendency to view alien cultures with disfavor, and a resulting sense of [one's own] inherent superiority"[37]—is a traceable feature in the imperialistic novels of the late nineteenth century. Paternalistic racism (good intentions coupled with white standards, a white perspective, and an assumption of white superiority) was apparent in both the ante- and postbellum eras.

"Romantic racialism" is, like paternalism, an inoffensive-sounding concept at first notice. The phrase is coined by Fredrickson to describe qualities attributed to Blacks by romantics and religionists, especially such qualities as patience under stress, meekness, and a New Testament approach to forgiveness. At one extreme, romantic racialists endorsed the idea of Blacks as innocent children, an attitude not very dissimilar to that of proslavery paternalists. At the other extreme, the romantics decreed that Blacks constituted a superior race—a conclusion based on what they saw as the predominant Christian virtue, docility.[38] In early works for children, it is not only a tone of condescension that separates such writings from less prejudiced narratives; there is also, in many examples, an admixture of romantic racialism and "blackface" humor.

The terms "chauvinism" and "jingoism" are also used in these pages in connection with the white supremacy myth. Chauvinism has the following dictionary definition: "prejudiced belief in the superiority of one's own group."[39] Jingoism is slang for the same thing. The origin of "jingo" is unknown, except that it can be traced to a British music hall ditty of 1878: "We don't want to fight, yet by Jingo! if we do,/ we've got the ships, we've got the men, and got the money, too."[40]

"Myth" is used with two meanings in mind. First, it indicates "one of the fictions or half-truths forming part of the ideology of a society."[41] Second, it refers to a theme that appeals to collective consciousness by embodying cultural ideals or that gives voice to impressions sustained at an emotional level.[42] The second definition is especially pertinent to a study dealing with childhood because it suggests that the "fictions or half-truths" of an ideology can be presented at a level where they become internalized—become practically ineradicable.

The terms "race," "racial," and "interracial" have been used in this book in accordance with common usage, although more precise terms would be "racialized" and "racialized relations." Race is a fluid social construct, as sociologist Stephen Small suggests when he writes that "while 'race' as a biological concept is spurious, racialized identities as social phenomena have become entrenched, and are embraced by various groups for different goals."[43] These goals and uses are an aspect of American intellectual history.

"White Supremacy" and Intellectual History

The conviction that the Caucasian "race" was superior did not originate in the 1830s, but this idea became systematized and more fully articulated at about that time. In earlier eras a specific rationalization and defense of slavery had been less urgent; organized opposition to the institution was relatively weak. By 1830, opposition was mounting. Influential people were attributing the degraded status of slaves to environmental causes. As Henry Clay put it, the problematic nature of the "free people of color . . . is not so much their fault as a consequence of their anomalous condition."[44] But even those supporting the manumission of slaves were ambivalent toward any real change in status for Blacks and the following contradictory images were shared by pro- and antislavery groups: Blacks as perennial children, as bumbling buffoons, as impassioned brutes, as docile Christians.

One link between these disparate images was the notion that extremism was intrinsic to Black identity. This fallacy served the needs of the dominant population, for it was then easy for one overgeneralization about Blacks to be exchanged for another in the White mind. The consistent feature remained the same—that is, that Black extremism was undeniable and warranted either management, containment, or in the case of the saintly image, indifference toward conditions on a human plane. The saint stereotype (the "romantic racialism" described above) was subtle but self-serving in the mainstream; a perception of Blacks as mystical figures obviated any responsibility in the realm of social action. On a pragmatic level, the saint stereotype was as unpromising as the custodial attitude that was adopted toward so-called brutes, innocents, and clowns. As the nineteenth century wore on, these misrepresentations were buttressed with elaborate rationalizations in the fields of religion, science, and history.

Western religious leaders had been interpreting the Bible selectively in relation to race for some time. Historian Marion Berghahn notes that the biblical association of Satan with darkness served as a justification for slavery, as it had also served as an excuse in the Puritan mind for turning Native Americans into adversaries.[45] Proslavery debaters invoked passages from Genesis about Noah's son, Ham, reasoning that God had cursed Blacks with perpetual servitude when Ham (as the story goes) was cursed in that manner.[46] Other detractors of African culture placed Blacks among the "beasts of the field" mentioned in Genesis 1. Variations on these themes multiplied with amazing ingenuity. God made the continents, contended the proslavery group, and intended them to serve as His "color line." God appointed Southerners as caretakers of slaves in order to bring them into contact with civilization. God planned for eventual emancipation, but abolitionists messed things up by interfering with God's timing.[47]

Members of the scientific community were as active as the religionists in improvising on the theme of Black inferiority. Charles Darwin said that "lower races" would be eliminated, a conclusion drawn from his belief that an environment selected some biological variations for continuance and rejected others. The most extreme racists translated this to mean that there was an ultimate cosmic advantage in mistreating Blacks. They watched the census figures to see whether Blacks were progressing toward their expected demise.[48] There was a theory among geographers that Blacks would inevitably drift toward the equator because they had a type of open nostril that could not tolerate cold air. Physiological theories were ubiquitous. There was the notion that size and surface fissures in the craniums of Blacks were significantly different from those of Europeans or their American descendants. Physiologists maintained that Blacks had pointed ears, large mouths, gluttonous appetites, and such thick skin on their hands and feet that they were insensitive to pain. Their bodies supposedly matured to the stage of adult sexuality, while their minds stopped developing at puberty—an explanation, said the scientists, for Black licentiousness.[49]

Such myths sound bizarre to a modern reader, but according to historian Idus Newby, these notions were casually endorsed by leaders in history and economics, as well as in the sciences. Support for these beliefs did not begin to lessen substantially in the scientific community until the 1930s.[50]

Among the postbellum historians, there was a race-purist group that worked at post–Civil War reunification on terms of strict White solidarity. Harvard-trained historian Lothrop Stoddard maintained that democracy would weaken race purity and consequently weaken civilization.[51] Between 1886 and 1922 William Archibald Dunning, a historian at Columbia University, trained a generation of scholars to rewrite Reconstruction history: to make slavery appear benign, Black enfranchisement appear reckless, and lynching appear reasonable as a response to alleged rapes.[52] Newby has concluded, after examining the works of many American intellectuals, that North/South unification "was facilitated [from the 1890s to the 1920s] by the respectability of racist thought in all sections of the country, and . . . produced more widely read anti-Negro literature than any other period in American history."[53]

Historians, scientists, religious leaders—these were the intellectual compatriots of the book writers and gatekeepers. Their views have been relatively easy to extract from the public record. Children's books have had less scrutiny. My eclectic approach enables me to situate the history of children's literature within history at large.

Applying an Eclectic Approach

In this study of nineteenth-century children's literature, a book sample has been selected that reveals which specific ideas about Blacks were circulating widely. Dorothy Broderick attended to some of the culling process in her bibliographic study: *The Image of the Black in Children's Fiction*.[54] She drew upon listings in the library guide, *Children's Catalog*, and in Jacob Blanck's *Peter Parley to Penrod: A Bibliographical Description of the Best-Loved American Juvenile Books, 1827–1926*.[55] I concentrate on popular and eminent writers because I am interested in a work's broad impact. I include, however, a few lesser names, especially for the 1830–1865 period, since materials from this era are scarce. I also use Jane Bingham and Grayce Scholt's extensive listings in *Fifteen Centuries of Children's Literature*[56] to locate dime novels and series books.

The choice of 1830 as the beginning of my time frame stems from the fact that 1830 has been identified by George M. Fredrickson and other historians as the approximate time when a white supremacist ideology became easily traceable. Also the nineteenth-century offers two contrasting eras: a slavery period that was becoming destabilized and a postemancipation period in which the idea of citizen status for Blacks rapidly deteriorated. Ambivalence toward Blacks, as seen in nineteenth-century children's books, points to the link between these seemingly disparate eras.

From the field of cross-disciplinary history, there are studies of nineteenth-century ideas that have influenced me (e.g., Fredrickson's *The Black Image in the White Mind: The Debate on Afro-American Character and Destiny, 1817–1914*,[57] and Rayford W. Logan's *Betrayal of the Negro, from Rutherford B. Hayes to Woodrow Wilson).*[58] Both Fredrickson and Logan interweave literary and political history and through this process, cultural patterns are illumined. The chapters that follow in my own study are somewhat similar. But many observations that could be made about a text's artistic features or an author's life story have been left unsaid unless they were likely to shed additional light upon the mainstream's white supremacist convictions. My major concern has been with juvenile books that provide social historians with evidence vis-à-vis American racialized relations. Additionally, I wanted this evidence accessible to educators—the group that works directly with children and teachers of children.

Children's literature specialists have argued, as Dorothy Broderick does, that "it is perhaps mundane to observe that the content of . . . books is directly related to the society in which the books are produced."[59] Or, contrariwise, specialists have insisted that an effort to establish links between books and society borders on vigilantism. Representing this latter viewpoint, *The Horn Book Magazine* editor, Ethel Heins, wrote in 1977: ". . . an 'issues approach' to children's books is not literary criticism at all. . . . Using the methods of vigilantes to track down messages in children's books is an exercise in profound futility and a cruel misuse of literature."[60] Neither of these attitudes is apt to lead to an examination of social/literary connections. One opinion holds those connections to be obvious, and the other opinion treats the search as misguided. But the difference in perspective can be mediated by describing exactly what society was doing to influence attitudes in books, and what books were like as they extended the life-span of social attitudes.

Notes

1. A study of the white supremacy myth is not an antiquarian exercise. In April of
    1987, a grand jury indicted fifteen individuals for alleged criminal actions associ-
    ated with white supremacist beliefs. Each person was affiliated with the Ku Klux
    Klan or Aryan Nations—groups implicated in the "killing of blacks, Jews, Federal
    officials, [and] journalists . . . ," and committed to creating an all-White nation in
    the northwest corner of the United States (See Wayne King "10 Named in a Plot
    to Overthrow U.S.," *New York Times*, 25 Apr. 1987, sec. 1, pp. 1, 9; "Indict-
    ments charge plot against U.S.," *Gazette* [Cedar Rapids, IA] 25 Apr. 1987, sec. 1,
    1, 11). George M. Fredrickson mentions in *White Supremacy: A Comparative
    Study of American and South African History* (1981) that the state motto of Ala-
    bama proclaimed a white supremacist philosophy until recent times.
2. Gene Wise, *American Historical Explanation: A Strategy for Grounded Inquiry*
    (Minneapolis: University of Minnesota, 1980), 36, 37.
3. This approach is not entirely new. Parts of it can be seen in the 1929 study by
    Lorenzo Dow Turner, *Anti-Slavery Sentiment in American Literature Prior to 1865*
    (Washington, DC: The Association for the Study of Negro Life and History, Inc.,
    1929); and in another study of adult literature by John R. Cooley, *Savages and
    Naturals: Black Portraits by White Writers in Modern American Literature*
    (Cranbury, NJ: University of Delaware Press, 1982). Other parts of the model
    have already been developed in the field of children's literature—for example, in
    R. Gordon Kelly's *Mother Was a Lady: Self and Society in Selected American
    Children's Periodicals, 1865–1890* (Westport, CT: Greenwood Press, 1974); and
    in Anne Scott MacLeod's *A Moral Tale: Children's Fiction and American Culture,
    1820–1860* (Hamden, CT: Archon Books, 1975).
4. Malcolm Cowley, "Criticism: A Many-Windowed House," *Saturday Review* (12
    August 1961), 11.
5. Peter L. Berger and Thomas Luckmann, *The Social Construction of Reality* (Gar-
    den City, NY: Doubleday, 1966), 56.
6. R. Gordon Kelly, *Mother Was a Lady: Self and Society in Selected American
    Children's Periodicals, 1865–1890* (Westport, CT: Greenwood Press, 1974), xvii.
7. See Roger Lancelyn Green, "The Golden Age of Children's Books," in *Only Con-
    nect: Readings on Children's Literature*, 2nd ed., ed. Sheila Egoff, et al. (Toronto:
    Oxford University Press, 1980), 1–16.
8. The Council on Interracial Books for Children was founded by writers, librarians,
    teachers, and parents to promote antiracist and antisexist books and teaching
    materials. It carries out this function by analyzing forms of bias and suggesting
    alternative resources; until the mid-1980s it published consciousness-raising
    articles in *Interracial Books for Children Bulletin*. It also published lesson plans
    and audiovisual materials at its Racism and Sexism Resource Center for Educa-
    tors, and conducts workshops and conferences designed to combat racism and
    sexism.
9. Joyce A. Ladner, ed., *The Death of White Sociology* (New York: Random House,
    1973).
10. E. Franklin Frazier, "The Failure of the Negro Intellectual," in *The Death of White
    Sociology*, ed. Joyce A. Ladner (New York: Random House, 1973), 58.
11. Ronald W. Walters, "Toward a Definition of Black Social Science," in *The Death
    of White Sociology*, ed. Joyce A. Ladner (New York: Random House, 1973), 196.
12. Ibid., 212.
13. Nathan Hare, "The Challenge of a Black Scholar," in *The Death of White Sociol-
    ogy*, ed. Joyce A. Ladner (New York: Random House, 1973), 73–74.
14. Donald Dunlop, "Popular Culture and Methodology," *Journal of Popular Culture* 9
    (Fall 1975): 26.
15. Arna Bontemps, "Ole Sis Goose," in *The American Negro Writer and His Roots*
    (New York: American Society of African Culture, 1960), 51–52.

16.   Joseph Turow, *Getting Books to Children: An Exploration of Publisher-Market Relations* (Chicago: American Library Association, 1978).

17.   Lewis A. Coser, Charles Kadushin, and Walter W. Powell, *Books: The Culture and Commerce of Publishing* (New York: Basic Books, Inc., 1982).

18.   Nancy Larrick, "The All-White World of Children's Books," *Saturday Review* (11 September 1965): 63–65.

19.   John Townsend Trowbridge, *My Own Story: With Recollections of Noted Persons* (Boston: Houghton, Mifflin and Co., 1903).

20.   Peter Hunt, "Narrative Theory and Children's Literature," *Children's Literature Association Quarterly* 9:4 (Winter, 1984–85): 191.

21.   John Cawelti, "Notes toward an Aesthetic of Popular Culture," *Journal of Popular Culture* 5:2 (Fall, 1971). See also "Recent Trends in the Study of Popular Culture," *American Studies: An International Newsletter* 10:2 (Winter 1971): 23–27.

22.   Lois R. Kuznets, "Some Issues Raised by the 'Issues Approach,'" *Children's Literature Association Quarterly* 5:3 (Fall 1980): 19–20.

23.   Hoyt Fuller, "Towards a Black Aesthetic," in *The Black Aesthetic*, ed. Addison Gayle Jr. (New York: Anchor/Doubleday, 1972), 10.

24.   Julian Mayfield. "You Touch My Black Aesthetic and I'll Touch Yours," in *The Black Aesthetic*, ed. Addison Gayle Jr. (New York: Anchor/Doubleday, 1972), 26.

25.   Addison Gayle Jr., Intro. *The Black Aesthetic*, xxii.

26.   CIBC Racism and Sexism Resource Center for Educators, *Human- and Anti-Human Values in Children's Books* (New York: Council on Interracial Books for Children, Inc., 1976), 21.

27.   Gayle, xxiii.

28.   Aidan Chambers, "The Reader in the Book," in *The Signal Approach to Children's Books*, ed. Nancy Chambers (Metuchen, NJ: Scarecrow Press, 1980), 253–257.

29.   James P. Comer and Alvin F. Poussaint, *Black Child Care* (New York: Pocket Books, 1976).

30.   Janice E. Hale-Benson, *Black Children: Their Roots, Culture, and Learning Styles* (Baltimore: John Hopkins University Press, 1986).

31.   Comer, 82–83, 185.

32.   Samuel Pickering Jr., "The Function of Criticism in Children's Literature," *Children's Literature in Education* 13:1 (Spring 1982): 15.

33.   Ibid., 16.

34.   Stokely Carmichael and Charles V. Hamilton, *Black Power: The Politics of Liberation in America* (New York: Random House, 1967), 4.

35.   George M. Fredrickson, *White Supremacy: A Comparative Study in American and South African History* (New York: Oxford University Press, 1981), xi.

36.   Ibid.

37.   *Webster's New International Dictionary of the English Language Unabridged*, 3d ed., s.v. "ethnocentrism."

38.   George M. Fredrickson, *The Black Image in the White Mind: The Debate on Afro-American Character and Destiny, 1817–1914* (New York: Harper Torchbooks, 1972), 101–102.

39.   *The American Heritage Dictionary of the English Language*, New College Edition, 1978, s.v. "chauvinism."

40.   Ibid., s.v. "jingoism."

41.   Ibid., s.v. "myth."

42.   Ibid.

43.   Stephen Small, *Racialized Barriers: The Black Experience in the United States and England in the 1980s* (London: Routledge, 1994), 32.

44.   Fredrickson, *The Black Image in the White Mind*, 15.

45.   Marion Berghahn, *Images of Africa in Black American Literature* (Totowa, NJ: Rowman and Littlefield, 1977), 4–5.

46.   Thomas F. Gossett, *Race: The History of an Idea in America* (Dallas: Southern Methodist University Press, 1963), 63.

47. I. A. Newby, *Jim Crow's Defense: Anti-Negro Thought in America, 1900–1930* (Baton Rouge: Louisiana State University Press, 1965), 93–94, 98–99.

48. Fredrickson, *The Black Image in the White Mind.* 230, 239.

49. Newby, 39–44.

50. Ibid., 29, 21.

51. Ibid., 54.

52. Ibid., 65–67.

53. Ibid., 7.

54. Dorothy Broderick, *The Image of the Black in Children's Fiction* (New York: R. R. Bowker, 1973). Broderick uses materials listed in the following editions of the *Children's Catalog:* first edition through the eleventh edition, 1967 Supplement to the Eleventh Edition, and 1968 Supplement to the Eleventh Edition.

55. Jacob Blanck, *Peter Parley to Penrod: A Bibliographical Description of the Best-Loved American Juvenile Books, 1827–1926* (New York: R. R. Bowker Co., 1938; rpt. 1956).

56. Jane Bingham and Grayce Scholt, *Fifteen Centuries of Children's Literature: An Annotated Chronology of British and American Works in Historical Context* (Westport, CT: Greenwood Press, 1980).

57. Fredrickson, *The Black Image in the White Mind.*

58. Rayford W. Logan, *The Betrayal of the Negro, from Rutherford B. Hayes to Woodrow Wilson,* new enlarged ed. (New York: Collier, 1965).

59. Broderick, 177.

60. Ethel L. Heins, "Da Capo," *Horn Book Magazine* 53:5 (October, 1977): 502.

Part One

The Antebellum Years

*While the poor black is treated so contemptuously in, what are
called, the free states . . . it is not to be wondered that the cause of
negro-emancipation moves so slowly.*
        —James G. Birney, White abolitionist,1835

*The abolitionists were torn between a genuine concern for the
welfare and uplift of the Negro and a paternalism which was too
often merely the patronizing of a superior class.*
        —William H. Pease and Jane H. Pease, Historians 1965

*The central icon of abolitionism, the figure of a black kneeling,
hands folded and eyes cast upward, carried a clear message. It
made emancipation conditional—on condition of conversion, on
condition of docility and meekness, on condition of being on one's
knees.*
        —Jan Nederveen Pieterse, Cultural historian 1992

Chapter One
Ambivalent Abolitionism
A Sampling of Narratives

Racialized relations do not follow an inevitable course in any historical period. There are always choices, alternatives, issues that can be resolved in a variety of ways. During a period of active abolitionist agitation, from about 1830 until the conclusion of the Civil War, the movement was splintered because its adherents were making different choices.

The conviction that so-called Caucasians constituted a superior group did not originate in the 1830s, but it was increasingly systematized to counter the growing attacks of abolitionists. As the antislavery forces expanded and spread their message, slavery advocates were forced into a more defensive posture and became more vocal on behalf of their cause. Ironically, abolitionists seldom opposed the idea of white superiority, even when presenting strong challenges to the proslavery forces in the South. An examination of antebellum children's books provides clues as to how the radical abolitionists differed from the conservatives and why neither faction succeeded in sowing the seeds of a continuing egalitarian movement. Neither the Christian "brotherhood" argument against slavery nor the democratic "principles" argument could mitigate ongoing oppression unless these arguments encompassed an antiprejudice theme. That theme did not materialize in many abolitionist narratives.

A disjuncture between theory and practice in the antebellum period had a certain ludicrous slant. Both proslavery and antislavery forces found it convenient to invoke biblical teachings and American constitutional principles in support of their causes. By neatly canceling each other out, it became possible for the Northern antislavery argument to take the lead only when a range of sectional

conflicts were added to the debate about emancipation. These sectional differences were enough to lead to war, but this is not to say
that there were great differences between the Northern and Southern view of Blacks. Slaves and free Blacks were typically perceived as
having a lower place than "Caucasians" on a supposed "chain of
being." Children's books indicated that even White abolitionists subscribed to such a theory, or were, at best, ambivalent. (It should be
noted that the historiography of abolitionism concentrates on White
abolitionist activity. Free Blacks were important to this movement
and opposed the bigotry of the [White] abolitionists, the group described below.)

The Reformist Group

Stories that represent the most hopeful and radical end of the abolitionist spectrum did explicitly address race prejudice as well as slavery. They were reformist tracts by such well known political commentators as Lydia Maria Child, Eliza Lee Follen, and Samuel
Goodrich. Others such as Julia Colman and Matilda G. Thompson
were not public figures but were among the committed antislavery
operatives, people who created for even the youngest citizens images
of slavery's invidiousness (e.g., Colman and Thompson were contributors to *The Child's Anti-Slavery Book*). Even though these writers were in the vanguard of progressive thought, the mainstream's
ethnocentric currents sometimes washed over them. They did not
always resist that tide.

   Lydia Maria Child's antislavery agitation ranged from vehement
exhortations, to antiprejudice parables, to incidental remarks tacked
on to narratives. "Jumbo and Zairee" falls into the first category. It
appeared in Child's children's magazine, *Juvenile Miscellany*, in 1831
and is based on a true-life account that was originally published in a
Colonization Society publication.[1] It features "two pretty negro children" whose father is an African prince, the rescuer of a shipwrecked
Englishman. After enjoying the prince's elaborate hospitality, the
Englishman, Mr. Harris, returns to his home in England, but fails
to tell Jumbo and Zairee that he is leaving. As they search for him by
the seaside, they are captured by slavers and end up on a plantation
in the United States.

   The Middle Passage, the Africans' journey across the Atlantic, is the occasion for the author's first direct statement to the reader about the evils of the slave system. She speaks of the ship captain's regret when his captives die, but he is only aggrieved about the profit loss. Child continues:

You will ask me if this man was an American? One of our own country-men, who make it their boast that men are born free and equal? I am sorry to say that he was an American. Let us hope there are but few such.[2]

When Child first describes the plantation experiences of the two children, she gives the slavers the benefit of the doubt. She explains that slaves on the plantation were not abused, and she adds the footnote: "We believe this is generally the case with the slaves at the south; but the *principle* is wrong, even if there are nine hundred and ninety-nine good masters out of a thousand."[3] However, Child's narrative is full of instances of abuse. When Zairee breaks an earthen pitcher and is about to receive twenty lashes, Jumbo intervenes on her behalf, but this results in seventy-five lashes for him and forty-five for his sister. At this point the author comments: "Even a Christian would have found it very hard to forgive such injuries. . . ."[4] These injustices are compounded when Jumbo is sold because of his impudence, and Zairee, too full of grief to eat her meals, is given the choice of eating or being whipped. Here Child vents her indignation before concluding the story optimistically. She writes:

This was in the United States of America, which boasts of being the only true republic in the world! the asylum of the distressed! the only land of perfect freedom and equality! Shame on my country—everlasting shame. History blushes as she writes the pages of American slavery, and Europe points her finger at it in derision.[5]

The narrative winds down with a series of coincidences. Jumbo is assigned to a different plantation, and it proves to be the home of his father (who has since been enslaved). Mr. Harris has immigrated to America and owns the neighboring plantation. These three are reunited and Mr. Harris arranges to buy Zairee at an inflated price. Apparently it is only his encounter with the very same African who saved his life that causes Mr. Harris a pang of conscience. At any rate, he suddenly frees all his slaves except two who refuse this change of fortune (they are old men, we are told, and too attached to Mr. Harris to part with him). Mr. Harris buys a ship for the freed Blacks and they return to Africa.

Even though Child emphasizes that the principle underlying slavery is wrong, she depicts Mr. Harris, the slave owner, as a paragon of virtue. The contradiction may not be inadvertent, since for many abolitionists it was a tactical maneuver to treat slave owners as suffering from a momentary moral lapse. In any case, Child's intermittent antislavery speeches are among the most direct and potent that children's books and magazines of the antebellum period offer.

While slavery is the chief target of "Jumbo and Zairee," Child suggests indirectly her opposition to race prejudice when she alludes to the American creed. As she states, those who uphold that creed "boast" of their convictions vis-à-vis the "perfect freedom and equality" of all peoples. In another short story, Child concentrates her attention upon prejudice, upon attitudes lacking the benefit of knowledge or reason.

In "The Little White Lamb and the Little Black Lamb," Child addresses the bigoted prejudgments of individuals rather than the slave system. This tale features a Black nurse, Nancy, who cares for a European American child, Mary Lee, but this story is unlike the plantation "Mammy" stories that were published in some quantity following the Civil War. In the stereotypic "Mammy" story, the Black surrogate mother is often depicted as someone with great disdain toward Black children. But Nancy is presented as a loving parent of Thomas, her own child. The author puts these words in Mary Lee's mouth: "I am my mother's little white lamb, and Thomas is Nancy's black lamb; and God loves us both."[6] Then she editorializes about God's love of children and God's love of lambs, irrespective of color, and the withdrawal of that love when children are naughty. "Mary" continues as the narrator:

I suppose lambs are always good. But little children are naughty sometimes. Henry Pratt struck good little Thomas, and called him a nigger; and that made me cry. My little white lamb loves the black lamb; but

Henry Pratt struck good little Thomas, and called him names. That was very naughty.[7]

A third type of story makes fewer references to race conflict, but does not miss its opportunity to suggest an egalitarian outlook. "Lariboo" has two primary thematic strands: first, the tragedy of intertribal warfare in Africa and its accompanying slave trade; and second, the possibility of a mystical, supportive relationship between a human and a wild animal. A young woman, "Lariboo," experiences grief over her child's death while on a forced march to a slave market, but her own life is sustained by a panther that befriends her after she is abandoned for dead. Early in the tale the author describes Lariboo's tribe. The reader is encouraged to think constructively about cultural differences, to adopt the relativism of a latter day anthropologist (even though Child unfortunately repeats the fallacy that an African nation is invariably "merry").

The Tibboos are a good-natured merry race, extravagantly fond of singing and dancing. Lariboo was reckoned quite a belle among them. I don't suppose you would have thought her very good-looking, if you had seen the oil streaming over her face, coral passed through her nose, and broad brass rings on her arms and ancles [sic]. But she thought herself dressed very handsomely; and I do not know why it is considered more barbarous to bore the nose for ornaments, than to pierce holes through the ears, as our ladies do. As for the dark tint of her complexion, it would be considered beautiful by us, as it was by the Tibboo beaux, if we had been accustomed from infancy to see all our friends of that color. The Africans, who never see white men, or see them only as enemies, who come to carry them into slavery, consider the European complexion ghastly and disagreeable. When they describe the spirit of wickedness, usually called the Devil, they always paint him as a white man.[8]

In the end Lariboo comments on the flawed human race in a general sense. She has been reunited with her husband, and has moved with her tribe to a safer region (this group is not so happy-go-lucky as to remain in the locale that is vulnerable to slave hunters). However, the most poignant lines in the concluding scenes are about the heroic, sacrificial panther as it dies in agony. It has intercepted an arrow that it believed aimed at Lariboo, and the young woman "sobbed like a child." "'My guardian of the desert,' she exclaimed, 'you saved my life; you protected me from the fury of your own species; but I could not save you from mine.'"[9]

Although Child's writings are not completely devoid of stereotypes, her plotlines reveal the kind of consistent political idealism and cultural relativism that were generally in advance of the times.

Another carrier of antislavery sentiments in early children's literature was *The Child's Anti-Slavery Book: Containing a Few Words about American Slave Children and Stories of Slave-Life* (1859). This work may or may not have been tied to a religious organization. According to historian John C. Crandall, "the American Tract Society and the other Sabbath School agencies did not see fit to make a concentrated attack on slavery in their relentless campaign against evil."[10] *The Child's Anti-Slavery Book* was, nonetheless, issued by Carlton and Porter, a publisher with a Sunday School Union address.

The book's introduction invokes both religious and democratic ideals:

I want you to remember one great truth regarding slavery, namely, that a slave is a human being, held and used as property by another human being, and that it is always A SIN AGAINST GOD to thus hold and use a human being as property! . . . God did not make man to be the property of man. . . . On the contrary, he made all men to be free and equal, as saith our Declaration of Independence. Hence, every negro child that is born is as free before God as the white child, having precisely the same right to life, liberty, and the pursuit of happiness, as the white child. . . . Children, I want you to shrink from this sin as the Jews did from the fiery serpents. Hate it. Loathe it as you would the leprosy. Make a solemn vow before the Savior, who loves the slave and slave children as truly as he does you, that you will never hold slaves, never apologize for those who do.[11]

Three short stories detailing the torments of slavery constitute the body of the work. A brief narrative fragment is added at the end that points to a precedent (emancipation in the West Indies), while also emphasizing the Christian devotion of a newly freed West Indian. Only the first tale, Julia Colman's "Little Lewis," concludes with the liberation of the hero. The slaves in Matilda G. Thompson's "Mark and Hasty" and "Aunt Judy's Story" end up either dead or destitute.

The introduction's antiprejudice content is not repeated in the fictional narratives with the same potency. But the experiential aspects of fiction generally engage a child reader, especially if the scenario centers on parent and child. The main thrust of the argument against slavery in "Little Lewis" centers on the breakup of families. Lewis's mother is nearly driven insane by her separation from her children, and in a moment of complete derangement, tries to murder Lewis by throwing him down a well. She then attempts to stab herself to death, but does not succeed. In fact her mind is restored after Lewis escapes to the North and she is reunited with her husband. But her tormented existence is vividly portrayed and comes across as a powerful indictment of slavery. She is a strong character.

Most of the minor Black characters are, however, noticeably unhelpful. For example, there is the cook, Aunt Sally, who calls Lewis "nigger" and chastises him for his studiousness; and there is a neighbor, Sam Tyler, who could teach Lewis to read with little risk to himself, but refuses because he will undertake nothing that is not explicitly approved of by the "white folks." While the story is therefore strong on pathos (centering on the mother), it is lacking in a positive or balanced treatment of the slave community in general.

The protagonist's opening monologue appears to be an expression of self-deprecation, a self-image that is not surprising given the treatment he receives in his formative years. But this white-is-best comment can also be interpreted as an acknowledgement of the prevailing power structure—that is, Little Lewis may be saying that white *power* is best:

. . . wont I be just so good as ever I can, an' learn to read, an' when I get to be a man I'll call myself white folks; for I'm a most as white as Massa Harry is now, when he runs out widout his hat . . .[12]

Little Lewis's story can be viewed as typical of the way White abolitionist writers tended to glorify the sacrifices of antislavery operatives (the White woman who helps Lewis is imprisoned). Such a focus on White heroics is also noticeable in Matilda G. Thompson's "Mark and Hasty." This second narrative in *The Child's Anti-Slavery Book* features a family breakup that occurs when a husband is sold "down the river." He had stood watch through the night at the bedside of his sick child, and then incurred the anger of his master by going to sleep on the job. A White abolitionist does everything in her power to save the situation, but is unable to influence the hardhearted White men who have all the authority. The wife of the "shipped-out" slave dies of grief, and only the child survives, thanks to the abolitionist's intervention. The narrator comments:

To the slave, the affections are the bright spots in his wilderness of sorrow and care; and as an Arab loves the oasis the better that it is in the midst of the desert, so the slave centers the whole strength of his nature in his loved ones, the more so that he is shut out from the hopes of wealth, the longings of ambition, and the excitements of a freeman's life.[13]

Thompson places the story of Hasty alongside an epic tale about "Aunt Judy," a Black woman who is alternately enslaved, freed, bound-out, and reenslaved. In "Aunt Judy's Story" there is a frame narrative in which an affluent White mother instills in her children a sense of sympathy for the neighborhood beggar, "Aunt Judy," by recounting events in the Black woman's life. This device serves to underscore the disparity in opportunity between the European American and Black families. Other injustices exposed in this story are similar to those in "Little Lewis" and "Mark and Hasty," except that Judy is presented as a freed slave who is tricked out of her freedom. The vulnerability of any Black person, while the slave system remained intact, was thereby emphasized. This kind of knavery comes across in the narrative as a powerful antislavery theme, although the overall tone is marred by the exaggerated, minstrel-like dialect attributed to Judy, and by the description of both Africans and Indians as cruel, warlike, debased heathens.[14]

Except in its Introduction, then, much of *The Child's Anti-Slavery Book* contains mixed signals with regard to the humanity and equality of Blacks. This is less true in the works of abolitionist Eliza Lee Follen, a writer whose poem, "The Slave Boy's Wish," was included in *The Child's Anti-Slavery Book*. Follen contrived some explicit antiprejudice narratives, as in *May Morning and New Year's Eve* (1857). This work includes a series of object lessons presented by a mother, "Mrs. Chilton," to her sons. The first one is about the annual May Day celebration in Washington, D.C., a joyous occasion, says Mrs. Chilton, when "all [children] have an equal right to go, ignorant and educated, poor and rich." At this point she qualifies her statement, noting that slaves and other Negroes were not invited and telling the traumatic adventures of "Harry," a Black child in a small country village. He is an elaborately delineated "model child." He is generous, brave, and true; he does his lessons well, confesses his faults, loves beauty, offers assistance to lame children, rescues baby birds, and faithfully refrains from treading on ant hills. But his "young heart ached" when village children ostracized him, and he tried to rub off his brownness in a little stream. During this latter episode Harry asks the narrator, "Why, if God is good, did he not make me white?" and the narrator speaks for the author, ". . . God is good; it is man that is not good; it is man that is cruel."[15] In addition to this direct denunciation of prejudice, Follen has her alter ego, Mrs. Chilton, give her young listeners this message: "When you are men and women . . . you may do much for the poor slaves. Remember them then, and do not forget them now. All can do something for them, even little children."[16]

But despite this sense of sympathy, Follen gives her evangelical message, rather than her interest in little Harry, a central position at the end of the tale. The child is ecstatically happy in the closing scenes because he has "tasted of the pleasure of doing good for evil" (he has been kind to the bully who called him "nigger" and tried to beat him up). The village children do become friendlier after Harry helps them find a supply of May Day flowers, but they do not invite him to take part in the May Day dance and other festivities, and Harry's jubilation seems out of proportion to his actual gains.

In the 1840s Follen edited a juvenile periodical, *The Child's Friend,* and used this opportunity to attack slavery. One device was to report to her readers the opinions of English acquaintances, especially their view that America's democratic pretensions were a sign of hypocrisy given the continuation of slavery. Even British children made this charge, according to Follen, and she was mortified to hear it from a fourteen-year-old. "But I could not but feel ashamed that one, almost a child, should throw this disgrace of my native land in my face, and I have not a word of defense to utter."[17]

Follen, like Lydia Maria Child, could exert influence over an extended period of time through her role as an editor, but it is likely that neither of these authors had as much impact as Samuel Goodrich, creator of the "Peter Parley" books, and Jacob Abbott, author of the "Rollo" books. These writers became "institutions." Using the "Peter Parley" pseudonym, Goodrich began in 1827 a series of fictionalized travel and science books designed for American audiences. In his zest for counteracting things foreign, he often promoted blatantly chauvinistic and biased attitudes about non-American and non-Christian peoples. However, in the title that concerns us here, *Peter Parley's Tales of Africa* (1830), Goodrich took an explicit stand against both slavery and race prejudice. Despite his bigoted generalization that in the four Barbary states, "the inhabitants are for the most part cruel, vicious, and unprincipled," he makes a plea for the elimination of race prejudice directed at free Blacks:

We very often hear people speak and act, as if they were under no obligation to treat blacks with as much kindness, humanity, and charity, as they owe to white people. . . .
Now those people who treat free Negroes with harshness, unkindness, or inhumanity, are just as much to blame, as if they treated white people so. The color of the skin makes no difference. The obligation is universal, to do to another, as you would have another do to you.[18]

It is hard for Goodrich to present uncomplimentary views of the United States, but he does condemn the slave system, even while he is far too generous in describing it. First he softens his criticism:

As there are people among us, who cruelly overwork and beat their horses; so in all slave countries, there are people of bad passions and cruel tempers, who abuse their slaves. But in the United States they are usually well fed, and well sheltered. . . .
There are no doubt many good people who have slaves.[19]

Then Goodrich attacks the institution:

But slavery is a bad system, it always brings great evils along with it. Instead, therefore, of defending slavery, every good person should condemn it, and use his efforts on all proper occasions, to hasten the time, when there shall be no slavery in the land.[20]

The Cautious Group

Antislavery storytellers were often cautious about moving Blacks beyond their enslaved status. Writers such as Jacob Abbott, William Adams, John Townsend Trowbridge, and Harriet Beecher Stowe would not take their ex-slaves beyond new posts as servants, new homelands as repatriated Africans, or new spirits in the afterlife!

Jacob Abbott was one of the less forthright commentators on slavery, but his influence extended up to 1900 and beyond. Abbott did not voice an explicit opinion about the plantation slave culture, but instead created contradictory images of African Americans and implied the need for ongoing servitude. His earliest works illustrate an extreme ambivalence about Black identity. To Abbott's credit, it can be shown that he did progress slightly from 1857, when he wrote the explicitly white supremacist *Congo, or Jasper's Experience in Command*, to 1860–1861, when he wrote the five-volume series of novels about "Rainbow and Lucky."

"Congo" is a free Black adolescent who goes to work for Jasper, a White farmer's grandson. Jasper is being instructed by his grandfather in business entrepreneurship, and is allowed to hire a helper as he transforms an unkempt island into a handsome garden. Part of Jasper's education is in learning to understand his Black workman, and to that end Grandfather describes Congo and his allegedly simple aspirations:

I think [Congo] is likely to spend his life as a laborer, or perhaps as a coachman or footman in some gentleman's family. Such a kind of life as that is the one that he is best qualified for, and that is undoubtedly what he would like the best. It is one of the characteristics of the colored people to like to be employed by other people, rather than to take responsibility and care upon themselves.[21]

With respect to book learning, Grandfather warns Jasper about the folly of viewing Congo as a fellow student:

I don't think I would do that [teach Congo to write]. You see, in at-
tempting to teach him to write, you don't expect he will ever make much
of a penman. All you can hope for is that he will learn to write his name
and make figures, so as to calculate an account or something of that
sort.[22]

Congo is then required by the author to validate his own simple-
mindedness in his own words:

[Congo] said that he never expected to have any letters to write, and
beside, there was such an infinite number of words in the language that
it would take him an immense while, he said, to learn how to write
them all, and unless he really learned them all, he never could be sure
but that some of these that he did not know would be the ones that
would come in his letters.[23]

Jasper and Congo are treated as opposites with respect to learning capability and aspiration, and the disparity is emphasized further when the two boys are trapped in a burning building. The bud-
ding gentleman-farmer is a model of courage and composure. Congo
is "almost beside himself" and "ready to faint with terror."[24] The
African American is so totally dependent upon his Anglo-Saxon counterpart that young readers probably feel relieved to see Congo employed as Jasper's mother's coachman at the end of the tale. There is
nothing in the novel to indicate that Congo has the normal human
capacity to mature, excel, or identify himself outside the strictly rou-
tine realm of servitude.

"Rainbow" is Abbott's other black character, and he also ends
up in the role of coachman. However, Rainbow has a stronger, more
viable personality in many respects. If he does not aspire to the fulfillment of the "American Dream" in *The Three Pines* (1860), the
novel does, nonetheless, make it appear as if this is his choice and
not the result of serious mental limitations. He is wise, gracious, and
astute, whether serving as a carpenter's assistant, a trainer and rescuer of animals, or a role model for younger children.

It is true that Rainbow is not the same kind of paragon as his
White employer, Handie—a veritable sage at the age of nineteen.
Handie has inherited a farm that is in disrepair, and the property's

trustee has sent Handie and Rainbow to make renovations even though Handie will not be old enough to take possession for several years. Handie is portrayed as a master craftsman and a master of human-relations problems with his neighbors. He is also Rainbow's reading and writing teacher, and his infallible adviser. But much of the time Handie is kept in the background. Abbott uses the novel to highlight various character flaws, including race prejudice. And he offers this remedy: the victim is to make no reply to bigots, but instead let their abusive and biased words echo around them until they are condemned by their own conscience and goaded by guilt to make amends. Abbott arranges the plot to demonstrate how effective such a course would be. He does not point out the self-serving nature of such advice to members of the White Establishment. That is, passivity in Blacks would be highly strategic for a master/employer such as Handie.

Yet Abbott takes up the "color line" issue and appears to be on Rainbow's side. To point up the illogic of a "line," Abbott includes in Rainbow's remarks an analogy to the black colt, Lucky:

I'm a colored boy, it is true, Lucky; but then you can't complain of that, for you are blacker than I am and nobody likes you the less on that account.[25]

Despite Abbott's antiprejudice theme, his portrayal of Rainbow is such that he appears lazier, duller, more skittish, and more excitable than Handie (and it is probably safe to say that Abbott would not have considered comparing *Handie* to a horse). The white supremacy message here is less pronounced than in *Congo, or Jasper's Experience in Command*, but the later novel suggests that Abbott had ambivalent attitudes even on the eve of the Civil War. In one scene Handie decides to walk the remaining two miles to the farm for the sake of the exercise, but not Rainbow. "Rainbow *was* perfectly comfortable. He was always comfortable when he was riding."[26] To suggest that Rainbow is a trifle "slow," the author devises some banter between Rainbow and the wagon driver and then observes: "Rainbow was not particularly quick in taking a joke."[27] After arrival at the abandoned farm, Rainbow is said to be unperturbed by spooks, but wary of possible ruffians and "squatters" until after

Handie has explored the rooms and proclaimed them safe. In the climactic episode about a burning barn, "Rainbow was getting too much excited" until Handie instructs him to "work quietly."[28] Handie illustrates by his own composure that self-control is the best response to an emergency.

A range of mixed messages appeared in Abbott's novels and in abolitionist narratives generally. Some authors introduced a messianic Black figure—a type that had symbolic usefulness, but was nonetheless so dehumanized that it could be easily exchanged for a satanic Black figure, depending upon what the national agenda was calling for at the time. In other instances, authors combined antislavery preachments with a variety of stereotypes, the messianic stereotype being placed alongside blackfaced minstrel figures. The antislavery theme is thereby coupled with a proprejudice theme (and, as we will see in the literature of the post–Civil War period, there is almost nothing left, following the war, but the latter message).

A case in point is *Hatchie, the Guardian Slave; or, The Heiress of Bellevue: A Tale of the Mississippi and the South-West* (1853). Author "Oliver Optic" was really the New England school teacher and administrator, William Taylor Adams (although he calls himself Warren T. Ashton when he writes *Hatchie*), and this was the first book to establish Adams as a professional author. Its Introduction contained a curious complaint directed at Harriet Beecher Stowe, that is, Adams noted that *Hatchie* was actually *drafted* before *Uncle Tom's Cabin* (1852), "before negro literature had become a mania in the community."[29] His reference to "Uncle Tom" is significant because Adams created in "Hatchie" a secular messianic figure in contrast to Stowe's evangelical "Tom." We might say that to some degree it was that evangelical theme as much as the antislavery theme that gave *Uncle Tom's Cabin* such instant and extraordinary success. Stowe's novel is an intricate set of variations on slavery and religion, but "Hatchie" is a pristine example of a dehumanized savior, a male "mammy" figure. He is a forty-year-old body servant to the young heroine's father, "Colonel Dumont," and he watches over the heiress "as a faithful dog watches over a child intrusted to its keeping."[30] He is a mulatto of great intelligence, humility, physical strength, and gentility. We are told that he worships Emily "with all a lover's fondness, without the lover's sentiment."[31] He refuses his manumission, explaining,

I have been near [Emily] from her birth, and though only a slave, I feel that I was sent into the world for no other purpose than to protect and serve her.[32]

Hatchie's reward for this sacrificial role (he has repeatedly risked his own life to save Emily) is to be able to shake her hand at her wedding. The author adds: "Nor did she shrink from him."[33]

Hatchie symbolizes the nobility of the slave by being saintly. Other characters are contrived to inform the reader about slavery when Emily is the victim of a disinheritance scheme. A fake document is produced that claims she is the Colonel's illegitimate quadroon and is to be manumitted if she will agree to leave the South. Hatchie helps to disentangle her from this plot. A "Reverend Faxon" also gives assistance and preaches that his services will not be lost on a quadroon because God accepts slaves as well as people of "noble birth."[34] The implication in the reverend's sermonizing is that Blacks have a status with God that they cannot expect in the human realm because their "nobility" is (in comparison with the "nobility" of Caucasians) somehow deficient.

Two additional Black characters are the stereotypical opposites of Hatchie. First there is a hotel servant who speaks the fractured English often assigned to nineteenth- and early-twentieth-century Black characters. He cannot grasp the language ("gentleman" becomes "genman") and in typical minstrel fashion he changes the name Mr. Dalhousie to "Massa Lousey" then "Dar Lousey" ("a new idea [was] penetrating his cranium, Dar Lousey, dat's de name").[35] The other African American is the drunken servant of the villain—a woman who is both a clown and a reprobate. Although she is not literate,

Vernon presented the note to the negress, who, with a business-like air, opened it; and though he could perceive that she held it up-side down, she examined it long and attentively, sputtering with her thick lips, as though actually engaged in the to her impossible operation of reading it.[36]

The range of characters from minstrel buffoon to messiah figure is repeated in Harriet Beecher Stowe's *Uncle Tom's Cabin*, but

Stowe appears to be intermingling evangelical and antislavery propaganda in roughly equal proportions. The abolitionist content seems
to be a channel for expressing her religious views, and her sermonizing seems to be a weapon marshaled on behalf of emancipation.
Many critics have analyzed this dual agenda, but our purpose here is
to examine the novel in the context of juvenile literature as well as
social history. As a children's book, it was in line with the many
about child "Christ figures" who make a short sojourn on earth to
convert irreverent adults. Stylistically the moral preachments are
treated with the same explicitness and excess that is typical in a juvenile moral tale. Stowe once commented that she planned all her
works so as to make them not inappropriate for a child reader.[37] As
for the abolitionist content in the novel, it would have been familiar
to young readers of Lydia Maria Child's story, "The Quadroons," a
poignant tragedy published in Child's *Fact and Fiction* (1846),[38] and
to readers of the antislavery publications described above.

"Uncle Tom" is, of course, the central figure, and it does not
take a reader long to see what role he will play in advancing Stowe's
anti-Calvinist religious views. To a modern reader, he is an annoying
character because he is so obviously set up to proselytize the author's
moral philosophy. But with the exception of Tom, the young couple,
George and Eliza, and Cassy (the ex-mistress of Simon Legree), Blacks
in this novel are used primarily for comic relief, and Stowe's comic
devices are those of the demeaning "blackface" variety. Alongside
these minstrel comedians, and even alongside George (who chooses
a colonization plan for Blacks), Uncle Tom comes across as anything
but an "Uncle Tom" in the modern pejorative sense. He is a model
of moral courage and selflessness. He is a dauntless fighter at the end
of his life—combating the slave system through his own self-immo-
lation. Given Tom's religious convictions, this is the method of combat he would necessarily choose; and from a secular standpoint, he
was devising a strategy to save Black lives. If he had decided to kill
the villainous Simon Legree, a number of Blacks may well have been
charged with conspiracy and executed, not Tom alone. When Tom
allows himself to be beaten to death, his submission is purposeful, as
was often the case in the slave community when its members used
obsequiousness as a mask. Historian Wilson Jeremiah Moses makes
this point in *Black Messiahs and Uncle Toms*. He writes, "Loyal and

steadfast in his dealings with the other slaves, heroic and unflinching in matters of principle, the literary Uncle Tom was in no way symbolic of the racial treason with which his name has more recently become associated."[39] However, Stowe's perception of Tom as "the old child" in juxtaposition with Little Eva as "the young child" suggests ambiguity on Stowe's part, even while Tom's actions exhibit both inner and outer strength.[40] It is other Black characterizations, however, that give the white supremacy myth its most noticeable support.

The first minstrel-like clown to appear in the novel is Black Sam. He is given a clown's mannerisms and costume (pantaloons held up with "a long nail in place of a missing suspender-button, with which effort of mechanical genius [Black Sam] seemed highly delighted," and a palm-leaf hat that "like the sword of Coeur De Lion, which always blazed in the front and thickest of the battle, . . . [could] be seen everywhere when there was the least danger that a horse could be caught . . .").[41] His fractured English is purely a farcical device ("I'se 'quired what yer may call a habit o 'bobservation, Andy").[42] He is the quintessential boaster, bumbler, and opportunist.

"Mr. Adolph," the body servant of the master, "St. Clare," is the minstrel dandy. "Conspicuous in satin vest, gold guard-chain, and white pants . . . [he is] a very *distinqué* personage, attired in the ultra extreme of the mode, and gracefully waving a scented cambric handkerchief. . . ."[43]

St. Clare's cook, "Dinah," is depicted as irrational as well as vain. Everything in Dinah's kitchen is absurdly incongruous (not to mention unsanitary), a point that Stowe underlines by cataloguing the contents of one of the drawers:

Miss Ophelia . . . found a nutmeg-grater and two or three nutmegs, a Methodist hymn-book, a couple of soiled Madras handkerchiefs, some yarn and knitting-work, a paper of tobacco and a pipe, a few crackers, one or two gilded china-saucers with some pomade in them, one or two thin old shoes, a piece of flannel carefully pinned up, enclosing some small white onions, several damask table-napkins, some coarse crash towels, some twine and darning-needles, and several broken papers, from which sundry sweet herbs were sifting into the drawer.[44]

The child, "Topsy," is another minstrel figure—a kleptomaniac whose thievery is presented stereotypically, not as a strategy induced by an unjust economic system.

Even though there is sometimes a degree of shrewdness in these comic characters, Stowe's overall tone as she describes the Black community is mocking and supercilious. Topsy is goblin-like, a "sooty-gnome from the land of Diablerie."[45] Tom's wife, "Aunt Chloe," takes a "goodly pile of cakes . . . and began alternately filling [the baby's] mouth and her own. . . ."[46] Animal images are often used in relation to Blacks as they are portrayed with the usual array of "stage Negro" qualities: gluttony, vanity, impulsiveness, irrationality, boastfulness.

The messianic "Uncle Tom" is a mouthpiece for religion in Stowe's novel, but there are other types of messianic Blacks in children's books—the eunuch-like "Hatchie," already described, and the "natural man" represented by "Pomp" in John Townsend Trowbridge's *Cudjo's Cave* (1864). Stowe drew upon two literary conventions: the buffoonery of minstrels in her minor characters and romantic racialism in Tom. A dozen years later Trowbridge seems to have a more fully developed white supremacy myth upon which to draw. In any case, racism takes shape in a greater variety of forms in *Cudjo's Cave*.

Trowbridge's novel is a quintessential collection of white supremacist beliefs. Its cultural distortions are scarcely matched by any other book in this study, an ironic fact since Trowbridge viewed the book as part of the Union war effort. Besides the mythically proportioned Pomp, there is "Cudjo," a slave who has reverted to the so-called bestial nature of his African ancestors. And there is "Toby," a male "mammy" figure who sees himself as the sole protector of the White protagonists: a blind clergyman and his two daughters. When Toby is not clucking over his brood, he is having superstitious fits in the manner of the "blackface" stage clown. A fourth Black character is "Barber Jim," who represents a middle ground but is nonetheless given the role of rum-seller, a business that would not likely be assigned to a White character in such a sanctimonious novel as this one.

Trowbridge treats Pomp and Cudjo as opposites as he illustrates the potential for White acculturation under a "good master." Pomp has lived in Paris with a master who has been "his friend," and who has imparted the qualities that make Pomp "a perfect specimen of a gentleman."[47] He is described as "grand and majestic . . . always cheerful, always courteous . . . a lion of a man."[48] Cudjo, on the other hand, has had a good master but a bad overseer and has become animal-like in mind and body: his was "a body like a frog's, and [he had] the countenance of an ape . . . more like a demon . . . than a human being. . . petulant and malicious. . . ."[49] The pointed distinction made between Cudjo's kind master and hateful overseer is in line with the elitism in much abolitionist writing.

Cudjo and Toby share the role of minstrel clown. They are frequently seen strutting, boasting, and contriving words such as "reckonoyster" and "carbunkum asses" (their versions of "reconnoiter" and "carbonic acid").[50] Toby is a free Black, but it is clear that he could scarcely have survived in society without constant supervision over "his foolish head and large tropical heart."[51] In the end he saves the family with his accumulated wages and dividends, but Trowbridge demeans him in his final scene:

Gold, sar! Gold, Miss Jinny! Needn't look 'spicious! I neber got 'em by no underground means! (He meant to say underhand.) . . . Ye see, Massa Villars, eber since ye gib me my freedom, ye been payin' me right smart wages,—seben dollar a monf! . . . An' you rec'lec' you says to me, you says, "Hire it out to some honest man, Toby, and ye kin draw inference on it," you says.[52]

Toby donates his life-savings to help the Villars family flee the impending war, but since Toby does not view himself outside the role of family retainer, he accepts no thanks. "'Tank yerself!' he tells Massa, for 'Who . . . 'pose to pay wages?'"[53]

Despite the antislavery arguments that punctuate the novel, Trowbridge brings the story to a close with images of a feeble-minded servant, a beast-like fugitive (Cudjo walking on all fours), and Pomp who is capable of reverting to a primitive state until tamed by the pleas of a compassionate White woman (". . . in [Pomp's] face shone a persuasive glitter of the old, untamable, torrid ferocity of his tribe . . .").[54]

Conclusion

Abolitionist children's literature supported an idea that circulated in the North as well as the South. Even though radical White abolitionists tried to prick the American conscience vis-à-vis slavery, many of their books would have injured the self-esteem of Blacks (and inflated the egos of European Americans) in about the same degree as proslavery texts. While the language of white supremacy evolved over time, the underlying message was audible in most white abolitionist writings—the message that European cultural values would always be the exclusive measure of what was best.

The storytellers were spread across the political spectrum: radicals were agitating for emancipation, and conservatives were cautioning that the antislavery movement was "extremist." Given this polarization, it is paradoxical that ambivalence toward Black identity existed to such a noticeable degree at both extremes of public opinion.

Various pieces of this puzzle will fall into place as we turn now to the sociopolitical and artistic contexts of the abolitionist children's narratives. Rhetorical positions vis-à-vis democracy were being put to the test as the nation faced the challenge of a more egalitarian society.

Notes

1. Carolyn L. Karcher, "Lydia Maria Child and the *Juvenile Miscellany*," in *Research About Nineteenth-Century Children and Books*, ed. Selma K. Richardson (Urbana-Champaign: University of Illinois Graduate School of Library Science, 1980), 77.
2. "Jumbo and Zairee," *Juvenile Miscellany*, n.s., 5 (January 1831): 291.
3. Ibid., 292.
4. Ibid., 293.
5. Ibid., 294–295.
6. L. Maria Child, "The Little White Lamb and the Little Black Lamb," in *Flowers for Children*, part II (New York: C. S. Francis and Co., 1854), 134.
7. Ibid.
8. L. Maria Child, "Lariboo," in *Flowers for Children*, part III (New York: C. S. Francis and Co., 1854), 156.
9. Ibid., 181.
10. John R. Crandall, "Patriotism and Humanitarian Reform in Children's Literature, 1825–1860," *American Quarterly* 21:1 (Spring 1969): 13.
11. [D. W.] "A Few Words About American Slave Children," in *The Child's Anti-Slavery Book: Containing a Few Words About American Slave Children, and Stories of Slave-Life* (New York: Carlton and Porter, 1859; rpt. Miami: Mnemosyne Publishing Co., 1969), 13, 14, 16.
12. Julia Colman, "Little Lewis: The Story of a Slave Boy," in *The Child's Anti-Slavery Book*, 2.

13. Matilda G. Thompson, "Mark and Hasty; or, Slave-Life in Missouri," in *The Child's Anti-Slavery Book*, 103.
14. Matilda G. Thompson, "Aunt Judy's Story: A Story from Real Life," in *The Child's Anti-Slavery Book*, 119–120.
15. Eliza Lee Follen, *May Morning and New Year's Eve* (n. p.: Whittemore, Niles, and Hall, 1857; rpt. Boston: Nichols and Hall, 1870), 14.
16. Ibid., 15–16.
17. Eliza Lee Follen, ed., *The Child's Friend* 13:2 (November, 1849): 53.
18. Samuel G. Goodrich, [Peter Parley]. *The Tales of Peter Parley About Africa* (Boston: Carter, Hendee, and Co., 1833), sig. 8.
19. Ibid.
20. Ibid.
21. Jacob Abbott, *Congo; or, Jasper's Experience in Command* (New York: Harper and Brothers, 1857), 102.
22. Ibid., 104.
23. Ibid., 109.
24. Ibid., 155–156.
25. Jacob Abbott, "The Three Pines," in *Stories of Rainbow and Lucky* (New York: Harper and Brothers, 1860), 83.
26. Ibid., 12.
27. Ibid., 14.
28. Ibid., 174.
29. William Taylor Adams, [Warren T. Ashton]. *Hatchie, the Guardian Slave; or, The Heiress of Bellevue* (Boston: B. B. Mussey and Co. and R. B. Fitts and Co., 1853), Intro. n. page.
30. Ibid., 44.
31. Ibid., 192.
32. Ibid., 112–113.
33. Ibid., 313.
34. Ibid., 53.
35. Ibid., 164, 170.
36. Ibid., 291.
37. Gayle Kimball, "Harriet Elizabeth Beecher Stowe," in *American Women Writers*, ed. Lina Mainiero (New York: Frederick Ungar Publishing Co., 1982), 177.
38. L. Maria Child, *Fact and Fiction: A Collection of Stories* (New York: C. S. Francis and Co., 1846), 61–76.
39. Wilson Jeremiah Moses, *Black Messiahs and Uncle Toms: Social and Literary Manipulations of a Religious Myth* (University Park: The Pennsylvania State University Press, 1982), 52.
40. Harriet Beecher Stowe, *Uncle Tom's Cabin; or, Life Among the Lowly* (Boston: John P. Jewett & Co., 1852; rpt. *The Annotated Uncle Tom's Cabin*, ed. Philip Van Doren Stern, New York: Paul S. Eriksson, 1964), 339.
41. Ibid., 93, 98.
42. Ibid., 99.
43. Ibid., 229, 230.
44. Ibid., 281–282.
45. Ibid., 318.
46. *Ibid.*, 73.
47. John Townsend Trowbridge, *Cudjo's Cave* (Boston: J. E. Tilton and Co., 1864), 122.
48. Ibid.
49. Ibid., 118, 119, 123.
50. Ibid., 373, 409.
51. Ibid., 422.
52. Ibid., 494.
53. Ibid., 495.

54.   Ibid., 468.

Chapter Two
Sociopolitical and Artistic Dimensions of Abolitionist Tales

The most active abolitionist period in American history, approximately 1830–1865, has been extensively examined by historians, but not in relation to children's literature. There are two parts of that history that have particular relevance to books for the young: the religious background of the movement and the political concerns that gave focus to abolitionist goals. These have meaning for the children's book historian because authors writing for young people during this period were typically explicit about their religious and democratic aims. Children were to come away from their story hours with rekindled godliness and patriotic fervor.

The religious and political contexts of the era shed light upon why children's books contained ambivalent messages about slaves and emancipation. This chapter focuses on these contexts, as well as upon the narrative conventions that influenced the shape of the messages. The overall theme that emerges is that spiritual and human concerns produced a unique antislavery dynamism; however, the egalitarian commitment was undercut by condescension toward people of color. Moreover, that conviction of superiority had an impact upon what the stories were like in a formalistic sense.

To a present-day reader, the early-nineteenth-century literature appears exceedingly superficial, perhaps because the themes were presented more as preachments than as part of lived experience. Black emancipation was handled without sufficient depth. The ambivalence of the message was due in part to the White abolitionists' social agenda, and to historic religious changes in particular. According to Anne C. Loveland, the new, nineteenth-century intellectual mix was primarily the result of a shift in religious thought.[1] The movement toward manumission was, to a degree, in the service of a changing religious culture.

Theological preoccupations did not, apparently, leave White abolitionists with much time left over to learn about Black experience. Or perhaps they simply did not have a strong compulsion to learn about the slave's dilemma at a level that reached beyond their own immediate cultural concerns and self-interests. As they created a blend of religion, gentility, and antislavery argumentation, they resorted to what was quick and easy in their portrayal of Black literary characters, that is, they drew upon conventions in popular art. They incorporated in their work minstrel humor, operatic sentimentality, and labored exhortation.

The stultifying sameness in abolitionist children's books (despite genre differences) is not surprising given this use of similar materials. An author's treatment of Black emancipation often resulted in a misrepresentation because the flat, surface treatment did little to ameliorate the potential for misunderstanding that was considerable in the society at large. The antislavery theme, then, became one of many themes in tales about religion and middle-class gentility. Yet it must be added that abolitionist writers challenged some conservative assumptions and did so unreservedly.

The Religious Context

There was a basic contradiction in the relationship between an abolitionist religious perspective and American political idealism. That perspective included for many the idea of millenialism, whereas the democracy taking shape in the United States involved slow and less-than-perfect processes. The utopianism of the religious revivalists went against the grain of that reality principle that remains uppermost in a democratic system of government.

Antislavery sentiment was viewed by many abolitionists as a means for "converting" the governmental system, a process more or less equivalent to the religionists' approach to conversion from sin. The complex democratic process that would have contributed to de facto as well as de jure liberation for slaves was apparently not a central theme in the antislavery movement. In any case, it can be argued that political idealism, as reflected in antebellum children's narratives, faded *after* the war because it was insufficiently grounded in egalitarian principles *before* the war. The antislavery theme could be genuine in children's literature (as I believe it was) and yet have a short-term effect.

The strengths and weaknesses of abolitionism are easier to understand when we note the changes that began to affect Calvinism in the early nineteenth century. Strict Calvinists viewed regeneration as a purely divine prerogative, an act of an inscrutable God. People were generally considered passive and infinitely sinful. By the 1820s, the religious thought of many New England clergymen had shifted to an acknowledgement of salvation as potentially within reach of everyone through free choice. Moreover, redemption could occur suddenly in people who achieved and professed a "new heart."[2] Anne C. Loveland notes that there were new connotations in the old religious vocabulary:

These developments [new views of personal reformation] infused the traditional vocabulary with new meaning which in turn compelled a new view of man's relation to God and his fellow creatures—one that emphasized ability rather than inability, activity rather than passivity, benevolence rather than piety.[3]

This changed perspective on selfhood, according to Donald M. Scott, was putting pressure on the Calvinists. For one thing, Unitarians were becoming a powerful rival because the style of their devotions accentuated the autonomy of the self. Scott makes the case that the accelerated movement of youths to the city in their premarital, precareer years made self-reliance and ingenuity necessities of life. This change had side effects that were pertinent to the antislavery cause: first, the youths' elders wanted them converted *now* (before the city's temptations got the upper hand), and second, the young people became a dislocated generation, caught between self-involvement and the old-time religion's censure of self-involvement.[4] This generation was ready for the revivalists' message of immediate conversion, solicitude for the unconverted, and a concept of church that was social as well as personal. Even Harriet Beecher Stowe's father, Reverend Lyman Beecher, advised a young minister that, "The state, the nation, the world demand your prayers, and charities and enterprise."[5] Beecher was not what one could call a fully reformed

Calvinist, yet he was among the traditional churchmen who could not hold back the rise of a new ministerial role and structure. That change included the service of large causes: evangelism and social improvement.[6]

Such an enlarged cultural purpose for the church made many New England ministers ripe for abolitionism. Unlike their predecessors, they emphasized personal responsibility, free will, the ability of people to change, and a social church. This was the program that gave many clergymen after the 1820s a well-defined sense of vocation and a means toward self-definition as well. This new emphasis led church leaders to stress works as well as words, take risks on behalf of others, recruit converts without regard to sect or region, and adhere to their principles with incredible stubbornness.

Such a "New Clergy" has self-evident strengths in relation to the antislavery cause, especially since slavery, in the eyes of this group, epitomized not only sin, but the "temper of sin."[7] "Immediatism" in the emancipation movement (the demand for instant manumission of slaves) was coordinate with an evangelical attitude toward sin, especially sin in its most standard nineteenth-century forms: self-gratification and selfishness. Slavery served as the ultimate symbol of these sins because the slave's whole being was a machine to feed the slave-master's self-indulgences. The plight of the female slave, moreover, was a symbol of universal concubinage. These are among the reasons why those in the religious community could easily associate moral activism with antislavery activism. It was not a matter of North versus South, but a question of sin's institution-based "tentacles [being] spread throughout society and [implicating] everyone, North and South alike."[8]

Because antislavery activities were so much a part of the culture of conversion—so deeply theological—abolitionists created problems for the emancipation movement while they also offered assistance. In children's antislavery narratives, the problems took form as White martyrdom complexes, as an emphasis on submissiveness in Blacks, and as an implied gradualism in social reform. Still suspecting that African Americans were inferior, abolitionists did not create a strong cross-cultural movement. At the planning and executive levels, White activists were usually in control, their notion of personal martyrdom giving them the impression that emancipation was their exclusive responsibility. While they did not always call themselves gradualists with regard to a sin such as slavery, they did call themselves relativists, which amounted to the same thing. They had a tendency to view all kinds of repentance from a religious angle and hence as gradual or relative. This posture was one of inward soul-searching rather than humanitarian action, and thus "progress" was to be measured more by its "redeemed" slave-holders than by its liberated slaves. Abolitionist pamphleteer Elizur Wright Jr. made sure that his explanation of "immediatism" did not raise the frightening specter of extremism. "A *doctrine* is one thing," he said, "and a *plan* is another."

When we say that slave-holders ought to emancipate their slaves immediately, *we state a doctrine which is* true. *We do not propose a* plan. *Our* plan . . . *is simply this: To promulgate the true* doctrine *of human rights*. . . .

By prosecuting the plan described, we expect *to see the benevolent, one by one at first, and afterwards in dense masses, . . . rushing to the standard*. . . .[9]

Religious leaders in the movement equivocated in this manner and over-emphasized abstractions. Historians William H. Pease and Jane H. Pease have made the latter point:

Endemic was the abolitionists' tendency toward abstractions. Frequently they so abstracted both the "Negro"and the "Crusade" that they dealt not with people in a situation but only with intellectualizations in a vacuum.[10]

To some extent, the strength of the combined slavery/sin symbol was in its unification of two concepts: the hatred of sin and the love of the victim of sin. However loving the victim was, as the Peases note, not a vivid awareness of "people in a situation."[11] Abolitionists did discuss and execute "plans," but much of their preaching was about "heart," "will," and "disposition."[12]

Religion, then, in the mainstream community, is perhaps best viewed as a problematic element in the antislavery cause. It had tremendous rallying power and emotional depth. But at best it was naive in relation to a political problem, and at worst it was self-interested and self-involved, a White cultural drama with Calvinists, Unitarians, and a generation of dislocated farmers as central players.

The Black clergy, on the other hand, had a pragmatic program centered on concrete forms of relief—on the "underground railroad," on night schools and Sunday schools, on benevolence auxiliaries. According to Carol V. R. George, abolitionism in local Black churches developed Black consciousness through antislavery activity, protests against discrimination, and free religious expression.[13]

Unfortunately, the children's literature establishment provided no channels for the Black perspective. In examining the juvenile books of this period, we find that they reflected only the White orientation, and more often than not they were an expression of the "white man's burden" concept. Writers seldom overlooked an opportunity to portray Northerners as martyrs. In *The Child's Anti-Slavery Book*, a White teacher and two White housewives are featured, all of whom relinquish their time, resources, or freedom on behalf of the emancipation cause.[14] In *Cudjo's Cave*, an abolitionist schoolmaster is willing to be tarred and feathered for his beliefs.[15] Little Eva, in *Uncle Tom's Cabin*, departs this world altogether rather than breathe the polluted air of a slave-ridden society.[16] In "Jumbo and Zairee," the Englishman-turned-plantation-owner sees the error of his ways and abandons the labor-free plantation life for the sake of his slaves' liberation.[17]

There are also stern words for clergymen and others who fail to bear the burdens of the antislavery movement. In *The Child's Anti-Slavery Book*, Lewis's mother cautions her son:

There are some young missies with tender hearts that do take a good deal of pains to teach poor slaves to read; but she isn't so, nor any of massa's family, if he is a minister. He don't care any more about us than he does about his horses.[18]

In children's books slaves are typically advised to quietly submit to their fate. In "Aunt Judy's Story" in *The Child's Anti-Slavery Book*, the idea that cruel masters should be punished is quickly countered by a White parent's explanation: "Do you forget what our blessed

Savior said about returning good for evil?"[19] And Harry, in *May Morning and New Year's Eve*, is depicted as a model Black because his highest pleasure is "doing good for evil."[20] Likewise the free Black, Rainbow, is counseled to remain silent in the face of discrimination in "The Three Pines."[21]

Submission for Blacks and heroism for European Americans is perhaps the most common expression of White self-interest in children's abolitionist fiction. But there are also passages that indicate how slavery is perceived as a theological testing ground. In *Cudjo's Cave*, the venerable clergyman makes this comment:

"Prejudice," said the old man, "is always a mark of narrowness and ignorance. You might almost, I think, decide the question of a man's Christianity by his answer to this: 'What is your feeling towards the negro?'"[22]

In another scene, the same character refers to God "who, by means of this war that seems so needless and so cruel, is working out the redemption, not of the misguided white masters only, but also of the slave."[23] In the vignette that closes *The Child's Anti-Slavery Book*, "Me Neber Gib It Up!" an ex-slave is struggling with his reading lessons and the narrator tells us:

He then pointed to these beautiful words in his Testament: "God so loved the world that he gave his only begotton [sic] Son, that whosoever believeth on him should not perish, but have everlasting life." "There," he added, with deep feeling, "it is worth all de labor to be able to read dat one single verse!"[24]

Here we see another focus in abolitionist texts: the desirability of teaching Christianity to Blacks. Emancipation is associated with religion, but it is not the religion of Moses as he rains down plagues on Pharaoh, or the religion of Jesus as he drives moneychangers from the temple. It is a theistic doctrine that makes patience and humility the chief virtues.

Ironically, when slavery as a religious symbol ended with emancipation, its significance seems to have come to an end in White culture. Mainstream groups moved on to other issues and other metaphors. But the use of political arguments against slavery should have resulted in a different scenario. Since activists in the children's book field opposed the antidemocratic nature of slavery, we might have expected them to be equally vocal about antidemocratic practices during and after Reconstruction. But this was not the case. A look at the political scene supplies us with clues as to why democracy, as well as socially focused religions, became almost invisible in the post-bellum children's books.

The Political Context

The realities that children's book writers concealed are as indicative of the national climate as anything they said openly. For example, the regional nature of the growing conflict over slavery was downplayed. A number of writers made it clear that children were not to condemn the South, per se, but rather those few greedy and licentious individuals who kept slaves and spoiled the region for everyone. Similarly, the tug-of-war over the West as either a slave or free region was rarely alluded to.

Class stratification, on the other hand, is much in evidence in the stories, and it is treated as a natural dimension of life, not as a problem. It seems clear that nothing will be told children about class or region that might cast doubt upon the overriding nationalistic myth: that the United States was God-ordained as a corrective to European classism.

Instead of tampering with this myth, authors found ways to present a few central democratic principles. Just as abolitionists used the traditional religious vocabulary and infused it with new implications, so the antislavery writers were able to take traditional ideas about property and power and put them to new uses. Property, they said, was first of all "ourselves," and thus no one could properly own another. As for the questions of autonomy versus arbitrary power (as formulated at the time of the American Revolution), this issue was addressed by interpreting those principles minus a color line. As *The Child's Anti-Slavery Book* put it, "Every negro child . . . is as free before God as the white child, having precisely the same right to life, liberty, and the pursuit of happiness, as the white child."[25] By means of such interpretations, the intellectual arguments countering abolitionism were, to a degree, overcome. Antislavery activists were able to refute with solid logic those who held (1) that the right of individual property was a natural right and (2) that the nation was destined to be exclusively white.

However, race consciousness was a problem that abolitionists themselves did not deal with adequately. Race consciousness is probably at the heart of much ambivalence in antislavery narratives. Authors such as Harriet Beecher Stowe, Jacob Abbott, and even Lydia Maria Child in the 1820s, were in sympathy with the ideas of the American Colonization Society—the group founded in 1817 with the principle of race separation underlying its policy of African resettlement.[26] Even when colonization was not advocated, the theme of separateness is suggested in various subtle ways. For example, such phrases as "African soul," "tropical soul," and "tropical heart" (always used flippantly and derisively) made the slave population appear to be almost a distinct species.

This deep-seated cultural divide may be interpreted as underlying the political ironies of both Jacksonian democracy and radical abolitionism. Or conversely, it could be argued that the cultural rationale was just a spinoff of the White self-interest that characterized the age. It was probably some of both. For our purposes, it is the ironies themselves that are revealing.

There was the paradox of the Jacksonian Party, a proslavery political party that nonetheless advertised itself as a democracy of the popular will. Jacksonian democracy can be interpreted as a misnomer on several levels because the more important advances in democratization occurred prior to Jackson's election in 1828. As historian Frederick J. Antczak points out, universal White male suffrage was adopted in six new western states between 1812 and 1821, and during this period four older states either lowered or dropped property qualifications for voters. Similarly, most states had changed to the direct election of delegates to the Electoral college, and Congressional caucuses had, by this time, been replaced by national party conventions as the presidential nominating system.[27]

What transpired during Jackson's two terms was primarily a new utilization of populist symbolism. Jackson himself represented the self-made-man ideal, having profitably switched during his lifetime from merchant to lawyer, to military commander, to planter, to speculator, to office holder. He opened his inauguration party to the crowds

in the streets, acknowledging the importance of the increased number of voters. He announced a policy of "rotation in office"—a plan
to allow all "men of intelligence [to] readily qualify themselves."
However, he was articulating here an ideal that never materialized in
any significant degree. "Rotation" became a spoils system, a way to
reward cronies for their undeviating political loyalty.[28] There developed, according to Robert V. Remini, a change in the political process, but that transformation consisted of a "wildly extravagant cam-
paigning style,"[29] and a "highly structured pyramid [in the convention
system] from local groups on up through county and state organizations."[30] The party system became respectable and integral to the
election process; the presidency would, ideally, come to symbolize
the entire democratic audience.[31]

Government under Jackson symbolized rule by popular will,
yet the Jacksonians, says Remini, were "singularly unresponsive towards women's rights, prison reform, educational improvements,
protection of minors and other forms of social betterment."[32] He
continues:

*Their treatment of the Indians . . . constitutes one of the most frightful
examples of bigotry and greed in American history. . . . Furthermore,
the Jacksonian record on slavery was abysmal.[33]*

The popular will excluded Blacks, as indeed they had been excluded from the political process by the Founding Fathers (e.g., in
calculating congressional representation, a Black was counted as three-
fifths of a person).

Radical abolitionists behaved in the real political world in a similarly contradictory manner. According to Merton L. Dillon, they
did not afford to Blacks full equality at the decision-making level of
the local abolitionist societies, they had no appreciation of Black
culture, and those in business reserved menial jobs for Blacks.[34] They
showed a distinct preference for light over dark skin hues, and they
retained conservative social views over a range of subjects, from adop-
tion and intermarriage to questions of deportment.[35] Richard Hofstadter interprets the nineteenth-century evangelists as so intellectually reactionary that he is able to treat the radicalism of revivalist

Charles G. Finney as little more than an aberration in Finney's doctrinaire temperament.[36]

Given these less-than-liberal attitudes in the North, the South was perhaps overhasty in reacting so bitterly to abolitionist pamphleteering. Their actions only exacerbated the sectional nature of the conflict. They succeeded in initiating censorship of abolitionist publications in the Postal Service. They helped enact congressional gag rules—a means by which Congress could table antislavery petitions (414,471 such petitions were sent and tabled between May 1837 and May 1838).[37]

The Mexican War (1846–1848) caused regional distrust to be further aggravated. The war was perceived by many Northerners as contrived by the slave states to protect legal servitude (Mexico, like Canada, was a refuge for runaways) and to extend the slave-holders' power in the territories and thereby in Congress. The South saw the dispute as allied with its ongoing effort to prevent a Northern three-fourths majority in Congress. Abolitionist poet John Greenleaf Whittier expressed the antislavery sentiments about the war in an unequivocal indictment: "Christian America, thanking God that she is not like other nations, . . . goes out, Bible in hand, to enslave the world."[38]

The Mexican War was soon to be augmented by other actions that would exacerbate Northern radicalism and deepen sectional antipathies. For example, the Fugitive Slave Law of 1850 made penalties stiffer than those in earlier fugitive laws. The territory of the free states became an open hunting ground for Southern agents who were allegedly pursuing missing slaves. In effect this turned the North into a theatrical stage upon which everyone was an actor. The importance of this change—the ensuing turbulence as alleged runaways were apprehended—can hardly be overestimated. The problem was seen as not solely an injustice to Blacks, but also as an unconscionable violation of the civil rights of mainstream groups. The new fugitive law wiped out all semblance of due process for those Whites who were said to be harboring or assisting runaways.

Then in 1854 the Kansas-Nebraska Act nullified the Missouri Compromise of 1820 that had prohibited the extension of slavery into new western territories (i.e., into those areas acquired in the Louisiana Purchase and north of 36° 30'). The bloodshed that ensued in Kansas, as proslavery and antislavery forces vied for control, exposed the futility of a "popular sovereignty" principle in relation to the expanding frontier. The legislative bills to organize Nebraska and Kansas had stipulated that these areas would be designated by Congress as neither slave nor free; the issue would be resolved by the territorial voters. Both the North and South established emigration societies to skew the percentages in the elections and each side accused the other of cheating.

In 1857 Northerners were enraged by yet another ruling. The Supreme Court upheld a lower Missouri court that maintained that Dred Scott, a Black, was not a United States citizen and on racial grounds could be disallowed the usual citizenship rights. The court also ruled that the Missouri Compromise had been unconstitutional, having violated the tenet that a person could not be deprived of any "property" without due process. By denying, in effect, Congress's right to regulate slavery in this way, the path seemed clear for increasing Southern dominance.

While these events indicated to antislavery Northerners that their cause was losing ground, John Brown's raid at Harper's Ferry in 1858 validated for Southerners their worst fears. When the raid was criticized in the North for its methods, but not for its motives, many Southerners interpreted that response as a prediction, a hint of how appalling their fate would be if an antislavery political party should win control of the government.[39]

Avery Craven has analyzed the antebellum period in relation to such sectional rivalry and its interlocking connection with the broad themes of territorial expansion and humanitarianism. He describes a political context of exceeding complexity, involving demographic factors, problems of tariffs and banking, the emergence of cotton as a leading staple, homesteading opportunities, soil erosion, and much more.[40] The struggle over slavery, as he interprets it, served as a symbolic center for a great variety of tensions and contests. Its association with religious revivalism tended to elevate all disputes to a cosmic level where compromise became unthinkable.[41] In the day-by-day politicking of legislators and officials, the debates over territorial expansion opened the way for some unusually effective fence-straddling. In Craven's words:

Opposition to the expansion of slavery *began to replace opposition [in the 1840s] to slavery* per se. *The issue became a practical one to be dealt with by practical men. . . .*

The politician could now be a practical abolitionist and yet deny the charge that he was one.[42]

It is not surprising that children's books expressed the simple polarities, while at the same time suggesting that the issues were not so clear-cut after all, that authors were themselves confused about race and about rights of citizenship. As already noted, children's book authors downplayed anything as intricate and potentially disillusioning as political sectionalism. Literature for the young emphasized only a few patriotic themes, perhaps the most important being personal liberty as alluded to in the Declaration of Independence, "possessive individualism" or the idea that we own only ourselves, and humaneness in human relations.

These principles were presented in various ways in children's abolitionist fiction. In *Cudjo's Cave*, freedom is identified with saving the Union, liberating the slaves, and contributing to the salvation of the whole world. The schoolmaster, Penn, refers to secessionists as aiming to destroy "Liberty," and he shakes the hand of the African American, Pomp, without hesitation and in full view of his more bigoted comrades. The prejudices of the other Union patriots are set at rest as Penn lectures them:

We are all men in the sight of God!. . . . He has brought us together here for a purpose. The work to be done is for all men, for humanity. . . . I believe that upon the success of our cause depends, not the prosperity of any class of men, or of any race of men, only, but of all men, and all races. For America marches in the van of human progress, and if she falters, if she ignobly turns back, woe is to the world![43]

Pomp is given the job of dismantling the "property" argument of the slavers:

. . . a man's natural, original owner is—himself. No, I never sold myself. My father never sold himself. My father was stolen by pirates on the

coast of Africa. . . . The man who bought him bought what had been
stolen. By your own laws you cannot hold stolen property.[44]

Pomp's legal mind is applauded in this scene, but the description of his general demeanor calls up a primitivist image: "There was something almost wicked in the wild, bright glance with which the negro repeated ['property']."[45]

Cruelties such as beatings, tortures, and the breaking up of families have strong thematic importance in many narratives, as when Aunt Judy's slave husband is whipped, weighted with heavy irons on his legs, and forced on a six-day march with bleeding feet through the snow.[46] However, in this story from *The Child's Anti-Slavery Book*, as in *Cudjo's Cave*, there is reference to African cruelty, and this trait is described as a sweeping generalization. The political nature of children's literature is particularly obvious in the passage that compares African and American Indian "treachery"; a White parent in "Aunt Judy's Story" turns the Indians into inveterate treaty-violators:

. . . my son, when you began the argument you said that you thought the
Indians were more deserving of compassion than the Africans. Now this
is the difference. The Indians were always a warlike and treacherous
race; their most solemn compacts were broken as soon as their own pur-
poses had been served. And they were continually harassing the settlers;
. . . at the present time they are . . . murdering the traders who cross the
plains. . . . Now the Americans had never this cause of complaint against
the Africans, for, although like all heathen, they were debased, and were
cruel and war-like among each other, they never annoyed us in America.[47]

Sociopolitical ambivalence is seen in some tales even while they are sympathetic to the antislavery cause. *Congo; or, Jasper's Experience in Command* is devoid of positive democratic messages, issuing instead some brief but emphatic declarations of white supremacy.[48]

Political tenets in children's books were not handled with subtlety, as the examples here indicate. Direct exhortation was not frowned upon as a literary device, nor was sentimentality viewed as a flaw. Political and social content was influenced by prevailing literary forms, especially by the conventions of minstrelsy and the juvenile moral tale. As I turn to the entertainment aspects of abolitionist fiction, these two genres will be the main points of reference.

The Art of Abolitionist Fiction

Nineteenth-century writers for children were interested in engaging the attention of their audience, as well as benefiting them morally and intellectually. To this end they devised playful, reassuring incidents and settings. Picnics, holiday celebrations, fireside story hours, outings in the snow, rambles on the seashore—these were among the appealing environments that were firmly in place before the young readers encountered the tragic slave trade or life on a plantation. However, this solicitude for young readers did not reduce the influence of the popular art forms of that era, especially minstrelsy.

"Blackface" minstrelsy can be characterized as a highly political art, although it was probably not consciously analyzed as such by nineteenth-century audiences. Alexander Saxton has written a detailed description of its political import—its relation to the Jacksonian proslavery program and to the economic and cultural tensions of the age. He reports that it was initially a theatrical event with all-male casts and audiences, and it served as a psychological outlet for several generations of dislocated men. It made fun of the new urban existence of these men (the city's looser moral standards, in particular) and at the same time it offered a symbolic journey back to the farm and even further back to the years of childhood. Playful innuendoes (exchanged between an interlocutor and two "end men") about sex, booze, and urban "stuffed shirts" made city life a bit more bearable. Songs eulogizing an idyllic Old South served as reminders of an innocent and pastoral life.[49]

But this image of a lost paradise included the idea of a perennial Black serving class. Therefore, while childhood would be lost, the hope of living among the leisured classes would *not* be lost so long as Blacks could be relegated to a low caste status. Thus the minstrel skits and songs about African Americans represented for European Americans both nostalgia and the desire for a higher position in the pecking order. Andrew Jackson's political agenda accommodated that hope in its white supremacist orientation.

According to Saxton, it was the Southern wing of the Jacksonian Democratic Party—the first mass political party—that demanded the organization's adherence to proslavery principles. The minstrel tradition was congruent with the wishes of these Southern Democrats.[50] Thus while some features of the plays, especially the dances, authentically reflected the slave culture, other features turned that culture on its head. Such a distortion is evident in the following example:

Old Massa to us darkies am good
Tra la la, tra la la
For he gibs us our clothes and he gibs us our food. . . .[51]

The slaves in a typical minstrel act loved "massa" and dreaded freedom. They could not imagine a more benign environment than the plantation, for they were neither self-possessed nor capable of normal human emotions. Such were the messages constituting an indirect justification for slavery—a justification that was largely monolithic.[52] The exceptions were antislavery connotations that could be attached to some African American music and to some European-style ballads about parted lovers or lost children. But according to Saxton, a conceivable antislavery theme in a song would be "disguised [on the minstrel stage] by shifting specific griefs to the generalized sorrows of time and distance, or by emphasizing the troubles Blacks were likely to encounter in the North."[53]

Without venturing further into an inquiry of the minstrel theatre, it is worth noting that images of a Southern slave utopia were combined during the 1850s and early 1860s with attacks against the groups that would, if they could, upset that plantation system—namely the abolitionists. It is ironic, therefore, that abolitionist writers themselves appropriated the white supremacist techniques associated with the "stage Negro."

In my sample of abolitionist writing, it is the novels extensively populated with Blacks in which the minstrel tie-in is most clear. In *Uncle Tom's Cabin* and *Cudjo's Cave* nearly every scene with Black characters is reminiscent of a minstrel skit, except those scenes featuring the saintly characters (Uncle Tom or Pomp). In *Hatchie, the Guardian Slave*, there are few Black characters, but everyone except the hero, the "guardian slave" himself, is a minstrel type. Jacob Abbott, in his book about Rainbow and Handie, makes Rainbow an appealing character in most respects, yet he is just a bit lazier and more skittish than the White characters—staple traits in the minstrel clown.

The most pervasive image of Blacks on the minstrel stage was one suggesting an innately deficient mentality. Sometimes this idea was manifested as a slave's inability to comprehend some simple thing and sometimes as a general proclivity for disorder. Both means of projecting imbecility are included in scenes about Black religious behavior in *Uncle Tom's Cabin*—a puzzling inconsistency given Stowe's efforts to characterize Uncle Tom as a holy man. In an episode where residents of the quarters are preparing for a prayer meeting, we see how futile it has been for the plantation owner's son to try to teach Black children the stories in the Bible. Tom's wife is arranging seating for everyone and suggests the use of some barrels:

"Well, ole man," said Aunt Chloe, "you'll have to tote in them ar bar'ls."
"Mother's bar'ls is like dat ar widder's, Mas'r George was reading 'bout, in de good book,—dey never fails" said Mose, aside to Pete.
"I'm sure one on 'em caved in last week," said Pete, "and let 'em all down in de middle of de singin'; dat ar was failin', warnt it?"[54]

Stowe's audience would have been familiar with the biblical basis of this joke—Elisha's miracle of providing an oil supply that could not be depleted (II Kings 4:1–7).

Depicting the prayer meeting in full swing, the author quotes lines from several spirituals and adds a commentary on "the negro mind":

[T]he negro mind, impassioned and imaginative, always attaches itself to hymns and expressions of a vivid and pictorial nature; and, as they sung, some laughed, and some cried, and some clapped hands, or shook hands rejoicingly with each other, as if they had fairly gained the other side of the river [Jordan].[55]

Stowe follows these remarks with a monologue by a Black woman that suggests a ludicrous literal-mindedness about the religious symbolism in a song and a general dimwittedness in the speaker.[56]

Elsewhere in the novel a cook, Dinah, "indulged the illusion

that she, herself, was the soul of order," while Stowe presents to the
reader the reverse image:

"What's this?" said Miss Ophelia, holding up the saucer of pomade.
"Law, it's my har grease;—I put it thar to have it handy."
"Do you use your mistress' best saucers for that?"
"Law! it was cause I was driv, and in sich a hurry;—I was gwine to
change it this very day."
"Here are two damask table-napkins."
"Them table-napkins I put thar, to get 'em washed out, some day."
"Don't you have some place here on purpose for things to be washed?"
"Well, Mas'r St. Clare got dat ar chest, he said, for dat; but I likes to
mix up biscuit and hev my things on it some days, and then it ain't
handy a liftin' up the lid."
"Why don't you mix your biscuits on the pastry-table, there?"
"Law, Missis, it gets sot so full of dishes, and one thing and another,
der an't no room, noways—"
"But you should wash your dishes, and clear away."
"Wash the dishes! said Dinah, in a high key, as her wrath began to
rise. . . ."[57]

Dinah, we realize later, was slovenly but with a difference. She
had an occasional "clarin' up" time. Then she would dress up in her
best outfit and "would contract such an immoderate attachment to
her scoured tin, as to insist upon it that it shouldn't be used again for
any possible purpose,—at least, till the ardor of the 'clarin' up' period abated."[58] "Immoderate" and "ardor" are terms that apply in a
general sense to the "stage Negroes." A blend of irrationality and
intemperance was attributed to Blacks and suggested that here was a
group to be isolated, managed, and denied citizenship. The import
of this clownish figure in abolitionist fiction was the way it undermined the theme of Black emancipation—a theme that antislavery
writers prided themselves upon sharing with both adult and child
readerships.

While minstrel devices added to works of fiction an element of
ambivalence toward the Black community, the conventions of the
moral tale provided a means for expressing emancipationist sentiments. The moral tale was unabashedly didactic, and thus an aboli-

tionist writer could say straightforwardly, "Shame on my country" (as Lydia Maria Child exclaims in "Jumbo and Zairee").[59] However, a less committed antislavery author (Jacob Abbott, for example) could also indoctrinate the reader with direct unequivocal pronouncements. The revered grandfather figure in *Congo; or, Jasper's Experience in Command* speciously pronounces that "it is one of the characteristics of the colored people to like to be employed by other people, rather than to take responsibility and care upon themselves."[60] Direct admonition could, as a literary device, cut two ways.

Rhetorical characteristics of the moral tale, such as the positioning of a fictional child to receive pearls of wisdom from an all-knowing adult, reduced the verisimilitude of a story, but the tales appear to have been no less engaging for that reason. Anne Scott MacLeod, using the evidence gleaned from nineteenth-century autobiographies, states that "early nineteenth century children both read and enjoyed, selectively, the fiction written for them. . . . A fervent concern with morality was simply part of the nineteenth-century outlook. . . ."[61]

Reaching a young, antebellum readership was not a problem, then, despite a narrative's two-dimensionality. But it can be argued that this highly underdeveloped treatment of characterization had a baneful effect upon biracial fiction. It was easy for the dominant culture to portray Blacks superficially—even as pure abstractions. It was only a short step, from that point, to the more serious distortions of identity that were prevalent in antislavery children's books.

Conclusion

To declare that abolitionists were racists, when nearly everyone in that nineteenth-century epoch could be labeled a racist by modern standards, would not be saying much. Instead, the basis of this inquiry is the attempt to pinpoint images and messages that may have contributed to the perpetuation of the white supremacy myth. As noted in these pages, there was a religious message: that slavery was a sin. But apparently this did not mean that it was sinful to treat Blacks as destined to remain separate from the White community. There was also a political message: that civic activism was the domain of Whites, whereas the correct posture for Blacks was passivity, service, and possibly a return to Africa. Neither the religious nor political movements included consistent, unequivocal refutations of the notion of innate Black inferiority. And it was not unusual for prevailing literary conventions, as in minstrelsy and the moral tale, to reinforce that myth.

Every type of taletelling was infused with a point of view that was either ambivalent or openly hostile. Therefore, it seems unlikely that injustices in the postbellum era would be adequately addressed by abolitionists or their descendants. Moreover, it would be virtually impossible for Blacks to achieve a power base and sustain it, for the new balance of power would not lead to democratization in any practical sense. In the realm of publishing that we are dealing with here, a North/South White "coalition" would emerge after 1865, and it would not cause writers to alter the now engrained portrayal of Blacks as perpetual outsiders.

Before turning to this exceedingly regressive period of White-authored books about Blacks, we need to consider biographical information and examine such "gatekeeping" institutions as schools, churches, and the press. We can round out our picture of antislavery children's literature by noting the impulses in lives and institutions that affected the emancipationist cause.

Notes

1.   Anne C. Loveland, "Evangelism and Immediate Emancipation in American Anti-slavery Thought," *Journal of Southern History* 32:2 (May 1966): 174.
2.   Donald M. Scott, "Abolition As a Sacred Vocation," in *Antislavery Rediscovered: New Perspectives on the Abolitionists*, ed. Lewis Perry and Michael Fellman (Baton Rouge: Louisiana State University Press, 1979), 54.
3.   Loveland, 174.
4.   Scott, 55.
5.   Ibid., 62.
6.   Ibid.
7.   Ibid., 66.
8.   Ibid., 68.
9.   Elizur Wright Jr., "Immediate Abolition," in *Slavery Attacked: The Abolitionist Crusade*, ed. John L. Thomas (Englewood Cliffs, NJ: Prentice-Hall, 1965), 16–17.
10. William H. Pease and Jane H. Pease, "Antislavery Ambivalence: Immediatism, Expediency, Race," *American Quarterly* 27:4 (Winter 1965): 693.
11. Ibid., 683.
12. Scott, 721.
13. Carol V. R. George, "Widening the Circle: The Black Church and the Abolitionist Crusade, 1830–1860," in *Anti-slavery Reconsidered: New Perspectives on the Abolitionists*, ed. Lewis Perry and Michael Fellman (Baton Rouge: Louisiana State University Press, 1979), 89–92.
14. *The Child's Anti-Slavery Book: Containing a Few Words About American Slave*

Children, and Stories of Slave-Life (New York: Carlton and Porter, 1859; rpt. Miami: Mnemosyne Publishing, Co., 1969).

15. James Townsend Trowbridge. *Cudjo's Cave* (Boston: J. E. Tilton and Co., 1864).

16. Harriet Beecher Stowe. *Uncle Tom's Cabin; or, Life Among the Lowly* (Boston: John P. Jewett and Co., 1852; rpt. *The Annotated Uncle Tom's Cabin*, ed. Philip Van Doren Stern, New York: Paul S. Eriksson, Inc., 1964).

17. "Jumbo and Zairee," *Juvenile Miscellany*, n.s., 5 (January 1831).

18. Julia Colman. "Little Lewis: The Story of a Slave Boy," in *The Child's Anti-Slavery Book*, 41.

19. Matilda G. Thompson. "Aunt Judy's Story: A Story from Real Life," in *The Child's Anti-Slavery Book*, 137.

20. Eliza Lee Follen, *May Morning and New Year's Eve* (n.p.: Whittemore, Niles, and Hall, 1857; rpt. Boston: Nichols and Hall, 1870), 24.

21. Jacob Abbott, "The Three Pines," in *Stories of Rainbow and Lucky* (New York: Harper & Brothers, 1860), 68.

22. Trowbridge, 42.

23. Ibid., 210–211.

24. "Me Neber Gib it Up!" in *The Child's Anti-Slavery Book*, 157–158.

25. "A Few Words About American Slave Children," in *The Child's Anti-Slavery Book*, 14.

26. Merton L. Dillon, *The Abolitionists: The Growth of a Dissenting Minority* (De Kalb: Northern Illinois University Press, 1974), 20.

27. Frederick J. Antczak, *Thought and Character: The Rhetoric of Democratic Education* (Ames: The Iowa State University Press, 1985), 27–28.

28. Ibid. 39.

29. Robert V. Remini, ed., *The Age of Jackson* (Columbia: University of South Carolina Press, 1972), xx.

30. Ibid.

31. Antczak, 29.

32. Remini, xix.

33. Ibid.

34. Dillon, 71–73.

35. Pease, 688–689.

36. Richard Hofstadter, *Anti-Intellectualism in American Life* (New York: Vintage Books, 1963), 111.

37. Dillon, 101–102.

38. Ibid., 160.

39. Some popular writers in the North went so far as to lionize John Brown and thereby helped direct attention to his lofty motivations. Emerson called him "a hero," Thoreau called him "an angel of light," and Louisa May Alcott dubbed him "Saint John the Just." See Avery Craven, *The Coming of the Civil War*, 2nd ed. (Chicago: University of Chicago Press, 1957), 408

40. Craven, 1–16.

41. Ibid., 15–16.

42. Ibid., 226.

43. Trowbridge, 397, 398.

44. Ibid., 226.

45. Ibid.

46. Thompson, 134.

47. Ibid., 119–120.

48. Jacob Abbott, *Congo; or, Jasper's Experience in Command* (New York: Harper and Brothers, 1857).

49. Alexander Saxton, "Blackface Minstrelsy and Jacksonian Ideology," *American Quarterly* 27:1 (March 1975): 8–14.

50. Ibid., 17.

51. Ibid., 18.

52. Ibid.
53. Ibid., 18–19.
54. Stowe, 75.
55. Ibid., 76.
56. Ibid., 77.
57. Ibid., 284–282.
58. Ibid., 184.
59. "Jumbo and Zairee," 294–295.
60. *Congo*, 102.
61. Anne Scott MacLeod, *A Moral Tale: Children's Fiction and American Culture, 1820–1860* (Hamden, CT: Archon Books, 1975), 15.

Chapter Three
Personal and Institutional Dimensions

Cultural history includes the life stories and institutional patterns that are strongly suggestive of impulses underlying artistic production. While such material provides no hard and fast conclusions, the struggles of abolitionist writers for children have probative value. Only a minuscule number of writers who entered the children's book field wrote antislavery tracts, and those who did rarely wrote a narrative or textbook that was not to some degree ambivalent in its attitude toward Blacks. What we need, then, is to probe the reasons why writers joined the emancipation cause, and why their works for children contained inner contradictions. The writers' personal experiences vis-à-vis emancipation offer clues about their willingness to participate in a tempestuous, divisive cause.

The "Agitators": Stowe, Child, Follen

An assumption of Anglo-Saxon superiority appears in the writings of Harriet Beecher Stowe (1811–1896) during her young adult years. In the children's geography book that she coauthored with her sister, Catharine, she downgrades the character of American Indians, Spaniards, South Sea Islanders, the Chinese, and, to a lesser degree, the "southern races" of Europe. Harriet was twenty-two years old when this book was published.

Her home life may have been instrumental in her acquisition of such ethnocentric notions. Her father, Reverend Lyman Beecher, would not allow his sons to associate with Blacks. When the Trustees of Cincinnati's Lane Seminary imposed a gag rule on antislavery discussions, Lyman Beecher (who was the seminary's president) assented. Catharine Beecher was strongly opposed to abolitionism because she believed that women should avoid controversy.[1] These early influences on Harriet Beecher Stowe might make us wonder how she came to write an antislavery narrative in her forty-first year. That she wrote *Uncle Tom's Cabin* at all may be more surprising than her ambivalence toward her Black characters.

In trying to understand her attachment to emancipationism, we can consider specific contacts that Stowe had with the slavery issue, and we can consider less concrete influences that may have made her susceptible to antislavery work.

The national debate over slavery must have been a particularly wrenching issue for the family of a clergyman who preached against the slave trade in his Boston pulpit, but then bowed to his proslavery bosses in Ohio. Reverend Beecher could maneuver his way out of this contradiction by proclaiming gradualism as the proper position vis-à-vis Black emancipation. But this did not prevent his children from coming into contact with emotion-filled happenings that made gradualism seem less than satisfactory. Stowe's aunt, for example, had been married to a merchant in Jamaica and had shared with her stories about the horrors of Jamaican slavery. Harriet was made keenly aware of proslavery mob violence when James G. Birney's printing press was destroyed in Cincinnati in 1836, and also when Elijah Lovejoy (a friend of Harriet's brother, Edward) was killed by a proslavery mob in Alton, Illinois, in 1837.[2] In 1836, Stowe's husband, Calvin, and another brother had helped arrange the escape of a runaway slave.[3]

When Stowe moved with her spouse (a professor of theology) to Bowdoin College in Maine, the antislavery rhetoric of the region must have kept such incidents vividly in mind. Historian Thomas F. Gossett sees the Stowe family's relocation as significant, coming as it did in 1850, the year of the revised Fugitive Slave Law. An antislavery position was not looked upon with horror in the far Northern states, and the new law energized antislavery sentiment. Furthermore, those sentiments would now be based on a new and important grievance: the judicial process for both Blacks and non-Blacks was to be abrogated in new ways. Federal commissioners would act upon slave-catcher affidavits, not upon court orders.[4] In a letter to her publisher, Dr. Gamaliel Bailey of the *National Era*, Stowe wrote: "Up to this year [1851] I have always felt that I had no particular call to meddle with this subject [slavery] . . . I feel now that the time is come when even a woman or a child who can speak a word for freedom and humanity is bound to speak. . . ."[5] Prior to voicing this new commitment, Harriet had been urged by a sister-in-law to forge her pen into a weapon, and she had had a lengthy conversation with her brother, Henry Ward Beecher, about what each one would pledge to do for the abolitionist cause.[6]

Besides these traceable events, there are less tangible reasons why Stowe may have taken up her pen against slaveholders. Several lines of speculation have been advanced. For one thing, Stowe may have identified with the mother/child separations in the slave community, especially after one of her babies died of cholera in 1849.[7] Stowe also felt deeply the painful economic insecurity of her married life prior to the commercial success of *Uncle Tom's Cabin* beginning in 1852.

Moreover, Stowe had a somewhat marginal status in her family and community. It is not possible to determine whether she would, on that account, be able to identify easily with the outside status of noticeably different others. However, it must have been mortifying when Stowe's father let it be known that because she was female, she had a less valued position in the family than his sons.[8] And there was apparently little relief from this second-class citizenship when Harriet was with her peer group in Cincinnati. She and her sisters have been described as misfits in that social circle.

It is difficult to calculate the importance of such social discomfiture. Harriet appears to have turned some of these problems into opportunities. For example, she could participate very little in her father's dialogues with his sons, but she could listen and absorb the exercises in logic that Reverend Beecher was providing his male offspring. Gossett makes a well-reasoned point in this regard: that logical argumentation became one of the literary and intellectual strengths of *Uncle Tom's Cabin*.[9] With regard to peer rejection, Stowe and her sister, Catharine, were busy enough as teachers and writers to develop some inner-directed self-respect. However, Stowe's later interest in fashion and material comforts suggests that she may have felt considerable anguish over early social ostracism. Historians have charged her with appropriating twenty thousand dollars collected in England and earmarked for the relief of ex-slaves—an unacknowledged and unproven theft that they associate with Harriet's struggle for status, ego-satisfaction, and acceptance.[10] John Townsend Trowbridge was on the scene in 1853, and in his memoirs treats Stowe's fund-raising as a well-known joke among the Boston elite. He writes about her: ". . . upon Mrs. Stowe's going abroad in 1853 on a supposed mission to collect funds for the anti-slavery cause, [Charles Graham Halpine, a columnist for the *Boston Post*] nicknames her, first among his friends and afterward in print, 'Harriet Beseecher Be Stowe.'"[11]

If Stowe's marginality led to empathy with other outsiders, this tie was probably not a strong feeling of identification. The egalitarian message about Blacks in her most famous novel is mixed with ridicule and condescension, and her canon as a whole reflects the ethnocentrism of her era. Gossett's analysis of Stowe's references to race indicates a consistent belief in white superiority throughout her career. When mixed with religious moralizations, this belief took the form of a supercilious sympathy for slaves. When touched by the indignation that swept the North over the Fugitive Slave Law, these racial biases changed in the direction of genuine sensitivity and political insight.

In explaining *Uncle Tom's Cabin*, we also need to factor in Stowe's intellectual acumen and talent as a writer. It is astonishing that the novel was cranked out in serial installments—that its numerous antislavery arguments were practically pulled out of the air as Stowe faced her weekly deadlines. Historian Philip Van Doren Stern notes that the book was not researched to any great degree in the course of its composition.[12] Stowe did have at hand, however, Theodore Weld's *American Slavery As It Is: Testimony of a Thousand Witnesses* and Frederick Douglass's *The Narrative of the Life of Frederick Douglass*. It seems that Stowe could absorb and give voice to the White abolitionist consciousness with few tools except the pen in her hand, and with a deadline that she rarely missed. This accomplishment is extraordinary because her plan initially was to write a mere three- or four-part sketch for the *National Era;* the sketch turned into a forty-part serialized novel.

The momentum behind all this effort may have partially stemmed from Stowe's interest in the family as a cultural epicenter. This interpretation is suggested by historian Gayle Kimball, an interpretation that emphasizes Stowe's conformity rather than momentary radicalism. Kimball writes: "She was not a complex or sophisticated writer, but she mirrored and evoked common beliefs and concerns of her era: the desire to sanctify woman and the family, to provide solutions, first, to the problem of slavery and, then, to the corruption of industrial urban life."[13] From this perspective, it is possible to connect Stowe's themes with those of her sister Catharine (a pioneer in women's education and a reinforcer of conservative ideas about the glory of home and hearth). It was Catharine, an antiabolitionist, who took over the management of the Stowe residence for an entire year so that Harriet could complete her novel. This is not to suggest that slavery was not a powerful additional interest in Harriet's experience in the 1850s, but unlike her contemporary, Lydia Maria Child, she was accustomed to making no more than a passive response to it. As she said: slavery was "so utterly beyond human hope or help, that it was of no use to read, or think, or distress one's self about it."[14]

Lydia Maria Child (1802–1880) can be viewed as representing the other end of an antislavery spectrum. Her actions and writings reveal an ongoing concern over the irrationality of race prejudice. When Stowe was writing her ethnocentric geography book in 1833, *Primary Geography for Children,* Child was editing *The Juvenile Miscellany,* a periodical for children that included intermittent attacks on bigotry. Perhaps the most telling single image that emphasizes a contrast between Stowe and Child is one that relates to their generosity. Whereas Stowe (as already mentioned) may have appropriated funds earmarked for slave relief, Child drew $100 from her meager account and asked Wendell Phillips to forward it to a freedmen's fund. Phillips returned the check, saying in effect: "You cannot afford this now." Child promptly wrote one for $200 and told Phillips to do as instructed![15]

In some important dimensions of their lives, Stowe and Child were similar. They were both women with intellects in search of an outlet. They were deprived of high levels of formal education because they were female, and they felt this injustice and other gender-related frustrations. Stowe's letters suggest a sense of burden and anguish over heavy domestic duties (she gave birth seven times between 1837 and 1850), over her melancholy husband, and over her anxiety as she tried to do the breadwinning work for her family. Child remained childless throughout her life, but she was eventually forced to deal with an even greater financial strain than Stowe.

At first Child's literary endeavors paid off. Writing was one of the few occupations women could undertake in the early nineteenth century, but an opportunity dependent upon the concealment of the author's female identity. (Child did not disclose her identity when publishing her first two novels.) The success of her first books, plus the intervention of an Athenaeum library member, resulted in her admittance to this all-male Boston institution. But ultimately her research activities led to her ouster. She had been one of only two women ever granted Athenaeum library privileges until her book, *An Appeal in Favor of That Class of Americans Called Africans*, was published in 1833. That display of skill and radicalism turned the trustees against her.

Both Stowe and Child took action to counter educational deprivation. As Stowe had listened in on her father's educational dialogues with his sons, Child tapped her brother's lessons as he prepared for the Harvard Divinity School. Like Stowe, Child felt both antislavery and proslavery influences in her childhood and young adult years. Her brother, Convers, cautioned her against abolitionism. But Maria (she dropped the "Lydia") heard tales from her father, a village baker, of fugitive slave captures and escapes.

In 1828 when Lydia Maria Francis married David Lee Child (a diplomat, lawyer, and antislavery lobbyist), he converted her to abolitionism by sharing reports of legal cases in Southern courts.[16] As a couple, the Childs seem to have enjoyed a considerable singleness of mind on political issues, a fact that seems overshadowed in William S. Osborne's analysis of friction in the Child family. Osborne claims that David Child was like Bronson Alcott, that is, he was a "stubborn idealist, whose appalling lack of common sense caused his wife as much anguish as Alcott caused his wife and daughters."[17] Such a comparison with Alcott seems plausible only if one fails to take account of the antislavery activism of the Childs. The financial debacle that became increasingly disastrous was primarily due to a courageous scheme that both David and Maria supported; it was a plan to introduce the beet sugar industry into America (a successful sugar-producing enterprise in Europe) and thereby undercut the lucrative sugar monopoly in the South. From the perspective offered by modern times, it is possible to assess such a plan as visionary. But its importance in the early nineteenth century must be evaluated within the context of the abolitionist movement. It was part of a number of produce-boycotting schemes. At least potentially, it was a more potent plan to launch against slavery than plans for pamphlets or new legislative petitions. Unfortunately, the beet sugar enterprise would require a significant outlay of capital (Maria's father had advanced her only $3,000 for a dilapidated farm site in Northampton, Massachusetts), and the Childs could never produce a crop large enough to cover expenses. Still, the idea was sound, as the history of the beet sugar industry later proved.

There is every indication that Maria was tolerant of personal poverty, but her indebtedness to others finally became too stressful. She wrote to a friend: "Poverty is a light thing to me, but a sense of dependence on others is galling."[18] Speaking of the bankrupt beet sugar experiment: "To pump water into a sieve for fourteen years is enough to break the most energetic spirit. I must put a stop to it, or die."[19] At this juncture, David Child was urged to come to New York to edit the *National Anti-Slavery Standard*, a new publication of the Garrisonian wing of the movement. But since he could not easily abandon his beet experiment, Maria agreed to go in David's place. She was the first woman to hold such a post on the staff of a national newspaper.[20]

For years Child labored to pay off the unpaid bills of the failed beet sugar business. But it was her father who again offered to help, allowing Maria and David to move in with him and willing his house to Maria after his death. This assistance was crucial, for the abolitionist movement was practically the only framework within which Maria and David could make a living. They were perceived outside that movement as extremists. They eked out an existence with Maria as chief breadwinner because she could write on many subjects. Her published works (none of which produced sufficient income) included anthologies of children's stories, biographies of famous women, manuals on homemaking and child rearing, an entertainment guide for girls, a coping manual for ex-slaves, books on religion, poetry, feature articles on life in New York City, romantic novels, and essays on behalf of both Black and American Indian well-being.

Despite the disruptive monetary problems, Child did not often waver in working for the abolitionist cause and in presenting democratic values to young audiences. But her uncompromising stance in *An Appeal in Favor of That Class of Americans Called Africans* led to the demise of her magazine for children, as well as to the cancellation of her library card and the ruin of a promising, well-launched career. Her subscription list for *The Juvenile Miscellany* practically vanished overnight after the publication of her *Appeal.* This latter work warrants some attention here because it points to the ideas that might have been forthcoming in stories for children had Maria not offended mainstream thinking. Even though *An Appeal* is generally objective in its presentation of data, it was vehemently denounced in all but staunch abolitionist circles.

The *Appeal* is a thorough, well-organized treatise. It contains information that could have been gleaned from the book collection of the Athenaeum, from the writings of the Black essayist, David Walker (whose *Appeal to the Coloured Citizens of the World* was published in 1829) and from the pages of William Lloyd Garrison's *Liberator,* an abolitionist weekly that began in 1831. But Child's book had a sardonic style that may well have infuriated those citizens who could conceivably tolerate antislavery arguments but not subtle ridicule. For example, Child responded in her *Appeal* to religious rationalizations:

To be violently wrested from his home, and condemned to toil without hope, by Christians, to whom he had done no wrong, was, methinks, a very odd beginning to the poor negro's course of religious instruction![21]

To highlight the interdependence of race prejudice and slavery, she wrote:

We first debase the nature of man by making him a slave, and then very coolly tell him that he must always remain a slave because he does not know how to use freedom. We first crush people to the earth, and then claim the right of trampling on them forever, because they are prostrate.

Truly, human selfishness never invented a rule which worked out so charmingly both ways.[22]

Replying to claims of slave passivity, she asked, in effect, "Where do such claims originate?" She directed attention to the forces behind the chronicling of Black history:

By thousands and thousands, these poor people had died for freedom. They have stabbed themselves for freedom—jumped into the waves for freedom—starved for freedom—fought like very tigers for freedom! But they have been hung, and burned, and shot—and their tyrants have been their historians![23]

She would not accept the notion that Southern humaneness mitigated the evils of the slavery system. She responded to that rationalization with a one-line truism: "The *laws* of a State speak the prevailing *sentiments* of the inhabitants."[24]

Given Child's incisive political commentary, it is paradoxical that Stowe was the popularizer who ultimately provided the emancipation movement with a powerful forward thrust. It can be argued that Child was the one who worked to change the more basic thought patterns that underlie political domination and cultural arrogance. But having said this in Child's favor, it must be added that she was not entirely free from white supremacist cultural influences. The negative side of her emancipationist writings is seen in her *Freedman's Book* published in 1865. It is an uneven anthology that includes patronizing lessons to ex-slaves on bathing, eating, and caring for domestic animals. It also contains Child's "A Meeting in the Swamp," an abridged version of an earlier story entitled "The Black Saxons." This narrative degenerates into typical minstrel characterization ("I'se *thought* a heap. . . . Sometimes I tink one ting, and sometimes I tink anoder ting: and dey all git jumbled up in my head, jest like seed in de cotton").[25] The book does, however, provide an outlet for such eminent Black poets as Phillis Wheatley and Frances E. W. Harper, and it contains well-written biographies of Black leaders.

Child's mainstream ties occasionally asserted themselves, as did the upper-class ties of another abolitionist radical: Eliza Lee Follen (1787–1860).

At this writing, no full-length biographical study of Follen has been published, but a picture of her life as an abolitionist can be pieced together from Follen's five-volume anthology of her husband's works and her memoir of his life. As she describes Charles Follen's active opposition to slavery, she shows us scenes in which she was present and deeply involved.

In the history of mainstream children's literature, Eliza Lee Follen was among the earliest American poets to write for children in a thoroughly modern manner. Her intention in writing poems for *Little Songs* (1832) and in collecting others from anonymous sources was "to catch something of that good-natured pleasantry, that musical nonsense, which makes Mother Goose so attractive to children of all ages."[26] Besides poems for children, and her lengthy tribute to her husband, Follen contributed to many genres of both adult and children's literature.

Follen was part of the prominent Cabot clan of Massachusetts, a sprawling family with connections in high social and intellectual circles.[27] She taught Sunday school in the Unitarian church of her friend and mentor, Dr. William Ellery Channing. Channing was one of the popular Boston ministers who broke his silence on the slavery issue after reading L. Maria Child's *An Appeal.* Eventually Channing wrote an exposé of slavery himself after (as Child reports) she had been "like a busy mouse, gnawing away the network which aristocratic family and friends are all the time weaving around the lion."[28] Follen was part of that network.

The lives of Follen and Child are parallel in several respects, although these women belonged to different social classes. They were both abolitionist activists in that epoch when an antislavery commitment was considerably risky. After Eliza Lee Cabot married Charles Follen in 1828, her life as a radical outcast intensified. Charles was a German emigre who was in exile for his liberal political ideas and activities. With the help of General Lafayette of Revolutionary War fame, he obtained a teaching job at Harvard and was later ordained by Dr. Channing as a Unitarian minister. However, in his efforts to earn a living—whether as Harvard's first professor of German or as pastor of the First Unitarian Church in New York City—he ran into opposition for his abolitionist views. Finding even the means of subsistence became a constant worry.

Eliza Follen therefore redoubled efforts to make money as a writer and as a tutor of Harvard-bound students. So thorough was the *persona non grata* status of the Follens by the time of Charles's death in 1840, that it took four months to locate a chapel in which a memorial service would be allowed.

Following the tragedy of her husband's death in a steamship disaster, Follen became the editor of a children's periodical, *The Child's Friend*, and an abolitionist annual, *The Liberty Bell.*[29] Like L. Maria Child, she worked continuously for the antislavery cause and in a variety of capacities: lecturing, writing, fund raising, and participating actively in abolitionist societies.

A description of one hostile meeting attended by the Follens will give the reader some idea of their central role. A committee of the Massachusetts Anti-Slavery Society was scheduled to meet with a committee of the Massachusetts House of Representatives in early 1837 regarding a proposed resolution to censure abolitionists. The South had been calling for laws in the North that would outlaw abolitionist societies, speeches, and writings, and although Massachusetts had not agreed to this breach of civil liberties, the governor had censured abolitionists in his inaugural address, and the legislature was considering an official reprimand of abolitionist societies and activities. A hearing had been arranged and Charles Follen addressed the House committee on the issue of guaranteed constitutional rights and said that the proposed censure would be "regarded by the mobocrat as a warrant for their outrageous proceedings."[30] (He is referring to antiabolitionist mob violence at Boston's Faneuil Hall at meetings of the Ladies' Anti-Slavery Society, and so on.) Follen claimed that a censure would do more damage than a penal law for it would encourage the proslavery group to "loose again their blood-hounds upon us."[31] At this point a legislator indignantly commanded Follen to be silent and accused him of being "very improper" and making remarks "insulting to this committee."[32]

Everyone then jumped in with charges and countercharges and the meeting almost broke up in total disarray. In recounting this experience, Eliza explains that abolitionists were "most hated, most reviled" at this time, and Charles's friends had reminded him often "that his being a foreigner made it peculiarly offensive in him to take any part in this [antislavery] question."[33] He was not impressed by this argument and went on to contribute some of the most eloquent speeches and monographs to come out of the entire movement.

Eliza Follen responded vigorously to the emancipation cause, and was, as well, a pacifier within the sometimes strife-torn abolitionist organizations. James Russell Lowell praised her as such a healer in these eulogistic lines from his poem "Letter From Boston":

And there, too, was Eliza Follen,
Who scatters fruit-creating pollen
Where'er a blossom she can find
Hardy enough for Truth's north wind. . . .[34]

The "Middle-Roaders": Abbott, Trowbridge, Goodrich

The entry of Abbott, Trowbridge, and Goodrich into the field of antislavery children's literature was the result of varied individual experiences. Jacob Abbott (1803–1879) began comparing Blacks with Caucasians and outlining "proper" Black behavior after the slavery issue began heating up in the 1850s. John T. Trowbridge (1827–1916) belonged to the next generation and was still a young man when he experienced directly the turbulence and violence caused by the 1850 Fugitive Slave Law. Samuel G. Goodrich (1793–1860) was a man of business and politics, adept at taking a middle-of-the-road antislavery position. Whereas Abbott and Goodrich were cautious in the face of controversy (including the slavery controversy), Trowbridge came into his adult years after the white supremacy myth had solidified as an ideology. His ambivalence toward the Black community may have been influenced by this ideology and its increasing diffusion in nineteenth-century American culture.

We are handicapped in our study of Jacob Abbott because he was eventually overshadowed in the chronicles of American history by his son, Lyman. As we can know something about Eliza Lee Follen from the five-volume tribute she paid her husband, so we can gain insights about Jacob through Lyman's biographical essays and full-length *Reminiscences*. Lyman called his father "radical," and he clearly thought of himself as the quintessential "liberal." Both terms, however, seem misapplied when attached to these men. Any comparison of Jacob and Lyman with the Childs, Follens, or other active emancipationists suggests that the Jacob Abbott family was generally of a

different mold. Lyman stated that his politics included an antislavery commitment, but that he was not an abolitionist. Tension over
these two distinct postures (as defined by Lyman) arose within Jacob
Abbott's immediate family. Lyman seems to have picked up from his
father a belief in the distinction between *supporting* emancipation
and actively *planning* for its achievement. Lyman offers the following explanation:

*The Anti-Slavery party . . . believed that the Nation had no more legal
right to interfere with slavery in the States than with serfdom in Russia,
but who also believed that it had an absolute constitutional right to
exclude slavery from national Territories; and that if this were done,
slavery, forbidden extension, would in time die in the Southern States,
with the consent of its present supporters, as it had previously died in the
rest of the civilized world.*[35]

This rationale is essentially one that Jacob adhered to before it was
more elaborately spelled out by Lyman.

Since Washington, D.C., was technically a "territory," Jacob
concurred in the abolitionist conviction that slavery as well as the
slave trade should be banned from this region. He believed that forced
labor within the "District" was "entirely inconsistent with the theoretical principles which this nation advances."[36] He did not see the
lameness of his logic: that policies within a ten-square-mile area
should conform to American democratic principles, while the rest
of America could justifiably remain at odds with those tenets. Jacob
seems to have recoiled from a consistent theory if it entailed bold
action. He encouraged Lyman to become a lawyer and thereby know
the right way to "strike . . . a blow for liberty," but he did not want
to see his son go to Kansas and engage in the struggle to ensure that
Kansas would become a free-soil state.[37]

In *New England and Her Institutions*, a book Jacob Abbott coauthored with two of his brothers in 1835, he identifies indirectly
with the position of the American Colonization Society, the group
that would attempt to resettle American Blacks in Liberia. "Most of
the moral and intellectual worth of the New England states," said
the Abbotts, was in accord with the colonizationists.[38] This stance
placed Jacob at odds with his sister Clara (a Garrisonian abolition-

ist), and with his brother John, who was so outspoken in his condemnation of slavery that he was removed from his Congregational pulpit in Roxbury, Massachusetts, in 1840.

Jacob's conservatism explains part of his ambivalence toward Blacks, but there is another side to his character that indicates why he may have decided to focus on race relations in six children's books. Jacob was a leader in educational reform and progressive child-rearing practices. His ideas about education stressed gentleness, self-knowledge, self-control, the importance of role models, and the importance of educational opportunities for young women. In educational circles he was a pathbreaker.

He had been left alone to complete the raising of four sons when his wife died in childbirth in 1843. He had had several careers by this time: Congregational minister, mathematics professor at Amherst, founder of a secondary school for girls, writer of books on theology and child rearing, author of children's tales, beginning with his twenty-eight-volume "Rollo" books. He had produced several series and gradually formulated a character-type that would be the model for his appealing Black teenager, Rainbow, a character he first developed in 1859.

Rainbow is the mentor of younger children and the carrier of numerous genteel values. As his employer, Handie, is the ideal teacher in an employer/worker relationship, so Rainbow is also an ideal educator, playing that role for many minor characters in the novels. Abbott's ambivalence is displayed in the irony of Rainbow's characterization. The fourteen-year-old Black protagonist is basically fitted for the same middle-class heroes in society as Abbott's Caucasian characters, but he is allowed to achieve no better position than that of a menial urban coachman, the same role assigned to Congo in Abbott's earlier novel about a Black. Congo, however, is frequently depicted as an inferior, whereas Rainbow comes close to being the ideal American youth. Rainbow symbolized the same abstraction that Abbott had been writing about for years, but the author changed his protagonist's skin hue on the eve of the Civil War without substantially correcting his own negative perception of Blacks as a distinct and inferior class.

Commenting upon Abbott as the author of the "first truly American child in fiction," Alice Jordan alludes to Abbott's

Rainbow-type characters as "all equally intelligent and . . . all trusted implicitly by the grownups to shoulder the responsibilities of maturity and take complete charge of the younger ones."[39] But whereas Rainbow is allowed to "shoulder responsibilities" like the other Abbott heroes (Jonas, Beechnut, Mary Bell), he will never be permitted to represent the American dream in its fullness. An unnamed writer in the *North American Review* makes reference to the symbols of that dream, using Abbott's white hero, Jonas, as a case in point:

Domestic and agricultural virtues adorn his sedate career. His little barn chamber is always neat; his tools are always sharp; if he makes a box it holds together, if he digs a ditch there the water flows. He attends Lyceum lectures and experimentalizes on his slate at evening touching the abstruse properties of the number nine. Jonas is American Democracy in its teens; it is Jonas who has conducted our town meetings, built our commonwealth and fought our wars.[40]

Rainbow could be almost substituted for Jonas if it were not for the many regions in America in which Rainbow would not be allowed to set foot in a town meeting for well over a hundred years.

The conservatism that is noticeable in Abbott's nature is not the source of racial ambivalence in John T. Trowbridge. Trowbridge is harder to understand, although it is not difficult to trace both abolitionist and antiabolitionist influences in his childhood. At the time he wrote *Cudjo's Cave* in 1863, he viewed himself as a most energetic emancipationist and as a committed fighter of race prejudice as well. His recollections dating from the 1850s and 1860s (which include the witnessing of outrageous abuses against ex-slaves in the postwar South) indicate no reason for his heavy use of demeaning stereotypes in *Cudjo's Cave*. Perhaps a study of Trowbridge's milieu is as close as we can come to a plausible explanation of his contradictions—a milieu that a popular magazine writer, playwright, versifier, and novelist such as Trowbridge could have easily imbibed without much conscious awareness. As a writer for the stage, he may have been particularly impressed by the "stage Negro" tradition of his day and by its many white supremacist implications.

In any case, he did employ minstrel portraiture on the one hand (especially by his depiction of the free Black, "Toby") while on the other he expressed the mood of a radicalized, post-1850 Boston. He credits his full conversion to abolitionism to the scenes he witnessed as slave-catchers tried to implement the 1850 Fugitive Slave Law. In particular, he was moved by the imprisonment and deportation in 1854 of Anthony Burns, an alleged runaway. Trowbridge describes the tension he witnessed in Boston: "a rallying cry . . . 'Another man kidnapped!' ran with electric swiftness through the city."[41] Trowbridge's eyewitness account is worth quoting at some length, as it evokes his new-found fervor and the revolutionary spirit that was reaching a crescendo level in the North.

> . . . *Boston was in a turmoil of excitement. Public meetings were held, an immense one in Faneuil Hall on the evening preceding the removal of the fugitive; and that night there was a gallant attack upon the Court House in which he was confined. A stick of timber was used as a battering ram against one of the western doors, which was broken in; there was a melee of axes, bludgeons, and firearms, and one of the marshal's guards was killed. . . .*
>
> *Reports of the Faneuil Hall meeting and of the assault on the Court House rallied an immense crowd to Court Square and the adjacent streets the next morning, to witness the final act of the drama. It was a black day for Boston, that 27th of May, 1854; the passions of men were stirred to their depths, and often friends were divided against friends. I remember meeting in the crowd one with whom I had been on intimate terms not long before. . . . Drawing me aside in the crowd, and opening his vest, he grimly called my attention to a revolver thrust into an inside pocket.*
>
> *"What's that for, Ned?" I asked, in the old familiar way.*
>
> *"I am one of the marshal's private deputies," he answered, with brutal frankness. "There are over a hundred of us in the Court House there and in this crowd. At the first sign of an attempt to rescue that damn nigger, we are going in for a bloody fight. I hope there'll be a row, for it's the top-round of my ambition to shoot an abolitionist."*
>
> *"Well, Ned," I replied, "you may possibly have an opportunity to shoot me; for if I see a chance to help that 'damned nigger' I'm afraid I shall have to take a hand."[42]*

Trowbridge continues with a description of the special contingents

of police and militia, the windows "draped in black in token of the
city's humiliation," and the march of the prisoner to the Long Wharf

*over the very ground where the first blood was shed preluding the Revo-
lutionary struggle, some of it the blood of a Black man. . . .*[43]

Prior to Trowbridge's move to Boston, he was not inclined to
make this kind of association between slaves and the patriots of
American independence. Slavery was a disagreeable subject because
his hometown pastor preached about it from the pulpit, and in
Trowbridge's mind, the frustrations of childhood were largely church-
related. His Calvinist family spent the entire Sabbath sitting in pews,
and for a child like Trowbridge, this was experienced as near-
torture. Moreover, while his father condemned slavery, in equal measure he condemned antislavery activism. There was no "moral earth-
quake" in the frontier farming community of Ogden, New York, as
there would be later in Boston. Trowbridge recorded his father's views
as follows:

*"Of course it's wrong; nothing under heaven can make it right for one
human being to own another. But what's the use of fighting it here at the
North? Leave it where it is, and it will die of itself. Any serious attempt
to abolish it will bring on civil war and break up the Union. . . ."*
*He often made use of these stereotyped words; but he would add, "I'm
opposed to the spread of it; we've a right to take that stand. . . ."*[44]

Such specific instances of indoctrination may be less important
to an understanding of Trowbridge than the overall complexity of
his life as a social climber. Like L. Maria Child, Trowbridge spent his
early years outside the boundaries of the genteel class. The hardships
of his adolescence may have produced in him some susceptibility to
abolitionism and some sympathetic feelings toward an underclass.
His life story resembles the plot of a Horatio Alger potboiler. He
took advantage of what bookishness there was on the farm (his mother
had been a teacher and his father subscribed to the local library).
When he was seventeen years old, his father died and he became
economically and intellectually adrift. He stayed with a relative so
that he could walk twenty-five miles per day to attend classes in

reading and elocution. He was self-taught in Latin and managed to learn French from a family in New York City that gave him lodgings when he journeyed there to make his fortune. At that time he was only nineteen, but he had already had a career as a teacher in Illinois and in New York. He lived on one meal per day and was sometimes forced to dispense with dinner altogether.

His move to Boston in 1847 proved entirely fortuitous. He was in his twentieth year and was equipped to meet an urgent demand felt by the editors of the Boston weeklies: "Stories, give us stories!"[45] Trowbridge had tried his hand in many genres, but was still submitting poems for the most part. He took the hint about "stories" and gained entry into the world of periodical publishing.

The story of Trowbridge brings us close to the history of Boston periodicals and other publishing enterprises. While he does not appear to be in the same class as Samuel Goodrich as an opportunist, he was venturesome, creative, and promptly adopted by the New England intelligentsia. His abolitionism was about as deep as one finds generally in this comfortable group. Like Harriet Beecher Stowe, Trowbridge could express indignation over injustice when it was flaring up on all sides.

He published *Cudjo's Cave* in 1863 when the war was approaching its concluding phase. The novel was his "own humble part in [the Civil War]"; it was "frankly designed to fire the Northern heart."[46] By this time, Northerners were beginning to think of the future, and Trowbridge rightly concluded that race prejudice would be a continuing problem.

The country had been but slowly awakening to a consciousness of the truth that the slave was not only to be freed; he was also to cease to be a merely passive occasion of the contest, and to become our active ally. Too many calling themselves patriots still opposed emancipation and the arming of Blacks. . . . The idol-house of the old prejudice was shattered, but not demolished. I was impatient to hurl my firebrand into the breach.[47]

Unfortunately, this foresight did not result in a work of fiction that attacked the white supremacy myth.

While Trowbridge has his tragic side, Samuel Griswold Goodrich is portrayed by even a sympathetic biographer as a somewhat ludicrous speculator in the education market. Trowbridge comes across as someone who used entrepreneurial as well as creative skills; Goodrich is characterized as having a single-minded penchant for lining his pockets. Such is the impression that often accompanies a popular cult figure—someone who is working every kind of angle, skillfully manipulating public taste, developing new forms of communication that may or may not catch hold of the popular imagination and result in a windfall. It is hard to study Goodrich without concluding that he had just one or two ideas, but could recycle them *ad infinitum* without antagonizing his incredibly loyal audience.

He has been called the father of the nonfiction series book, whereas Jacob Abbott is referred to as the American father of the story series books. But writing stories, that is, narratives with a fictional emphasis, requires a different kind of imagination. Goodrich could hire ghost writers, assemble data, and produce what appeared, on the surface, to be books of information. Some of his British critics accused him of dishing out a lot of "slip-slop" that had little scholarly credibility.[48] Certainly he gave voice to a stream of ethnocentric opinions. Yet he consistently opposed slavery. The path he charted for himself was, as he explained, the Americanization of literature, both juvenile and adult. Slavery was a major source of embarrassment in such a program.

Goodrich, therefore, scattered antislavery comments throughout his "tales" and his history and geography books for children. But simultaneously he stressed the inferiority and childishness of peoples in Asia and Africa, and the inferiority (and often the unscrupulousness) of the peoples of Europe. His racist and chauvinistic attitudes are so extreme that it would almost seem as if his opposition to slavery was a mere formality. Or it may have galled him that Great Britain, one of his favorite targets of criticism, had outlawed slavery in 1833; as long as the U.S. supported it, he was unable to make his Anglophobia sound convincing. To a modern reader, his overgeneralizations would be comical if it were not for the sobering fact that Goodrich wrote over 100 books, claimed to have supervised 50 more, and enjoyed a sales record that is estimated at 12 million copies. Twenty-eight Goodrich titles were still in print in 1902.[49]

A sampling of his cultural commentaries will suffice as a clue to his ethnocentrism. With respect to the Moors of Northern Africa, Goodrich provides the following description:

They have the same rudeness and austerity [as the Turks], while piratical habits, and an unsettled government, have rendered them more mercenary, turbulent, and treacherous.[50]

The central and southern African peoples are presented as the ultimate hedonists.

Improvidence, gentleness, and thoughtless gaiety, appear to compose the leading features of the negro character. The natives, in possession of a fertile soil, which supplies the necessities of life with little labor, . . . devote themselves wholly to pleasure.[51]

Both the British and the Chinese are characterized as thieves.

Let me . . . give you one piece of advice; if you ever go to London take good care of your pocket-book and your watch![52]
The Chinese are great fibbers, and very much addicted to cheating.[53]

Religious intolerance is pervasive:

The truth is that Chinese are an ignorant and superstitious people, and their religion is a system contrived by cunning priests to obtain influence over them. Like the religion of Mahomet, it is a false religion.[54]

In a dialogue about the pope, Goodrich gives full voice to his anti-Catholicism:

Ellen—*One thing astonishes me . . . that [Catholics] think it is pleasing to God for these monks and friars to spend their lives in idleness and beggary. It astonishes me to see them believe that they can save their souls by kissing the toe of a marble image in Saint Peter's, and by ascending a particular pair of stairs on their knees. How is it possible that they can be thus degraded?*
Merry—*Their priests teach them thus.*[55]

Attitudes of this sort were widespread in the nineteenth century, and would not have caused much comment among Whites within the proslavery or antislavery mainstream. It was one issue—emancipation—that led Southern writers to place Goodrich in the abolitionist camp, whereas antislavery periodicals condemned him for his equivocations.[56] He could sound like the most ardent emancipationist in one breath, and then reverse himself in the next. For example, he wrote in the *New York Evening Post* in 1856:

I direct your attention to the fact that slavery . . . has waxed fat, and kicks against the law and the Constitution; that it mocks the fundamental principles of our government; that it overturns the liberty of speech and press; that where it prevails it exercises a despotism, only to be paralleled in savage and barbarous countries; . . .[57]

But acting as if none of this mattered, he continued his public letter to "a friend in Kentucky":

We make no war on slavery where it is established. . . . We accept it as sheltered by the compromise of the Constitution. Within this boundary it is sacred. We desire to leave it, with all its good and evil, to those who are interested in it and responsible for it. . . . We war not against slaveholders, but slave extensionists.[58]

"Extension" became the ultimate rallying cry. For someone like Goodrich, opposing extension translated into the "middle road"—a position that did not require a fundamental revision of cultural preconceptions.

As a man of business, a Massachusetts state legislator, and United States consul in Paris, it is not surprising that Goodrich was a compromiser. He had a hard-won middle-class status that was probably accompanied by some bitterness. His struggle to the top may have made him empathetic toward other outsiders, or, contrariwise, energetic in keeping the "out" groups in their "place."

Goodrich was the son of a Congregational minister in Ridgefield, Connecticut, and therefore part of the solidly entrenched middle class. But being an indifferent scholar in childhood, he was denied the privilege of attending college. His parents could feel justified in not throwing good money after bad, but it placed their son, Samuel, in the awkward position of educating himself, sponging on friends, and playing the humiliating part of the fawning nephew vis-à-vis his influential and respectable uncles.[59] He was blessed, however, with a loyal and talented friend, George Sheldon, who supervised his self-teaching and joined with Goodrich in a book publishing and selling enterprise in 1816. They published an eight-volume octavo edition of Sir Walter Scott's works—all pirated! Goodrich thus started his long career of gauging the possibilities of a popular literary market. His works for children began at the same time with toybooks and school texts.[60]

"Peter Parley" was the idiosyncratic character devised by Goodrich for the role of friend and guide to young readers. Goodrich viewed this mythical figure as a device, "a principal part of my machinery," as he put it.[61] The character was a trademark, a marketing gimmick comparable to other devices Goodrich contrived for his many series and holiday gift books. His publishing activities proliferated steadily, even while he was a state legislator from 1837 to 1838 and consul in Paris from 1851 to 1853.

It is hard to assess Goodrich's commitment to the antislavery cause because it is so easy to view him as mouthing the platitudes of the American creed for some expedient purpose. His upward mobility was accompanied by stress, as we have seen to be the case with most of the other individuals profiled in this chapter. But we can probably never determine satisfactorily whether social marginality in these individuals made them receptive to a liberal cause, or conversely, made them ready and eager to keep the doors of the middle class closed to potential competitors, especially Blacks.

Looking back over the lives of these six authors, we see an ambivalence toward African Americans whether the writers were men or women. The men may have felt more threatened than the women by Blacks who could become potential business rivals. Still, the women engaged in stereotyping no less than the men, despite their concerns about family life and human rights. It must be added, however, that the connection between slaves and women in the abolitionist era existed at a level that reached far beyond concerns about family and business. The antislavery cause was like a spotlight illumining the many civil rights grievances of women.

Practically every antislavery meeting offered examples of the contradiction between democratic rhetoric and the oppressive muffling of female voices. Records of the meetings describe abolitionist women, who sat silently in the back of the hall as the prevailing social code demanded. The story of selected abolitionist women in Alma Lutz's *Crusade for Freedom: Women of the Antislavery Movement* highlights a constant theme: an evolving self-awareness and quest for self-liberation. "We would have the name of *Woman*," writes Elizabeth Chandler in the early 1800s, "as a security for the rights of the sex. These rights are withheld from the female slave; and as we value and would demand them for ourselves, must we not ask them for her?"[62] Angelina Grimké wrote to a friend: "I feel that it is not only the cause of the slave that we plead, but the cause of woman as a moral, responsible being."[63] Maria Weston Chapman admonished women:

we see that women, generally, cannot become other than abolitionists in the abstract, till their sentiments respecting the rights and consequent duties of women are the growth of their own minds.[64]

This emerging self-involvement may have diverted attention away from the emancipation movement, but in Chapman's view it was a case of "freedom begets freedom," as she said.[65] One double standard will inevitably illumine another.

As women found it ironic that abolitionist men would deny them freedom of speech, so they found it absurd that mention of immoral relationships between female slaves and male slave owners resulted in the charge that women emancipationists practiced "promiscuous conversation." Codes of conduct had a built-in male bias. Influential institutions buttressed these codes.

Institutions impacted directly upon both adults and children. The stand that an individual might take would likely be affected by trends in community organizations.

The School, Church, and Press

American antislavery writers for children had tie-ins with institutions that both strengthened and weakened their opportunities to oppose race prejudice. Schools, churches, and publishing enterprises helped them develop skills, gain experience with children, and make a living in a respected occupation. However, these community and business agencies were typically steeped in the white supremacist ideology of the period.

Self-development was perhaps the most important by-product of school teaching for L. Maria Child, Harriet B. Stowe, and John T. Trowbridge. They all wanted more educational experiences than they had been given, and they were all employed as teachers when they were still in their teenage years. Eliza Follen and Jacob Abbott had better academic opportunities in their young adult period, and they developed an interest in children that led to careers as educators and children's authors. As a means to an end, then, and as a viable career choice, schools were significant. But school was a place with a potentially negative influence upon a child's perceptions and behavior. For Black children, it could mean abusive treatment from the White community, and for European American children, it usually meant indoctrination in racist ideas.

Seven states had instituted systems of public education prior to the Civil War, and Massachusetts had passed a compulsory education law in 1852.[66] At the private level, some New England schools had been racially integrated as early as 1798, but Blacks sometimes requested a separate school because of the harassment of their children (e.g., such a request was issued in Hartford, Connecticut, in 1830).[67] Such protective action on behalf of the Black child could have been justified on other grounds as well. Teaching materials, for example, had a white supremacist slant.

School textbook writers resided overwhelmingly in the New England states, and there can be little doubt about the sociopolitical intentions that informed their work. In 1789 Noah Webster, in his *An American Selection of Lessons in Reading and Speaking*, said that his goal in writing schoolbooks was, in part, "to diffuse the principles of virtue and patriotism."[68] However, the "patriotism" of the schoolbook writers was such as to disallow positive traits in the portrayal of Africans and African Americans. Ruth Miller Elson, who has analyzed the cultural content in more than one thousand nineteenth-century schoolbooks, found just two exceptions to this rule: in the pre–Civil War period gaiety was sometimes attributed to

Blacks, and in the post–Civil War period the one positive feature was loyalty.[69]

The contradictions surrounding the slavery issue seem more blatant in the textbooks than in other genres, perhaps because slavery is explicitly condemned, yet there is an implied justification for slavery in the portraits of Blacks. They are assigned traits that are more openly degrading, as well as threatening to Whites, than the traits we have seen so far in the works of original fiction. For example, Elson documents the racist indoctrination that was experienced by children in the late eighteenth and early nineteenth centuries in their first eight years of schooling:

[Negroes] are a brutish people, having little more of humanity but the form. . . .
Their mental powers, in general, participate in the imbecility of their bodies. . . .
Africa has justly been called the country of monsters. . . . Even man, in this quarter of the world exists in a state of lowest barbarism. . . .[70]

One way that authors harmonized such attitudes in schoolbooks with the antislavery movement was by focusing almost entirely on the slave trade, and then blaming that evil on the French, English, Dutch, Portuguese, and Spanish! Elson notes that according to school texts, the antidemocratic institution of slavery was thrust upon the United States "before America had charge of its own destiny."[71] From this angle, Whites were absolved from any responsibility vis-à-vis slavery other than tutelage over the allegedly childish or brutish ex-Africans.

School textbook publishers, notes Elson, were notoriously slow about making revisions. But given the prevalence of white supremacist attitudes in the nineteenth century, it seems unlikely that changes would have meant advances in Black portraiture.[72] Attitudes within the school environment kept pace with mainstream opinion, as did attitudes in most major church groups.[73]

The organized churches had both a positive and a negative influence upon the drive toward emancipation. It is impossible to read an account of abolitionist activism (as in Alma Lutz's *Crusade for Freedom*) without being impressed by the number of Quakers who joined the cause. But, at the same time, we learn that the printer for the New York–based journal, the *National Antislavery Standard* was read out of the Friends Meeting because he was viewed as a Garrisonian extremist.[74]

Unitarians were also conspicuous as participants in abolitionism, yet William Ellery Channing, the leading antebellum Unitarian in Boston, had a lukewarm attitude toward antislavery activism. When he did speak out in *Thoughts of Slavery*, he condemned the militant wing of the antislavery movement so harshly that Garrison told his readers of the *Liberator* that Channing's book was deceptive, unrealistic, and inconsistent on at least twenty-four counts.[75]

One of the worst blows to antislavery organizations was the Pastoral Letter emanating from the General Association of Congregational Ministers in 1837. It condemned the discussion of abolition in the churches. Moreover, some statements seemed to suggest that ministers thought they were being upstaged:

Your minister is ordained by God to be your teacher, and is commanded to feed that flock over which the Holy Ghost hath made him overseer. If there are certain topics upon which he does not preach . . . it is a violation of sacred and important rights to encourage a stranger to present them.[76]

The Letter also criticized women in the role of reformers, stating bluntly that "the appropriate duties and influence of woman is in her dependence."[77]

In 1840 ministers with these misgivings were powerful enough to help split the main abolitionist organization into the American Antislavery Society and the American and Foreign Antislavery Society, thereby weakening the movement. Similarly, the organized Methodist and Baptist churches divided into distinct factions in the 1840s (the Southern Methodists joining the Methodist Episcopal Church South). Presbyterians engaged in an internal struggle over slavery until the beginning of the Civil War.[78]

Fratricidal behavior within the emancipation movement was so disillusioning to some members that L. Maria Child practically vanished from abolitionist circles between 1840 and 1852. Only the shock of "bleeding Kansas" and the martyrdom of John Brown aroused her to renewed participation.

Two interdenominational organizations, the American Sunday School Union and the American Tract Society (established in 1824 and 1825, respectively), may have affected the abolitionist movement, but their impact is hard to trace. According to Frank Keller Walter, "the slavery question was too delicate for most churches to handle as freely [as the temperance question]."[79] However, one of the main purposes of these organizations was the circulation of the Bible and its teachings, and the Bible can be read as a revolutionary book. Certainly the stories of Moses, Esther, Christ Jesus, and others are stories of civil disobedience. It can be argued that Jesus was more vitriolic in his Pharisee-directed criticisms than William Lloyd Garrison was in lambasting slaveholders.

Moreover, by establishing libraries for children (as many as 33,580 by 1870, with an aggregate of 8,346,153 volumes)[80] the Sunday School Union was a vital institution in young lives. It was such a Union that served as the locale for the publishing firm of Carlton and Porter, publisher of *The Child's Anti-Slavery Book.*

On the other hand, Edwin Wilbur Rice's history of the American Sunday School Union indicates a prevailing "white man's burden" concept. People of color were referred to by ministers as "Cuban bandits" and "Philippine negritos." Children in Sunday school, notes Rice, will bring the gospel home and "then the bandits will disband, and savages will become civilized."[81] As for Blacks in the American South, Rice quotes Dr. E. K. Bell on their potential for "redemption":

If the means were placed in the hands of the American Sunday-School Union to enable it vigorously to prosecute its work among the negro children . . . within ten years the crimes of rape and murder, the crimes of lynching by burning and mutilation, would practically cease.[82]

Bell continues with the declaration that "The regeneration and rehabilitating of the Black race can only be accomplished by . . . putting the gospel where the Holy Spirit can work before the flesh and the devil have pre-empted the occupancy."[83] Sunday School Union officials clearly saw Blacks as disruptive and inferior.

As a major socializing agency, the organized churches in the antebellum era missed an opportunity to contribute to improved "race relations" in succeeding generations. The churches were hopelessly divided on the slavery issue and could send only an ambivalent signal.

On the other hand, the inanimate machine had an unexpected importance. A technological revolution prepared the way for the press and the publishing industry to play a large role in abolitionism. Steam-powered printing presses (pioneered in Germany in 1810) created an efficient means for issuing propagandistic materials at an unprecedented rate. The possibilities of the "Adams Power Press" of 1827 were so quickly recognized that abolitionist lobbyists would soon be able to make a livelihood (although a meager one) by working for the organizations that published antislavery weeklies. This development led to an emerging organizational "hard core" between 1830 and 1865—a network that was morale building and relatively easy to coordinate. Every act of martyrdom or near martyrdom refueled the network and was put to service as consciousness-raising material. By being economically viable, the publishers of cheap weeklies, pamphlets, and books could oversee an ongoing movement with two important components: a stable corps of reliable workers, plus an endless supply of distributable antislavery messages. Children's writers were involved with this publishing phenomenon in several capacities—as writers, editors, publishers, and advisers.

The printing revolution in the 1830s (the new presses, paper-cutting machines, transportation improvements, and paper production techniques) resulted in the reduction of newspaper costs from six cents to one penny per copy. The number of possible prints per day increased from 2,000 to 55,000.[84] Until the public became used to these changes, it tended to overestimate the power of abolitionists—to view their antislavery printing activities as a sign of wealth and collusion with foreign powers and fund-raisers.[85] In fact the new technology was simply put to such good use that free pamphlets and other materials could be widely distributed.

While cheap publishing opportunities contributed to the vitality of the emancipation movement, there were also disadvantages connected with the new technology. Messages could be circulated quickly and widely, and angry antiabolitionist mobs could be rapidly assembled. Such mobs plagued antislavery workers and made it easy for the general public to judge antislavery viewpoints as fanatical and disruptive. Abolitionists charged several New York newspapers with inciting the riot in 1834 that demolished churches as well as Negro sections of New York City.[86] With such "respectable" journalistic backing, both upper- and lower-class groups could be successfully rallied against antislavery societies.

It can be argued that a very particular publishing event (the serialized *Uncle Tom's Cabin*) and a regional struggle ("bleeding Kansas") had to overlap before radical abolitionists could gain ground in their fight with proslavery forces. The new power of the press was not sufficient of itself to liberalize the community. However, the quick spread of antiabolitionist indignation was one of the underlying reasons for the rapid demise of L. Maria Child's journal, *The Juvenile Miscellany*.

Moreover, the antislavery press remained strictly in the minority. High circulation newspapers and magazines are geared to reflect majority opinion. Even a historian writing in 1953, Howard R. Floan, echoed the nineteenth-century attitude toward abolitionist authors (Garrison, Phillips, Whittier, Lowell, Emerson, Thoreau, etc.) and labeled them fanatical troublemakers. He commended the nineteenth-century New England magazines (*The North American Review*, *New England Magazine*, and *Waverly Magazine*) for being "balanced" and sympathetic toward the Southern view of slavery. For Floan, slavery was not an unmitigated evil, and he expressed approval of the mainstream New England periodicals for having taken this position.

An antebellum reviewer for *The North American Review*, for example, found portraits of the plantation system "truthful" when those portraits treated the system as beneficent. He was convinced when J. P. Kennedy, the author of *Swallow Barn, or A Sojourn in the Old Dominion*, claimed that slaves held the master in "profound reverence."[87] A correspondent for *The New England Magazine* reported that Blacks were better fed, clothed, and conditioned in Charleston than in New York. The reporter said that he wished he might "paint the cheerful, undescribed and indescribable negro, whose laugh is so ready, and is such an explosion of joy, that it is a pity, when it is so easy to make him laugh, that he should ever cry."[88] Mutual affection between slaves and slaveholders is a theme that was continuously reiterated in both of these periodicals, according to Floan's analysis.

As they editorialized about abolitionists, the mainstream periodical writers portrayed the antislavery activists as intolerant, mean-spirited insurrectionists. *The North American Review* was saddened because the "tone of [James Russell Lowell's] mind . . . [had] been injured by contact with them." John Greenleaf Whittier was condemned in the *Review* for his "virulent tone."[89]

In another representative periodical, *Waverly Magazine*, the treatment of the slaveholding South was entirely sympathetic. The editors praised a book written in response to *Uncle Tom's Cabin* called *Notes on Uncle Tom's Cabin* as being a logical answer to its allegations and influences against slavery and its institutions. *Waverly* readers were told that *Notes* "clearly disposes of many allegations in Mrs. Stowe's work," and furthermore, "it will serve to modify [the reader's] animosities towards our brethren of the South, for an evil which prudence would not require to be removed too hastily."[90]

It would seem from a sampling of major periodicals that the abolitionist press could do little more than repeat the role of the proverbial voice "crying in the wilderness." The antislavery editors did much to sustain a dissident movement, but they could hardly compete with a periodical like the long-lived *North American Review*, which has remained, for the most part, extant from 1815 to the present day.

Conclusion

The antislavery children's writers in America were closely associated with leading social institutions. But such institutions as schools, churches, and mainstream publications were not generally constructive in their portrayals of Blacks. The antebellum era presented a confused and turbulent social milieu in which to attempt the overthrow of race prejudice. It is not surprising, therefore, that the writers had different centers of emphasis. Abbott and Stowe could be called "religious moralists," authors who continuously stressed personal piety. Goodrich belongs with this group, also, for he punctuated his children's texts with the popular homilies of the times. Follen and Child are not indifferent to personal piety, but their sensitivity to problems of justice places them in what I call a "social moralist" category. Although Trowbridge is less consistent than Follen and Child, he also includes political argumentation in his writings in juxtaposition with platitudes about redemption.

Nothing has been included here about writers of narratives in *The Child's Anti-Slavery Book*, Julia Colman and Matilda G. Thompson. They did not achieve enough eminence in the nineteenth century to make them interesting to scholars in the twentieth, but they were among that huge corps of workers connected to the Sunday School Union movement.

Writers who became prominent after the Civil War expanded children's literature generically, but their concerns about North/South reunification did not lead them down an egalitarian path. Instead, Black characters were dehumanized in fiction with increasing severity. Abolitionist leaders did not foresee this problem at the children's book level, but they sounded warnings in the political sphere.

As the war drew to a close, Frederick Douglass, Wendell Phillips, and others predicted a still impending struggle for citizenship rights for Blacks, and they opposed Garrison's plan to disband the American Antislavery Society. In 1865, an alarm was also sounded by Susan B. Anthony about the possible failure of the quest for equal rights: Slavery, she said, "could readily be re-enthroned under the new guise of Negro disfranchisement"; and she added that "unless the Negro was given the vote, rebels would be put in office and a new code of laws apprenticing Negroes would be formed, establishing a new form of slavery."[91]

The intellectual underpinning for this "new form of slavery" can be traced in books for children throughout the period 1866 to 1900.

Notes

1. Thomas F. Gossett, *Uncle Tom's Cabin and American Culture* (Dallas: Southern Methodist University Press, 1985), 43.
2. Ibid., 45.
3. Ibid., 61.
4. Ibid., 87–88.
5. Philip Van Doren Stern, ed., *The Annotated Uncle Tom's Cabin* (New York: Paul S. Eriksson, Inc., 1964), 20.
6. Gossett, 91.
7. Gayle Kimball, "Harriet Elizabeth Beecher Stowe," in *American Women Writers*, ed. Lina Mainiero (New York: Frederick Ungar Publishing Co., 1982), 176.
8. Gossett, 15.

9.   Ibid., 4.
10. Stern, 32.
11. John Townsend Trowbridge, *My Own Story: With Recollections of Noted Persons* (Boston: Houghton, Mifflin and Co., 1903), 183. With regard to the missing funds, it needs to be noted that slave relief societies, with some frequency, allegedly lost track of the money they raised. This was an issue causing considerable anguish. Charges against Stowe need to be viewed in this context.
12. Stern, 30.
13. Kimball, 177.
14. Gossett, 63
15. Milton Meltzer, *Tongue of Flame: The Life of Lydia Maria Child* (New York: Thomas Y. Crowell Co., 1965), 185.
16. Margaret Farrand Thorp, *Female Persuasion: Six Strong-Minded Women* (New Haven: Yale University Press, 1949), 185.
17. William S. Osborne, *Lydia Maria Child* (Boston: Twayne Publishers, 1980), 23.
18. Meltzer, 70.
19. Osborne, 23.
20. Thorp, 233.
21. L. Maria Child, *An Appeal in Favor of Americans Called Africans* (Boston: Allen & Ticknor, 1833; rpt. New York: Arno Press and the *New York Times*, 1968), 3.
22. Meltzer, 39.
23. Ibid.
24. Child, 76.
25. L. Maria Child, *The Freedman's Book* (Boston: Ticknor and Fields, 1865), 108.
26. Bert Roller, "Early American Writers for Children," *Elementary English Review* 8:9 (November, 1931): 214.
27. Phyllis Moe. "Eliza Lee Cabot Follen," in *American Women Writers*, ed. Lina Mainiero (New York: Frederick Ungar Publishing Co., 1980), 58.
28. Meltzer, 43–44.
29. Elizabeth Bancroft Schlesinger, "Two Early Harvard Wives: Eliza Farrar and Eliza Follen," *New England Quarterly* 38:2 (June 1965): 164.
30. [Eliza Lee Follen, ed.], *The Works of Charles Follen, with a Memoir of His Life in Five Volumes.* Vol.1. (Boston: Hilliard, Gray, and Co., 1841), 390–391.
31. Ibid., 391.
32. Ibid.
33. Ibid., 388.
34. Schlesinger, 166.
35. Lyman Abbott, *Reminiscences* (Boston: Houghton, Mifflin Co., 1915), 98.
36. Mary E. Quinlivan, "Race Relations in the Ante-bellum Children's Literature of Jacob Abbott," *Journal of Popular Culture* 16:1 (Summer 1982): 29.
37. Abbott, 106.
38. Quinlivan, 28.
39. Alice M. Jordan, *From Rollo to Tom Sawyer and Other Papers* (Boston: The Horn Book, Inc., 1948), 76.
40. Ibid., 75
41. Trowbridge, 219.
42. Ibid., 221–222.
43. Ibid., 224.
44. Ibid., 214.
45. Ibid., 135.
46. Ibid., 262.
47. Ibid., 260–261.
48. Daniel Roselle, *Samuel Griswold Goodrich, Creator of Peter Parley* (Albany, NY: State University of New York Press, 1968), 43.
49. Ibid., 53–54.
50. S. G. Goodrich, *History of Africa* (Louisville, KY: Morton and Griswold, 1850), 15.

51. Ibid., 17.
52. S. G. Goodrich, *Peter Parley's Tales of Europe* (Philadelphia: Charles Desilver, 1860), 35–36.
53. [Nathaniel Hawthorne], *Parley's Universal History on the Basis of Geography*, vol. 1 (New York: Nafis and Cornish, 1845), 299–301.
54. S. G. Goodrich. *The Tales of Peter Parley About Asia* (Philadelphia: Charles Desilver, 1939), 55–56.
55. Peter Parley, ed. [S. Goodrich], *Balloon Travels of Robert Merry and His Young Friends Over Various Countries in Europe* (New York: Derby and Jackson, 1859), 191.
56. Roselle, 76.
57. Ibid., 139
58. Ibid., 140
59. Ibid., 21–24.
60. Ibid., 27.
61. Ibid., 39.
62. Alma Lutz, *Crusade for Freedom: Women of the Antislavery Movement* (Boston: Beacon Press, 1968), 12.
63. Ibid., 106.
64. Ibid., 117.
65. Ibid., 199.
66. Ruth Miller Elson, *Guardians of Tradition: American Schoolbooks of the Nineteenth Century* (Lincoln: University of Nebraska Press, 1964), 6.
67. Peter M. Bergman, *The Chronological History of the Negro in America* (New York: Harper and Row, 1969), 80, 139.
68. Elson, 2.
69. Ibid., 88.
70. Ibid., 87.
71. Ibid., 98.
72. Even in the 1970s, high school textbooks continued the dissemination of conservative interpretations of abolitionism and Reconstruction. See Patrick Groff's "Abolition in High School History Texts: The Latest Versions" in *Negro Educational Review* 32:2 (April 1981) and "The Freedman's Bureau in High School History Texts" in *Journal of Negro Education* 51:4 (1982).
73. The genetic assumptions about Blacks that are suggested in school books are also included in Horace Bushnell's guidebook for parents. His chapter entitled "The Out-Populating Power of the Christian Stock" in *Christian Nurture* deals with the way "education, habit, feeling, and character . . . become thoroughly inbred in the stock." He urges that piety be propagated, for God ordains a superior race to carry "the godly seed." After assuring his readers that civilization is "inbred," he then pinpoints savages, slaves, Jews, Mohammedans, Latin Americans, and American Aborigines as groups that are clearly outside the realm of civility. See *Christian Nurture* by Horace Bushnell (New York: Charles Scribner's Sons, 1861; original title: *Views of Christian Nurture and of Subjects Adjacent Thereto*, 1847), 212, 207, 213.
74. Lutz, 176.
75. Ibid., 69–70
76. Ibid., 115.
77. Ibid.
78. Craven, 200–201
79. Frank Keller Walter, "A Poor but Respectable Relation—the Sunday School Library," *Library Quarterly* 12:3 (July 1942): 737.
80. Ibid., 736.
81. Edwin Wilbur Rice, *The Sunday-School Movement and the American Sunday School Union* (Philadelphia: American Sunday-School Union, 1917), 411–412.
82. Ibid., 412.

83. Ibid.
84. Leonard L. Richards, *"Gentlemen of Property and Standing": Anti-Abolition Mobs in Jacksonian America* (New York: Oxford University Press, 1970), 72.
85. Ibid., 73
86. Ibid., 150.
87. Howard R. Floan, *The South in Northern Eyes, 1831–1861* (Austin: University of Texas Press, 1953), 90.
88. Ibid., 92–93.
89. Ibid., 102–103.
90. Ibid., 106.
91. Lutz, 294.

Part Two

The Postbellum Years

The Master he says we are all free, but . . . it don't mean we is equal.
— George King, Free Black from South Carolina

Our literature has become not only Southern in type but distinctly Confederate in sympathy.
— Albion W. Tourgee, Northern judge and novelist, 1888

Yankeeism took to its heart the Lost Cause.
— Historian C. Vann Woodward, 1971

Chapter Four
Children's Fiction
A Sampling

Post–Civil War cultural history is incomplete if it fails to take account of the one-sided delineations of African and African American character in books for the young. Occasionally in postbellum children's fiction there is a return to antebellum ambivalence about Black personality (e.g., in the protest fiction of Martha Finley when she is addressing the Ku Klux Klan problem or in the social satires of Mark Twain when he uses the slavery era as his setting). However, in the many plantation tales and adventure stories, there is seldom a thematic counterbalance to the depiction of a race hierarchy. Even in the protest novels and satires, a conviction of Black inferiority is embodied in the narratives through a one-sided treatment of slave and ex-slave characterization.

The irony in this handling of the Black image is readily apparent. The evil of slavery—the dehumanization of human beings—became the symbolic center of the war, yet dehumanization is now to be continued in a new guise. Either serfdom or imperial domination are hailed in the postbellum children's literature as entirely proper. In fact, slavery itself is to be refashioned as a benign (even blissful) lifestyle, as a life of constructive tutelage. Slavery was created by "the hand of an All-wise Providence," writes Joel Chandler Harris, and its design was "the scheme of a vast university. . . ."[1]

Authors of postbellum children's literature saw no need to call attention to forced labor, as such, and its anomalous character in a democracy. In books about Blacks, the focus was on personality and what was perceived as an implicit distance between European Americans and Blacks. Africans and African Americans were depicted as moved by instinct rather than logic, as prone to imitate rather than initiate action, as excitable and immoderate, as self-deprecating and clownish. The portraits can be summed up as variations on the theme of childishness, with the threat of brutishness often lingering in the background.

A widely used organizing device in these narratives is the plantation setting. Even an African war story (George A. Henty's *By Sheer Pluck*) contains a long interlude in which life on American plantations is depicted. Mark Twain uses the plantation setting in the important "Evasion" section at the conclusion of his picaresque novel, *Adventures of Huckleberry Finn*. The White imagination seemed at a loss when it mused over how to place people of color and Whites in the same space and pinpoint alleged personality differences. The solution of White writers was to mythologize the Southern plantation and treat it as a step up the civilization ladder for the Black laboring and servant classes. In such a fictional framework, authors could symbolically reunite the White Northerner and Southerner and suggest that there had *never* been any significant disagreement about what Blacks were like and where their place should be.

What the postbellum children's books are about, then, is a form of North/South disunity that scarcely existed. In other words, there is a joint perception that Blacks should remain more or less permanently outside the social and political mainstream. Generic features overlap in these books, but I separate them into three classes: plantation stories, adventure stories (including imperialist novels), and works of social satire and protest.

Plantation Stories of J. C. Harris, T. N. Page, L. Pyrnelle

The plantation myth was a collection of ideas that served to pacify the Southern anguish associated with the war. Louise-Clarke Pyrnelle states flatly that slaves were happy and defends that position in her preface to *Diddie, Dumps, and Tot, or Plantation Child-Life*. Joel Chandler Harris refers to mean-spirited slaveowners and thereby implies slave discontent in *The Story of Aaron* and its sequel; however, he claims that slaves left the plantation in droves when they faced abuse, as if they could simply walk off with no great fear of the consequences. Thomas Nelson Page was a spellbinding mythmaker who could turn the slave world into a noble, visionary realm.

As the plantation tale played down hardships among the enslaved, it also implied the need for slavery as an institution. One way to make this suggestion was by drawing frequent comparisons between Blacks and European Americans, or, as Harris does in some books, between Blacks and Arabs. These comparisons are at the expense of the Blacks. Another way to rationalize the institution was by using various means to imply simple-mindedness, including a thoroughly irrational self-deprecation on the part of Blacks. Another staple of the plantation story was the claim that sensible slaves did not really want the kind of freedom offered by the Emancipation Proclamation. In fact, freedom merely resulted in confusion in the Black population. This group is depicted as not understanding the meaning of the word "freedom"—as desiring nothing more in life than the freedom to be well fed. According to the plantation myth, slaves agreed that the prewar plantation system fulfilled that single-minded desire better than the postwar conditions.

Another tendency among writers of plantation stories was to create a special bonding between Northern and Southern mainstream characters, a relationship that transcended any kind of political dispute. Sometimes this theme entered into the plotline as a marriage, sometimes as a moment of mutual respect between two patriarchs or matriarchs, sometimes as a mutual exchange of favors. Joel Chandler Harris used all of these approaches.

Joel Chandler Harris has been characterized by his most comprehensive bibliographer, R. Bruce Bickley Jr., as "one of the most sensitive interpreters of the Southern Negro. . . ."[2] This assessment is hard to reconcile with Black portraiture in Harris's children's books, unless one starts from the premise that Black personality is, in fact, inferior when compared with the traits of lighter-skinned groups. Harris's acceptance of this premise put him in accord with the White mainstream of the North and South. By insisting that Harris's vision of Blacks is faithful to the reality of Black character, critics lend their weight to the myth of white superiority. (Critics in this tradition include John Herbert Nelson in the 1920s,[3] Walter Blair in the 1930s,[4] Thomas H. English in the 1940s,[5] and in recent decades, Louis D. Rubin Jr.,[6] and R. Bruce Bickley Jr.,[7] to mention only a few examples.)

Harris's vision, as it was passed along to children, can be seen in two separate story series: the Uncle Remus group and the six-volume set featuring seven-year-old Sweetest Susan, eight-year-old Buster John, and their twelve-year-old slave nurse and playmate, Drusilla. In the Uncle Remus books, the narrative featuring a White plantation family (especially its child member) is interwoven with sets of Black folk tales. Also original character sketches about Blacks are sometimes included. The traditional tales are given a more significant position than the framing story. In two of the six books about Drusilla, Sweetest Susan, and Buster John, Harris's own fictional creations predominate. In three other works, symbolic tales with European and African American roots have a major role in the overall narrative. In *Plantation Pageants*, Harris's animal anecdotes are naturalistic rather than symbolic.

In the Sweetest Susan/Buster John/Drusilla stories, the plantation myth is not contradicted by the presence of authentic Black folklore. Ethnic comparisons are almost entirely at the expense of the Blacks. Images of "the peculiar institution" are essentially benign. Freedom is depicted as a baneful imposition on slaves, and North/South White solidarity is shown as not seriously impeded by the hostilities of the war.

The series began in 1894 with *Little Mr. Thimblefinger and His Queer Country*, and a sequel *Mr. Rabbit at Home*. These two titles are about a magical land—"the country next door to the world." They are designed to accommodate a number of original and traditional fanciful tales, and except in the characterization of Drusilla, do not address interracial relations or other sociopolitical issues. The next two volumes—*The Story of Aaron* (1896) and *Aaron in the Wildwoods* (1897)—are Harris's main attempts to communicate the plantation myth to the young. *Plantation Pageants* (1899) opens with political commentary but changes to a collection of natural-history anecdotes, plus one Black folk tale.

The Story of Aaron is structured around four charming animal characterizations. A stallion, pony, track dog, and white pig are each brought into service as a narrator of Aaron's story (Aaron being a slave runaway and later a plantation overseer). In the novels about the post-war era, Aaron is a supervisor of tenant farmers. We learn about a villainous slave trader and neighboring plantation owner, but we are also encouraged to view Drusilla as a problem. We are reminded repeatedly of the intellectual distance between Drusilla on the one hand, and Aaron and the White children on the other. Aaron is an Arab, Son of Ben Ali; and, after a mystical encounter with the White children's crippled uncle some years before, he has emerged as a messiah figure. *Aaron in the Wildwoods* backtracks fifteen years to recount the relationship of Aaron and Little Crotchet, the crippled uncle of Sweetest Susan and Buster John.

It is clear that Harris views Arabs as a class apart from Blacks and racially more advanced. Aaron is described in *The Story of Aaron* with obvious approval in terms of physical features:

Now Aaron was the most remarkable slave in all the country around, not because he was tall and finely formed, nor because he carried himself as proudly as a military officer, but because he had a well-shaped head, a sharp black eye, thin lips, and a nose prominent, but not flat. Another remarkable feature was his hair which instead of being coarse and kinky, was fine, thick, wavy, glossy, and as black as jet.[8]

In contrast to Aaron's "military" bearing, the Black slaves are described as "very much afraid of him." Some see him as a conjurer "in league with the 'old boy.'"

In *Aaron in the Wildwoods*, Aaron is different from the Blacks because "he used his head, as well as body and limb."[9] He is contrasted with Chunky Riley in particular, a slave described as "chuckleheaded." The plantation Blacks themselves often comment on how Aaron is different, especially how he is more courageous and unselfish. Uncle Andy tells Aaron:

. . . you ain't no nigger, kaze you don't do like a nigger, en dey ain't no nigger in de roun' worl' what kin stan' up in dis boat an' shove it 'long like you doin'.[10]

And when Aaron urges a slave woman to report his whereabouts to his mean-spirited owner and thereby win favors for herself, she responds: "You ain't no nigger. Dey ain't no nigger on top er de groun' dat'd stan' up dar an' talk dat away."[11]

Although Aaron is the indisputable hero of both novels and used as the principal comparative device, there are also contrasts between the African American slaves and the White population. For example, the slaveowner, Mr. Abercrombie, speaks with a "cool, decisive voice" in an emergency, whereas the slaves cringe and manage to stay on the safe side of the fence. They resemble minstrel stage Negroes when they are sent to investigate a suspicious noise. A bug brushes the face of one of the scouts and he acts as if he is half-murdered; he exclaims foolishly: "Who flung dat rock?"[12]

Drusilla, the slave companion of Sweetest Susan and Buster John, is used in all six novels as comic relief. She is a character who sinks "to the floor, speechless," or gives "a piercing scream, and [falls] on the ground in a heap" in contrast to the mild trepidations experienced by the White children when in danger.[13]

Although Sweetest Susan is only seven years of age, she delivers this critique of Drusilla: "Don't mind Drusilla. . . . She doesn't mean anything she says, except when she asks for something to eat."[14] Drusilla herself is self-deprecating when she is told to return to the safety of the wagon if she is afraid to follow her young masters:

> "Go dar by myself!" exclaimed Drusilla, "no, suh! You don' know me! I would n't go 'cross dat hill dar by myse'f, not fer ham! Uh-uh! I know I ain't got much sense, but I got mo' sense dan dat. I would n't mo' dan git out er sight er you-all fo' dat ar White Pig would have me."[15]

By the end of the series, Buster John is five years older (thirteen years) and Drusilla is seventeen, but there is no evidence that this newly liberated slave has matured. When Buster John and his sister decide to approach a strange little old man who is acting oddly, Drusilla expresses her characteristic lack of self-control. The narrator tells us:

> Buster John wanted to laugh, but prudence restrained him. Drusilla, not knowing what prudence is, felt obliged to giggle. . . .[16]

Sweetest Susan chides her ex-nurse for this lack of courtesy, and Drusilla responds:

> I hear um say dat some folks kin keep fum laughin' when dey see sump'n funny, but dat ain't de way wid me. When I want ter laugh, I'm bleedze ter laugh er bust.[17]

A vivid treatment of the disparity between European American and Black children occurs in *The Story of Aaron.* The children are hearing about Little Crotchet's Northern-born tutor, a man who is about to be lynched when Mr. Abercrombie and Aaron intervene.

The White Pig had told all he knew. . . . So Buster John and Sweetest Susan amused themselves by wondering whether the Teacher was hanged or whether he was rescued. As for Drusilla, she very plainly said that she didn't much care. It was all past and gone anyhow. . . .
But Buster John and Sweetest Susan thought it made all the difference whether a man was hanged or saved.[18]

Harris also supports the plantation tradition with indications that slavery was an acceptable system within which interracial relations could develop. The kindly-managed plantations, for example, outnumber by far those that were in the hands of cruel and unscrupulous people. The good Mr. Abercrombie tells his son's tutor that he has seen a slave trader and his human cargo only twice in fifty years.[19] His neighbor, Colonel Gossett, is treated as the only churlish and venal character, as the owner of discontented slaves—that is, those that run away. The slave, Uncle Andy, describes the harmony that otherwise pervades the community:

You may go all 'round' here for forty mile, en holler at eve'y plantation gate en ax 'em how many niggers day got in de woods, en dey'll tell you na' er one.[20]

Aaron testifies to the benevolence of the system by being an individual who is "dignified and proud," whose "whole nature resented the idea of serving as a slave," and yet "he would have asked nothing better than to be Little Crotchet's slave; and he was glad to call Mr. Abercrombie master."[21] Despite the ill treatment he received at the hands of the Gossetts, he felt "no resentment against the Southern people."[22]

Such suggestions of well-being, with only an occasional aberrant type to spoil the reputation of the slave-owning class, is inconsistent with such plot incidents as the near lynching of the Abercrombie plantation's resident teacher. The lynchers consisted of a group of "paterollers" (night patrolmen) who routinely terrorized the region. Mr. Abercrombie does not file criminal charges against these dangerous people, even when he finds his son's tutor dangling at the end of a rope and close to death.

To make his point unmistakable, Harris arranges for this same tutor (Richard Hudspeth) to sum up the "beauties" of slavery. Since Harris places him at the center of the Lincoln administration as the president's closest adviser, Hudspeth becomes a convenient device for reinforcing the notion of North/South solidarity. The teacher exclaims:

Looking back on the history of the human race, let us hasten to acknowledge, while the acknowledgment may be worth making, that two hundred and odd years of slavery, as it existed in the American republic, is a small price to pay for the participation in the inestimable blessings and benefits of American freedom and American citizenship.[23]

In delivering this sweeping comment, Harris seems to be counting on the gullibility of a young readership. Yet the plantation myth is riddled with contradictions that escaped the notice of the reading public at large. A case in point is the treatment of the ex-slave. Southern leaders had assured the North that the end of slavery had been accepted in the South. Harris, therefore, shaped his stories so as not to contradict this point. At the same time, he tried to suggest that a slave society was among the best of all possible worlds. *Plantation Pageants* picks up the story of Sweetest Susan, Buster John, and Drusilla at the close of the war, and illustrates how Harris straddles the issue and still makes his own defense of the slave system unmistakable.

At first most of the Abercrombie slaves leave the plantation because they believe the assertions of neighboring slaves that they must "go ef we wanter be free sho 'nuff. . . ."[24] But they all return and express repeatedly their disillusionment over emancipation. Big Sal, however, voices some ambiguity: "Dem what went wuz big fools, an dem what stayed may be bigger ones, fer all I know."[25] On the following page, it seems clear that Big Sal is confused about the whole subject and is not being used by Harris as a reliable narrator. She converses with the children:

*"Grandfather says all the negroes are free now," said Sweetest Susan.
"Did he say dat? Did he say dat wid his own mouf? Well, I thank my
stars! I'm free, den! Me an' all de balance!. . . ."*
*"Well," said Big Sal, "ef I'm free, I better get up frum here an' go ter
work. Wat does Marster want us ter do? I'm gwine up dar an' ax
'im."*[26]

A free labor system, with its mutual agreements about what is
to be done and what wages will be paid is apparently not understood by this sixty-year-old Black woman.

The reasons given for dissatisfaction with freedom are twofold:
first, there are said to be too many sentimental attachments to the
plantation. Big Sal is too attached to the long-dead Little Crotchet
to leave; Drusilla's mother says "ef dis ain't my home, I dunner whar
in de roun' worl' I got any."[27] She feels rescued when the seven-year-
old White child leans against her: "It was as if a tramp steamer had
thrown out an anchor within sight of the lights of home."[28] Second,
the ex-slaves who scurry back give alarming reports about overwork.
The newly freed slave, Fountain, tells of being at the mercy of his
new employer's whip.[29] He tells Drusilla's mother about his messy
job lifting wagon wheels from a quagmire: "You can't call it freedom
atter you wade thoo dat mud an' water." "You'd 'a been sorry plum
ter yo' dyin' day,' [if you had left the Abercrombie plantation]" warns
Fountain for the sake of the slaves who had contemplated leaving.
Johnny Baxter chimes in, ". . . . de free white folks work harder dan
niggers."[30]

One of the most ironic aspects of the plantation myth was its
many variations on the theme that Blacks had an incurable distaste
for work. The irony lies in the fact that slaves were in an ideal position to see what the fruits of their labor consisted of; that is, they
could watch the products they produced being turned into a lifestyle
of lavish wealth. Even the most modest of dreamers would have left
the slavery era with a keen sense of the advantages of making and
selling things for American markets. Their experience in watching
this "system" operate was certainly as great as the experience of many
of the aristocrats they worked for.

Clearly insisting upon the unreliability of Black workers was a
self-serving tactic in the White-dominated economy. It was a rallying point in both the North and the South, and could be buttressed

by plantation storytellers, if they could only find a way to highlight North/South solidarity. In *The Story of Aaron*, the Abercrombie patriarch is visited by General Sherman as he marches through Georgia. The general speaks of the interruption the war is causing in both of their lives. He is then chided by Grandfather Abercrombie for being in the business of "dealing out death and destruction"; but, after the general had "placed his hand on the old gentleman's shoulder" in a gesture of sympathy, Harris implies reconciliation:

[General Sherman] resumed his seat as suddenly as he had left it, throwing one leg across the other with an easy familiarity that was not at all displeasing to the elder man.[31]

The novel concludes with a letter from the former tutor, Mr. Hudspeth, that the general reads aloud to Mr. Abercrombie. The teacher (Lincoln's confidante) requests that the general protect the plantation and refrain from foraging there for supplies. Hudspeth is repaying the debt he incurred when Abercrombie rescued him from the "paterollers."

The symbol of reconciliation used in the Uncle Remus books is the marriage between Remus's wartime slaveowner, Miss Sally, and a Union soldier whom Remus had wounded while protecting the plantation from Northern invaders. Remus boasts that although the skirmish cost the soldier one arm, it was not a bad exchange because the soldier gained the affectionate arms of Miss Sally; and moreover, "'I gin 'im deze'—holding up his own brawny arms."[32]

Harris's use of Uncle Remus for backward glances at history make his biases apparent. Referring to the twenty-one character sketches in *Uncle Remus: His Songs and His Sayings*, critic Robert Hemenway says that Harris had "primarily appealed to readers in need of a minstrel show."[33] *Uncle Remus and His Friends* includes twenty-one additional anecdotal vignettes with the same qualities. Despite his long experience in life, Remus is depicted as less aware of his evolving technological environment than a normal child would be. For example, he says to his employer at the other end of a telephone line:

"How in de name er God you git in dar, Mars John?"

"In where?"
"In dish yer—in dish yer appleratus. . . ."
"Mars John, kin you see me—er is she all dark in dar?"[34]

Harris's original sketches are about free Blacks in a post-war, increasingly industrial society; yet these characters are depicted as primitive throwbacks who cannot be expected to contribute to such a world.

Turning to Thomas Nelson Page and his use of the plantation tradition, we see again a North/South reunification effort. It was a highly visible theme in Page's stories for children. Page said that he had "never wittingly written a line which he did not hope might tend to bring about a better understanding between the North and the South. . . ."[35] The plantation myth as a whole owes much to Page's defensive attitude toward the South and his skills as a mythmaker. While Harris has been frequently called a sensitive portrayer of Blacks, Page is assigned an even broader significance in postbellum literature. He is called by literary historian Theodore L. Gross "the literary spokesman of the South during the 1880s and 1890s."[36]

Page's novel for children, *Two Little Confederates* (1888), is riddled with reconciliation, as well as with loyal slave characters. Page was twelve years old when the Civil War ended, and he uses his childhood home, Oakland Plantation, as the setting of this novel about small boys observing the war in Virginia. Much of the narrative provides a highly credible treatment of child psychology and childhood mannerisms and play. But a political statement is unmistakable when Northern soldiers readily befriend the Southern protagonists, when Northern and Southern mothers commiserate with each other about losing sons to the war, and when a Northern child (the son of a Yankee buried in Oakland's garden) promises to spend his vacations from school with Frank and Willy (the Southern children). According to this narrative, it is within hours of Lee's surrender at Appomattox that an intimate bonding occurs between wartime antagonists.

When the Yankee buried in the garden has his death scene, Page uses this incident to make an overt comment about North/South unity. The delirious, dying man utters a few words of the prayer

"Now I lay me down to sleep," believing in his feverish mind that he is putting his child to bed. When Frank and Willy join in the recitation, the narrator remarks: "They did not know that he was saying . . . the prayer that is common to Virginia and to Delaware, to North and to South, and which no wars can silence and no victories cause to be forgotten."[37]

The loyal-slave theme is repeated in the novel in several ways. When Union troops move into the vicinity, Oakland's mistress tells the slaves that they may leave, but Uncle Balla assures her, "Y'all sticks by us, and we'll stick by you."[38] The slaves are true to their word, helping to conceal Confederate officers, and assisting Mistress in burying the family silver. They pretend to want their freedom and use this ploy as a way to put the Yankee raiders off guard. When the father of Frank and Willy returns from military duty in the war, he has his body servant with him, a retainer who stayed at his master's side throughout the entire conflict. After peace is declared, Page does describe the departure of all but one lame slave, but before long a number "of the servants . . . had one by one come back to their old home."[39]

The theme of slave/master solidarity is one of the central elements in Page's short story for children, "Jack and Jake" (1891). Jake is a slave who is bestowed upon Jack when the White child is only a few years old. Their friendship, writes Page, "prevented either of them ever knowing that Jake was a slave. . . ."[40] The boys were inseparable and behaved more like comrades than master and servant. However, at the outset the reader is precluded from assigning any kind of equality to this pair. "Jake was dull," writes the author.[41] Jake joins Jack in the adventures the young master contrives, but the relationship rests upon bribery and threats. When Jack wants to catch a wild horse that is loose in the woods, Jake at first refuses because the venture would expose them to capture by Yankee troops. Jack uses a series of threats to induce obedience: refusal to play with Jake, refusal to share any more biscuits with him, and finally, "I'm going to tell [your mother] that you lost [her axe] and she'll cut you all to pieces."[42] The last tactic works because Jake's mother, we are told, often threatens to cut "him almost in two."[43] At the end of the tale, Jack is responsible for the circumstances that lead to the drowning of Jake, but Page treats the tragedy as an example of Jack's nobility since the White child does make an effort to compensate for his irresponsible actions and tries to rescue Jake after he falls into a stream.

There are actually three relationships that are developed in this story: the friends' relationship and the ties between Jack and Jake and their respective mothers. A contrast between European Americans and Blacks is obvious from the outset in Page's description of Jake as dull and Jack as having a "spirited look."[44] But the mother/ son interactions are another means of accentuating the contrast. It is hard to imagine a more ideal image of motherhood than the one Page creates for Jack's mother. Jack is treated as the ideal son, bravely stepping into his absent father's position as protector of the home. The relationship radiates warmth and mutual understanding. On the other hand, all of Jake's unwise decisions are based ultimately upon the terror Jake feels vis-à-vis his mother.

The ill treatment that Black children experience at the hands of Black adults in children's books can be viewed as a toned-down facet of the brute image often assigned to Blacks in adult books. Page asserts in his 1892 essay, "The Race Problem," that the racial superiority of Whites rests upon "constancy, . . . intellect, and the domestic virtues."[45] In nineteenth-century literature by White authors, Blacks are allowed scarcely any domestic peace, whether the relationship is between mother and child or husband and wife.

The mammy figure is a variation on the theme of faithful Black retainers, but ironically this seemingly benign character has a brutish dimension when Black children enter the scene. We can see this dimension in Louise-Clarke Pyrnelle's *Diddie, Dumps, and Tot, or Plantation Child-Life* (1882), as well as in works by Harris and Page.

Ordinarily it would be a thoroughly villainous character who would attack youngsters with the kind of insults and corporal punishment that Mammy directs toward Black children in Pyrnelle's novel. In the scene in which the following rebuke occurs, there is no apparent reason for Mammy's hostility, since it is the White children who first interrupt her as she tells a tale:

"[L]ook er hyear, yer kinky-head nigger, whar's yer manners?" asked Mammy, "'ruptin' uv eld'ly pussons. I'm de one w'at's struck'n dese chil'en, done struck de mother fuss; I'll tell 'em w'at's becomin' fur 'em ter know;

I don't want 'em ter hyear nuf'n 'bout sich low cornfiel' nigg?rs ez Club-foot Bill. "[46]

Elsewhere Mammy gives the Black children a sound whipping for mischief that is clearly instigated by the all-powerful White girls.[47] The slaves are in a no-win position since Mammy also thrashes them if they do not obey orders. In another scene, Dumps intervenes with her father for her Black companion's sake when Mammy is abusing the child.[48] There is a sharp contrast in the imagery here: Black women in hostile associations with Black children versus the image of Black women in warm, maternal relationships with a slaveowner's children. This dichotomy is perhaps indicative of a deep-seated possessiveness that the post–Civil War plantation establishment felt it must assert over the Black population. This emotion-charged symbolism hints at how resolutely the New South's citizens would try to restore aspects of the Old South's social structure.

Diddie, Dumps, and Tot contains other elements of the plantation story—for example, images of close master/slave relations and references to the wretchedness of free Blacks—and also draws upon the conventions of "blackface" minstrelsy. The sketches that resemble stage Negro routines were a means of mocking Black intellect. For example, Mammy tries to explain to her White charges the reasons for the Fourth of July holiday. She thinks it has something to do with fighting, perhaps the conflict between David and Goliath, or perhaps the warlike activities of the Bible's Samson. Another slave refutes her interpretation, explaining that there was a "Defemation of Ondepen'ence" (Declaration of Independence). He does not recall what "Defemation" means, but urges the girls to ask their mother to look up the word in the "squshionary" (dictionary).[49] The Fourth of July is celebrated, he explains, because of a man called "Marse Fofer July." For several pages the farcical repartees build with one piece of misinformation added to another.

Religion was often the center of a stage Negro sketch, and Pyrnelle includes a classic example of such a skit when she tells how Uncle Daniel has heard a passage from the Bible read by the overseer's wife and attempts to use it as the basis for a sermon. He devises an elaborate oration that concludes with a call for "monahs" to come to the "Monahs' bench" in crowds, in droves.

I want 'en laid 'pun top er one renudder, bredren, tell yer can't see de bottumus' monahs. I want 'em piled up hyear dis evenin'. I want 'em packed down, mun, an 'den tromped on, ter make room fur de nex' load.[50]

The lay preacher inspires such a commotion of shouting and falling in trances that he frightens the children. Everything that is happening in this scene is based on a foolish misinterpretation of scripture, and the parodied language of the sermon and of all the dialogues among Blacks is the fractured English of minstrel tradition.

It is not surprising that Pyrnelle's first novel was immensely popular with White audiences. It contains the kind of Black folk tales popularized by Joel Chandler Harris, the astute treatment of child perspective that would later appear in Thomas Nelson Page's works, and the sort of minstrel routines that Mark Twain would include in *Adventures of Huckleberry Finn* in 1884 and in *Tom Sawyer Abroad* in 1893–1894. *Diddie, Dumps, and Tot* and its many misrepresentations of Blacks remained in print until the 1940s. A sequel, *Miss Li'l' Tweetty*, was published in 1917.

It is not valid to associate such misrepresentations with Southerners and Southern history exclusively, despite the regional aspects of the first plantation stories. As we consider another genre in children's literature, the adventure story, we find writers from the North, as well as one from Great Britain, sustaining the white supremacy myth with as much zeal as Harris, Page, and Pyrnelle.

Adventure Stories of W. T. Adams, G. A. Henty, E. Stratemeyer

The generic label, adventure story, signifies a loose, catch-all category of children's literature. In the nineteenth century it was almost synonymous with the term "boys' story," and it is in this connection that it is used here. "Adventure" implies a noticeable level of danger and excitement in the narrative, and it also means that sometimes the author will give over a considerable amount of space to descriptions of tactical maneuvers in either a war or wilderness setting. Books of this sort were usually a mixture of types: partly about school, hobbies, friendships, first loves, and so on. But in many, battle tactics became a major focus of the narrative.

When the nineteenth-century adventure story included Blacks, it usually illustrated a number of ways in which authors contrasted Blacks with people of European descent. For example, it incorporated the "white man's burden" and "great white hunter" themes in narratives with foreign habitats; it utilized the plantation myth; it characterized Blacks after the model of the "blackface" stage Negro. The "boys' story" warrants specific attention here because it was the primary means of conveying the Black brute stereotype to the young. The adventure story included images of Blacks that ranged from Sambo minstrel figures (the staples of the nineteenth-century plantation stories, social satires, and social protest novels) to brute beast images. The latter made a frequent appearance in the propaganda of white supremacist organizations (e.g., the Ku Klux Klan), and it is not surprising that the growth and activism of such organizations would be reflected in symbolic ways in children's literature. It is not an overstatement to suggest that many children's authors constructed a solid intellectual foundation for KKK recruiters.

Some of the milder forms of stereotyping in a boys' book are seen in William T. Adams's Civil War story, *Brother Against Brother, or The War on the Border* (1894), the first novel in a six-volume series entitled "The Blue and the Gray on Land" and sometimes "The Blue and Gray Army Series." Adams had created in 1852 a male mammy figure in *Hatchie, the Guardian Slave* (discussed above). He creates in *Brother Against Brother* images of the genial, loyal slave, the comic Black, and the potentially ferocious primitive; but he does not emphasize brutish character traits as such. Adams represents the liberal fringe of mainstream Northern thought, the accommodation achieved between ethnocentrism and abolitionism.

Brother Against Brother is in large measure a plantation novel, although it includes the same kinds of adventures and military maneuvers that will be more in evidence as the series develops. It presents a view of sectional conflict prior to the Civil War. Its descriptions of battle tactics show the reader what local skirmishes might have been like when Unionists and Secessionists began to compete in a border state such as Kentucky. The author's bias is clearly a Northern Unionist bias, but the work is imbued with contradictions. Adams brings two brothers from New Hampshire, settles them in Kentucky, and portrays them as polarized in their lifestyles. Noah

Lyon is a prince among men, a "model" slaveholder (a role he assumes when a deceased brother wills him his estate as a means of protecting its slaves from the newly Southernized brother, Titus Lyon). The off-stage brother was an "ideal" slaveholder before his death. In William T. Adams's final years, the contours of the "peculiar institution" have been softened, and Adams faithfully duplicates the mythical plantation setting that has been shaped by prominent Southern writers.

When Noah arrives at his new home, Riverlawn, he finds "happy and contented" slaves with "neat and substantial dwellings."[51] There are fenced gardens beside each house, the Black women are "neatly dressed," the head cook is respectfully called Diana rather then the disrespectful Southern substitute, Dinah."[52] We are told that the deceased brother was "the best friend [his slaves] ever had" and that he hired an always "gentle and indulgent" overseer.[53] He was regarded by the slaves "as a father, guide, and friend rather than as a taskmaster."[54] When the new Colonel Lyon is about to be besieged by Secessionists, the slaves join his defense force crying "Glory to God! We all die for Mars'r Lyon."[55]

This new Colonel Lyon is apparently not bothered by his own contradictory attitudes. As a Unionist, he is "instinctively . . . opposed to human bondage. . . ."[56] However, "he had never been considered a fanatic or an abolitionist." Adams explains that statement when he voices the typical antislavery stance of the antebellum period—namely, that his hero opposed the extension of slavery, but "did not believe Congress had any constitutional right to meddle with the system as it existed in the states."[57] It is not explained why Noah thinks *he* cannot meddle with the system—why he cannot manumit the slaves he has inherited. There is a written request from his dead brother that no slaves be sold (selling slaves was the sure sign of a bad slaveowner although no one explains how slaves were obtained in the first place unless someone sold them). But nothing prevents Noah from freeing them. His failure to do so reveals the new, more conservative definition of Unionist adopted by an author of the 1890s.

The loyal slave stereotype is joined in Adams's novel by the comic "darky" figure. Even though the novelist paints Riverlawn as a veritable Eden, he does not erase the color line for his young readers.

The Blacks do not come across as individuals who could function as citizens. While the slaves do frequently behave bravely and sometimes competently, they do not lose their characterization as clowns. Both the old and new colonels use nicknames for their male slaves that are demeaning in the same way that minstrel show characters are often marked as clowns by their names. Among the Riverlawn slaves are General, Dummy, Rosebud, Woolly, Shavings, Gouge, and Clinker. General is described as quick-witted; but, on a dangerous mission to recover secessionist weapons, he is more interested in showing off what he has learned of nautical jargon than contributing to the mission at hand. The overseer must instruct him about doing the right thing at the right time.[58] And despite his gift for picking up a seaman's lingo, General is unable to say "officer" without turning it into the comical sounding "ossifer."[59] Dummy is depicted as a sensible preacher, but he never says a word unless he is in his pulpit and then "he could talk fast enough."[60] His behavior is inexplicably bizarre. Rosebud could "hardly say or do anything without laughing."[61] Woolly's hair is a "tremendous mop"; and Shavings and Clinker are named for their trades, carpentry and blacksmithing. All the Blacks, writes Adams, were "proud of their cognomens."[62]

Primitivism is added to humor when the slaves on a neighboring plantation enlist in the battles to protect their "Mars'rs." They are said to be good imitators, but unless firmly controlled, they become dangerous. The overseer explains: "They only obey their orders, but they rather overdo it."[63] They respect the commands given by an elderly Black preacher who had "the most terrible fighting character [the slaveowner] had ever seen."[64] Only the preacher's instructions to his fellow slaves (received from the humane White planters) restrain them from killing the "ruffians"—the Secessionists. One of the planters assesses his Black recruits for the reader:

From mild, peaceable, and even timid people, they suddenly became as brave as lions, and as ferocious as fiends.[65]

Other White soldiers refer to the Black warriors as "lunatics," as they watch the Blacks club the fallen Secessionists with pitchforks and other farm implements until they are too battered to move.[66] The novelist pays tribute to the Black recruits from a white supremacist perspective (as when he writes that "white men of average ability could hardly have done better . . ."), but he also highlights their unreliability. A slave who is sent to report on the proximity of the enemy says that "dar's more'n two tousand men comin' ober it [the bridge]. . . . Call it fifty or a hundred, Bitts," corrects the overseer.[67]

Adams included similar examples of stereotyping in his novel of the early 1850s, *Hatchie, the Guardian Slave,* but he created in Hatchie a messiah figure that has no counterpart in this Civil War tale. And the ambivalence in *Brother Against Brother* is also in contrast to the more supportive characterization of a slave in Adams's 1865 novel about the Civil War, *Fighting Joe, or The Fortunes of a Staff Officer: A Story of the Great Rebellion.*

In that narrative, the slave, Alick, has become the contraband and servant of a Union officer. Due to Alick's "cool, collected, and self-possessed" behavior in a battle with guerrillas, the hero of the tale is rescued. Elsewhere in the story, plantation Blacks are said to be invaluable to prisoners of war as they escaped from camps "where [Northern] officers and soldiers died by thousands of sheer inhumanity."[68] But despite Adams's straightforward defense of the Unionist cause, he does not include Blacks in the novel except at rare intervals, and finally he forgets that they are even there. He leaves Alick and other Black servants holding the horses of the hero and his companion while they get mixed up in another scrape with the double-dealing guerrilla bands. The war ends, the hero marries, and the novel winds down to its conclusion. Alick is holding the horses yet!

It would seem that Adams's inattentiveness to his Black characters changed to an attitude molded by white supremacist convictions. At least there can be little doubt that in *Brother Against Brother* he shaped each Black characterization so as to incorporate something either fierce or absurd.

George A. Henty's *By Sheer Pluck: A Tale of the Ashanti War* (1884) is also much more than a record of military advances and retreats. This British novel splits neatly in half—the first section dealing with schoolboy exploits, a young man's hobbies, and the anguish of being orphaned and impoverished, and the second half describing African wars and the British/Ashanti war of 1873–1874 in particular. In its treatment of Blacks, it offers a detailed portrait of African Americans as well as Africans. Both groups were at the center of the debate about imperialist foreign policies. The Henty novel is important in this study because it had an enormous American distribution, being pirated by many American publishers.

When a British schoolboy, Frank Hargate, secures a job as assistant to a famous naturalist and embarks for Africa, the novelist uses this character as the reader's eyes. Frank has his first glimpse of Africans and has many questions that his employer, Mr. Goodenough, is happy to answer. The latter explains to Frank, for example, that although there are Africans who are "splendidly muscular fellows," they are often not "plucky" enough for the work Frank will be doing. Goodenough remarks: ". . . they are notorious cowards, and no offer would tempt them to penetrate into such a country as that into which we are going."[69]

Yet the travelers do find the carriers and guides they need (the stereotypic faithful servants) and proceed into the African interior. They use warlike Houssas to carry breech-loading guns and help them intimidate the various chieftains. Without them, Goodenough explains, "I should be at the mercy of every petty chief who chose to plunder and delay me."[70] While most of the chiefs and their people are presented as either thieving or cannibalistic, there are also so-called superior tribes in Henty's novel—that is, those that have been Christianized. Such groups are "clad with far more decency and decorum than is usual among negro tribes," their lodgings have "an air of neatness and order," and the citizenry are "quiet and dignified."[71]

These Christianized Africans are treated by the novelist with less condescension than Sam, an African-turned-African American. The protagonists meet Sam in the African interior, and he is the means by which Henty outlines swiftly the entire Black diaspora (i.e., we see Sam enduring the Middle Passage, captivity in Cuba, enslavement on a "good" American plantation and then a bad one, life as a runaway, and so on). As an African prince returned to power, Sam is also used for comic relief. He spreads a "snow-white table-cloth . . . on the table," and apologizes for the negligible amenities of his household:

"You must 'scuse deficiencies, sar," he said. "We bery long way from

coast, and dese stupid niggers dey break tings most ebery day."
"Don't talk about deficiencies," Mr. Goodenough answered, smiling.
"All this is, indeed, astonishing to us here."
"You bery good to say dat, sar, but dis chile know how things ought to
be done. He libed in good Melican family. He know bery well how
tings ought to be done."[72]

Goodenough contributes some brandy to the festivities, and Sam
explains how he is never deficient in his supply of rum but that his
clumsy carriers had smashed many bottles on their last trip inland
from the coast.[73]

One of the most thorough summations of the traits of the "sable
mind" from the imperialist viewpoint, is provided in *By Sheer Pluck*.
Several Africans have been knocked into the water as they scaled the
side of a European ship.

So intense was the appreciation by the sable mind of this joke that the
boatmen rolled about with laughter, and even the victims, when they
had once scrambled into their boats, yelled like people possessed.
"They are just like children," Mr. Goodenough said. "They are always
either laughing or quarreling. They are good-natured and passionate,
indolent, but will work hard for a time; clever up to a certain point,
densely stupid beyond. The intelligence of an average negro is about
equal to that of a European child of ten years old. A few, a very few, go
beyond this but these are exceptions, just as Shakespeare was an excep-
tion to the ordinary intellect of an Englishman. They are fluent talkers,
but their ideas are borrowed. They are absolutely without originality,
absolutely without inventive power. Living among white men, their
imitative faculties enable them to attain a considerable amount of civi-
lization. Left alone to their own devices they retrograde into a state little
above their native savagery."[74]

In boys' series books, the image of savagery competes with the
image of Blacks as childish and habitually lazy. Frank positions himself "so as to avoid witnessing the horrible spectacle" when "a hundred [Ashanti] victims [are] sacrificed to the success of the expedition."[75] The Ashanti king commands his general to bring him the

head of his enemy so as to "place it on [his] drum by the side of that of Macarthy."[76]

Henty did not refrain from issuing strong criticisms of British military commanders when they broke faith with the natives. But his journalistic assessments of foreign policy did not mitigate his white supremacist premises. Henty's biographer, Guy Arnold, sums up the problem that this British author represents in children's literature:

The stereotype of Blacks as lazy, childlike, without capacity, and still more the feeling of contempt for them are glaring . . . and Henty must take a full share of responsibility for propagating the kind of views which have done such damage to British relations with African or Asian people during the present century. Nor is the retrospective defence of such attitudes—that they were normal for that period in history—really tenable. To suggest that Henty was expressing no more than what half his contemporaries felt is to denigrate his powers and influence. . . .
[His] views were not incidental to the story; as Henty often claimed, he set out to instruct as well as amuse. His books were still to be found on school shelves fifty years after his death and at least some of the racial arrogance which, unhappily, has been so marked a characteristic of British behavior in what is now termed "The Third World" can be attributed to his influence.[77]

Publishers in the United States made Henty's books readily accessible to American children, and this author's "racial arrogance" undoubtedly had some impact upon American intergroup relations.

Edward Stratemeyer in *Tour of the Zero Club, or Adventures Amid Ice and Snow* (1894–95) goes as far in the direction of qualified support for an African American character as any writer goes in my sampling. While he treats the Black protagonist, Pickles Johnsing, as an instrument of comic relief, he nonetheless makes Pickles a noble and talented fool. Stratemeyer (like Twain when he shapes the character of the slave runaway, Jim) creates a thoroughly inconsistent character in Pickles. Pickles performs many rescues during his participation in a camping expedition organized by four White friends, but he also endangers lives by his lack of judgment or attentiveness. Even in scenes in which Pickles is clearly the hero of the hour, he is laughable. Stratemeyer seems to be making a positive statement about a Black adolescent in this novel, while also being careful to sustain the color line.

In *Tour of the Zero Club*, Stratemeyer uses a variety of means by which to suggest Black inferiority. First he has Pickles disparage himself by announcing his second-rate status and stating the proper role distinctions between himself and young Whites. After Pickles has helped the Zero Club members recover their ice boat from a group of town bullies and has protected a club member from assault, he requests limited membership in the club:

"Say, why can't yo' fellahs take me along!" he burst out suddenly. "Ebery fust-class camp hab got to hab a cook an' general util'ty man around, pap sez, an' he sez I kin go along if youse will hab me. I don't want no pay fo' gwine along, an' I'll do wot I kin to help fill up de larder. I ain't much wid a gun, but I kin trap t'ings, and yo' all knows wot I kin do fishin' an' spearin'. It an't fo' delikes of yo' to wash de dishes and sech, an'—an', to tell de truf, I wants to go powerful bad!"[78]

Pickles's comment about "de likes of yo'" is not based on economic distinctions, for the primary hero of the tale is a boy whose family is in serious financial straits.

Pickles is allowed to join the tour, but his separateness from the other travelers is underscored by the narrator when sleeping arrangements are described (Pickles is always in a corner by himself) and when the group is invited to a country dance (Pickles is permitted to join the farm hands in the barn, but can enter the house only as an entertainer). These segregated arrangements are, however, not the author's chief methods of dehumanizing Pickles. He lets Pickles's unusual behavior and speech pattern serve as an implicit signal of otherness. For example, Pickles degrades himself with the disrespectful epithets of his era. After everyone has been badly shaken up by an encounter with a wounded fox, Pickles says about himself: "Dis coon is werry glad he is alibe jess about now, boys!"[79] And when the campers joke about keeping up the fire to ward off bears, Pickles joins in the banter: "'Gee, shoo, no!' put in Pickles. 'Dat would make dis yere coon turn white, 'deed it would!'"[80]

Pickles is unlike the others because he was "a firm believer in spirits."[81] Although a hoax by the town bullies causes a White member of the group to refer to ghosts, this youngster is soon talked out of his fears by the others. Pickles cannot be reassured and will not go back to bed for the rest of the night. He huddles so close to the campfire that he singes his hair.

There is no consistency in the characterization of the Black club member. On one hand, he is so self-possessed that he can prevent a disaster, but, on the other hand, so forgetful and imprudent that he can cause chaos. He saves the life of one camper by emerging from the safety of a hollow log and shooting a wolf that is about to pounce. But he nearly causes the demise of the whole group by building the campfire too close to the sleeping hut and setting it alight. When he accidentally loads his gun twice, the discharge knocks him flat, and we are told that he is first wild-eyed and then perplexed (scratching "his woolly head").[82] Pickles's physical reactions and his features in general are similar to those described in other works of fiction about Blacks: he rolls his eyes intermittently and his overall portrait is treated stereotypically:

Pickles Johnsing was a stout, round-faced colored boy, with big red lips, and teeth which reminded one very forcibly of double-black dominoes set in twin rows.[83]

The speech pattern devised for Pickles is, in many respects, similar to the dialects assigned to characters in novels of this period. Non–Anglo Saxon characters, unschooled rural inhabitants, and toddlers were typically assigned a distinctive dialect. The speech of the stereotypic comic "darky" was, however, consistently different. Blacks in the role of clowns did not only speak with a regional accent, as when "sure" becomes "suah" when Pickles is speaking; they also spoke in a manner that suggested muddled-headedness. Pickles is not able to remember correct prefixes and turns "exactly" into "persackly," "insult" into "consult." The comic effects are obvious, as when he is enraged by an insult and shouts indignantly to the offending party: "Yo' can't consult me dat way, yo' low down white trash!"[84]

It is not surprising that a character with this qualitatively different speech problem will be separated from the White youths at the end of the tale. In *Tour of the Zero Club*, Pickles is left in the employ of the father of one of the club members, while the other young men go off to high school and college.

Stratemeyer does, however, oppose race prejudice when he associates such prejudice with the novel's villains (as when the town bully enters a bobsledding race with Zero Club members and complains, "I expected to race white fellows").[85] Also Stratemeyer sounds liberal when he sums up the feelings of Pickles's companions: "I'm glad he came along."[86] But the novel conveys unmistakable white supremacist assumptions; Pickles is depicted as innately and significantly different from White mainstream characters. While he is a better fisherman than his companions, this trait cannot be expected to elevate Pickles in any significant way in the eyes of this book's intended middle-class readers.

In *The Young Auctioneer*, Stratemeyer introduces Blacks into the story as minor characters, and in juxtaposition with an array of unscrupulous types. These Blacks are depicted as drunks and thieves who are parasites in the community. White drunks and thieves populate this novel also, but they are presented within a context of orderly community life. They are aberrations, people who for various personal reasons went astray. The African American miscreants are not counterbalanced by positive images of Blacks; in such a vacuum they suggest that Black culture is entirely problematic, having no redeeming characteristics.

When the four Blacks appear in the auctioneering store of the heroes, Matt and Andy, they are "ugly-looking," "loud and coarse," careless of property (they break a display case), and under the influence of alcohol. In this scene, the feature that makes them different from White ruffians who similarly threaten the protagonists is that they charge Matt and Andy with race prejudice when they break the glass and try to avoid paying damages. One of the four says, "Maybe yo' think yo' kin lay it on us just because we is colored, hey?"[87] Andy denies having any such bias. A later scene treats the Blacks as a general menace in the community, not just one of any number of "occupational hazards" that this novel highlights for the reader. Matt unwittingly calls at the home of this foursome when he is seeking advice on how to find the right road to a neighboring town. They assault him and attempt to rob him. Matt and Andy explain this to a farmer, after they have made their escape, and the boys are told that the men plague the area with their petty thievery. The farmers, who insist that they have been tolerant and long-suffering, are about to ask the constable to put the marauding Blacks behind bars. It is never explained why four men, without families or any means of support for themselves, live in an isolated cottage and in constant danger from the police and from the people in the area who are infuriated by their lawlessness. As far as the reader of the novel can tell, Black people just behave in that disruptive and inexplicable way.

These Blacks are not used by Stratemeyer as comic relief (as he uses Pickles). The only lightening of tone occurs when a broad dialect is assigned to some German immigrants. They are angry at traveling auctioneers who have defrauded them, and they explain to Matt that the hiding place of the con men is unknown: "Ve ton't know. Of ve did ve vould tar an' fedder dem, by chiminy!"[88]

It is argued by Stratemeyer scholar John T. Dizer Jr. that Stratemeyer is "unusually objective and liberal for the times in his literary treatment of blacks." His use of dialect, says Dizer, is the same for Blacks and others.[89] Similarly, he maintains that Stratemeyer's handling of African American villains does not differ from his handling of White villains, and that the menial roles assigned to Blacks are realistic and unbiased, that they are not roles relegated solely to African Americans. To make such a claim is to overlook the uniquely minstrel-like quality in the dialect of some Black characters, to overlook the different communal contexts in which the villains operate, and to ignore the upward mobility theme connected to White characters but not to African Americans.

The most that can be said in Stratemeyer's favor is that he occasionally creates an ambivalent character, a personality that intermittently transcends the image of the minstrel fool or the community parasite. Paul C. Deane, who has made a comprehensive study of children's series books since 1899, concludes that the traditional stereotypic image of Blacks did not change substantially over the first half of the twentieth century.[90] Stratemeyer was among those writers who reinforced the assumption that Blacks are second-rate citizens and are flawed in their very being.

"Protest" Fiction by Mark Twain and M. Finley

Mark Twain was without doubt a pathbreaker, but not with regard to Black portraiture. His most famous African American character—the runaway slave, Jim—is a cross between a male mammy figure and a "blackface" minstrel clown in *Adventures of Huckleberry Finn*. In *Tom Sawyer Abroad* (1893–1894), he is just a minstrel clown. If we discount the features drawn from the minstrel tradition, we can see a forerunner of Jim in William T. Adams's *Hatchie, the Guardian Slave* (1853) and a successor in Joel Chandler Harris' characterization of "Aaron, Son of Ben Ali" in *The Story of Aaron* (1896) and *Aaron in the Wildwoods* (1897). At the end of the nineteenth century, Edward Stratemeyer used a blend of nurturing and clownish characteristics in his youthful Pickles in *Tour of the Zero Club* (1894–95), and to some extent that combination is evident in Jim's predecessors: Harris's Uncle Remus and the slave friends of Pyrnelle's Diddie, Dumps, and Tot.

The elevation of Jim as a kind of personified social conscience in the writings of Twain scholars has at least two bases. First, critics have been generally inattentive to the white supremacist implications of the characterization. Second, critics have seen Jim as having a crucial role in relation to theme. He is, for example, often credited with being a catalyst for Huck's emerging moral position vis-à-vis slavery. Twain, however, undercuts the antislavery theme in so many ways that there is cause to look elsewhere for an explanation of Jim's importance. I will argue here that Jim is the catalyst for Huck in another sense: he helps the youngster break loose from the provincial, hypocritical conditioning of his social environment. With that break comes a new range of humanistic sensibilities. Twain apparently viewed the social conditioning of a child as a powerful form of bondage, and it is no small triumph when Huck (in certain ways and with Jim's help) rises above it.

In short, then, Jim is important in terms of theme and plot, but the characterization of this slave gives him a largely negative import in relation to Black identity. To make this argument, we need to consider the compromised antislavery theme, the specifics of the minstrel characterization, and the way Jim fails to represent a credible adult Black male. In each case, Jim becomes a means of lending support to the white supremacy myth.

The antislavery theme is prominent at that point in *Huckleberry Finn* when the general outline of Huck's socially conditioned beliefs has been laid before the reader. To Huck, slavery is good, the capture of a runaway slave is good, and any conscious neglect in forwarding the purposes of good is a sin against God. The joint efforts of Huck and Jim to survive on the river, and their joint appreciation of nature, undercuts such definitions of "good." Huck abandons them even though he believes he is risking damage to his soul. Once the change in Huck's outlook has occurred, abolitionism remains an ostensible thread in the plot, but Twain contradicts it. The many times when Jim could escape into the free states but does not do so are left unexplained; he seems to have lost interest in his emancipation and the potential good that could ensue from it. He is just a sidekick for Huck as Huck reports on rivertown corruption and charlatanism. Then he becomes the pawn of Tom Sawyer as Tom plays his romantic, bravado-inspired games. Finally, we learn that his owner has liberated him in her will. As Leo Marx notes, Jim's owner was the very sort "whose inhumanity first made the attempted escape necessary."[91] Twain seems to be reinforcing what Southerners, as well as a good many Northerners, had been insisting all along: that slaveowners would do the right thing if abolitionists would just leave them alone.

The minstrel content in the narrative is distributed in about the same proportions as in Pyrnelle's novels. The narrative progression stops intermittently for repartees or monologues that are pure farce and accentuate the alleged inferiority of Blacks. Jim becomes a "blackface" caricature when he goes into a long spiel about witches riding him around the world, about a banking swindle and a "chuckle-headed" slave named Balum's Ass, and about "Sollermun" and the Scriptures. When he is locked in a shed and accepts Tom's views of proper escape tactics, he is the ultimate buffoon.

The dialogue that concludes with the Balum's Ass character will suffice as an example of typical stage Negro repartees. Jim is explaining to Huck about his one-time wealth:

"Wunst I had foteen dollars, but I tuck to speculat'n', en got busted out."
"What did you speculate in, Jim?"

> *"Well, fust I tackled stock."*
> *"What kind of stock?"*
> *"Why, live stock. Cattle, you know. I put ten dollars in a cow. But I*
> *ain' gwyne to resk no mo' money in stock. De cow up 'n' died on my*
> *han's."*
> *"So you lost the ten dollars."*
> *"No I didn' lose it all. I on'y los' 'bout nine of it. I sole de hide en taller*
> *for a dollar en ten cents."*
> *"You had five dollars and ten cents left. Did you speculate any more?"*
> *"Yes. You know dat one-laigged nigger dat b'longs to old Misto*
> *Bradish? Well, he sot up a bank, en say anybody dat put in a dollar*
> *would git fo' dollars mo' at de en' er de year. Well, all de niggers went*
> *in, but dey didn' have much. I wuz de on'y one dat had much. So I*
> *stuck out for mo' dan fo' dollars, en I said 'f I didn' git it I'd start a*
> *bank mysef. Well o' course dat nigger want' to keep me out er de busi-*
> *ness, bekase he say dey warn't business 'nough for two banks, so he say*
> *I could put in my five dollars en he pay me thirty-five at de en' er de*
> *year."*[92]

At this point in the sketch, Jim tells how a "nigger" sold him a wood-flat (a raft for transporting timber), Jim promising him thirty-five dollars for it when his investment matured at the end of the year. But the wood-flat is stolen and Jim is left with ten cents for his next "speculatin'" venture. He gives the money to a "chuckle-headed" slave, Balum's Ass, who gives it in turn to the preacher because he hears the preacher say "'dat whoever give to de po' len' to de Lord, en boun' to get his money back a hund'd times.' 'Nuff'n' never come of it,'" explains Jim.[93]

In such exchanges, Huck plays the straight man and his speech pattern is standard English rather than the yokel dialect that is assigned to him elsewhere.

Instead of noting any stage Negro connections in such a dialogue, critic Michael Patrick Hearn interprets the biblical allusion about Balum as a light-hearted attempt by Twain to characterize Jim as someone with prophetic powers. "Of course," writes Hearn, "Twain is burlesquing Jim's abilities as a seer. . . ."[94] The white supremacist assumptions in what is, in essence, a minstrel sketch are not examined by Hearn. Instead he urges the reader to "read between the lines of these deceptively light debates; in each instance, Jim wins the argument through his good common sense."[95] But it is hardly an instance of common sense when Jim concludes the "Balum's Ass" sequence with the comment, "I's rich now. . . . I owns mysef, en I's wuth eight hund'd dollars."[96] The idea that Blacks are property and see themselves as such is Twain's reversion to the plantation myth. Hearn's "reading between the lines" is no satisfactory response to nineteenth-century racism.

Typically, critiques of *Huckleberry Finn* have not successfully separated Mark Twain's use of ironic and minstrel-inspired forms of humor. Perhaps the desire to see Black and European American populations symbolically unified in the Huck/Jim relationship has led readers to interpret as ironic scenes disparaging to Blacks. Critics have often grouped Twain's ironic dialogues (as when Huck responds to the query, "Anybody hu't?" with the reply, "No'm. Killed a nigger.") with Jim's minstrel antics and called them the same kind of humor. In fact, Twain was marshaling a number of comic devices, sometimes with an eye for how a scene would play in one of his live stage performances (i.e., readings).[97]

Besides the treatment of Jim as muddled-headed, he is portrayed as a nurturing mammy. Some critics have even called him a shaman.[98] But Jim is hardly ever a credible Black adult male. Because of the minstrelsy, as Ralph Ellison has noted, Jim appears to be the child figure on the raft and Huck the adult.[99] As he ministers to Huck and cries over him, Jim is closely associated with nineteenth-century females and the traits reserved for them.[100]

As Southern and Northern writers busily contrived stories to help reconcile the two regions after the war, they brought together White Union and Confederate patriarchs, matriarchs, lovers, and child playmates. But what was to be done to show African Americans and European Americans in the same harmonious space? A common method was to show Black adults and White children as united. The fiction of regional reconciliation is replete with such pairings. But if the white supremacist assumptions in these groupings were to be overcome, some realistic adult Black males had to be depicted. Such was not to be the case in Twain's works.

In *Tom Sawyer, Abroad*, more than in *Adventures of Huckleberry Finn*, Jim is a juvenile among juveniles, as well as another typical example of the stage Negro. Twain structures *Tom Sawyer, Abroad* as a picaresque narrative that will enable him to comment about the enigmas of nature and about humanity's inhumanity. The three protagonists sail blissfully above the Sahara Desert in a balloon and observe the aftermath of destructive storms and warlike clashes. Jim sometimes bears the brunt of Huck's and Tom's jokes and sometimes is himself an unwitting comedian. He delivers the following oration about the origin of the Great Desert:

I b'lieve it uz jes' like when you's buildin' a house; dey's allays a lot o' truck en rubbish lef over. What does you do wid it? Doan' you take en k'yart it off en dump it onto a ole vacant back lot? Course. Now, den, it's my opinion hit was jes' like dat. . . . He measure out some rocks en yearth en san', en stick 'em together en say "Dat's Germany," en pas'e a label on it en set it out to dry; en measure out some mo' rocks en yearth en san', en stick 'em together, en say, "Dat's de United States," 'en pas'e a label on it and set it out to dry. . . . Den He notice dat whilst He's cal'lated de yearth en de rocks jes' right, dey's a mos' turrible lot o' san' lef' over. . . .[101]

Critics have been quicker to comment upon the racial biases in *Tom Sawyer, Abroad* than in *Adventures of Huckleberry Finn.* Albert E. Stone Jr. points to *Tom Sawyer, Abroad* as an example of how Twain uses a childhood perspective to filter some of his primary existential concerns (e.g., instinct versus intellectualism, the coexistence of good and evil, etc.); but he also notes the way in which the clownish antics of Jim for the amusement of two White boys suggests "Twain's and Huck's jaundiced view of humanity" in the 1890s.[102] Kenneth S. Lyon points to the minstrel connection in *Tom Sawyer, Abroad:* ". . . the compassionate figure of the slave in *Huckleberry Finn* is barely recognizable in the minstrel-show darky of the later book."[103] In fact, the characterization of Jim does not shift substantially in the two books. The only noticeable difference in *Huckleberry Finn* occurs when Jim intermittently assumes a mammy function. It is too generous to call the runaway slave a "compassionate figure" while minstrel dimensions are so noticeably woven into the texture of both novels.

Switching from Twain's ironies to Martha Finley's sanctimonious exhortations, we find many paradoxes. If we could discount Twain's portrayal of Blacks, it would be easy to honor him for his stylistic achievements, his indignation over corruption and pretentiousness, and his clever handling of irony. Finley, on all counts a mediocre writer, attacked the Ku Klux Klan (KKK) in *Elsie's Motherhood* (1876)—a courageous and timely act in the postbellum era. Twain attacked slavery with his acerbic ironic mode, but slavery was a dead issue at the time he made his thrust, and had been for two decades. Twain goes after an obsolete political target; Finley (after studying the Congressional Ku Klux Klan Reports) writes a tedious, senti-mental tract about sociopolitical conflicts of great import and im-mediacy. Yet these writers are on a par when they attempt Black portraiture.

Elsie's Motherhood is part of a lengthy series of girls' books about a character named Elsie Dinsmore. There is so much overt preach-ing in these novels that it is hard to view them as anything but a channel for evangelical zeal. However, *Elsie's Motherhood* is also full of political debate. Finley explains in her preface that this was inten-tional, that someone had suggested that she weave an anti-KKK theme into one of her novels, and in preparation she studied the record of Congressional hearings.

The setting of the story is a Southern plantation where Elsie lives with her husband, Edward Travilla, her children, and her husband's former slaves (now wage-earning laborers). Some of Elsie's relatives on neighboring plantations are KKK activists; and, while they are terrorizing the region, Elsie and Edward are trying to find ways to convert them. Both the KKK and anti-KKK positions are spelled out in some detail.

On the KKK side, we are told that people in these vigilante groups are angry because farmers like the Travillas have "put up the price of labor" by paying ex-slaves high wages and that they have no right to do so.[104] Moreover, the KKK is serving a useful purpose as a protection against carpetbaggers and potential Black insurrection-ists. It is clear that the KKK supporters have no notion of what a contractual labor system consists of, for they complain that Blacks demand their wages when they are due and that they are sometimes dissatisfied "with what one chooses to give."[105]

Finley also reveals the residual bitterness over the Civil War and Reconstruction. Some of Elsie's pro-KKK relatives insist that the

Confederate cause was "as righteous a cause as that of our Revolutionary fathers," that the Fugitive Slave Law was ignored in the North, and that abolitionists secretly raided the South and enticed the slaves to escape.[106] But the emancipation and enfranchisement of Blacks is presented as the main point of contention when one Klan leader speaks of how the South has been shamed and adds: "It is a thing hitherto unheard of in the history of the world, that gentlemen should be put under the rule of their former slaves."[107]

Those arguing against the Klan include Elsie's father, who explains that the KKK exists for the purpose of denying Blacks their new constitutional rights. Also a neighbor who has migrated from the North tries to defend the federal government by reminding disgruntled Southerners that the postwar period included no executions for treason and no confiscation of lands. Moreover, he boasts that the government generously repaired the war-ruined Southern railroad lines. He blames any flaws in Reconstruction on Southern landowners because, he said, you "refused to take part in the . . . reorganizing [of] your State government." Thus "the Blacks acquired the right to vote . . . and fell prey to unscrupulous white men, whose only care was to enrich themselves by robbing the already impoverished States, through corrupt legislation."[108] According to this character, Finley's chief anti-KKK mouthpiece, the Fourteenth Amendment left power to State governments and enabled them "to limit suffrage and office to the white race."[109] This passage implies that Finley was not a supporter of the Fifteenth Amendment with its guarantee of the suffrage for both Black and Caucasian males. Her characterization of the Black population includes such strong images of inferiority that there is little reason to believe that she objected to Black disfranchisement.

The ex-slaves behave like loyal children who cannot master the English language. They believe that devils are attacking them when the KKK riders enter their cabins. And they readily accept Elsie's facile solutions for their anguish. When the invaders fatally wound an infant, Elsie comforts the grieving mother with the words, "If you love Jesus, you will go to be with him again some day." An elderly victim of the raid is preached the doctrine of atonement in Jesus and told: "You are almost home, Uncle Mose."[110] Elsie does not appear insincere when she quotes Scripture, but her Black listeners do appear less than human because their dependence upon the aristocratic Travillas is all-encompassing.

By the end of the novel there can be little doubt that Finley is strongly opposed to the violence of the KKK, but there is little in the texture of the novel that is supportive of social equality. There is an unabashed white supremacist strain in Finley's works that is clearly expressed in the following lines of dialogue from *Elsie's Womanhood* (1875). Elsie has been instructing a Black child about God:

"Does He lub niggahs, missus?" queried one grinning little wooly [sic] head.
"Yes, if they love Him; and they won't be negroes in heaven."
"White folks, missus? Oh dat nice! Guess I go dar; ef dey let me in.[111]

Finley's Northern roots did not insulate her from such racist attitudes, nor keep her from becoming an active propagandist for the plantation myth. African American shiftlessness is a trait emphasized in *Elsie's Womanhood*. Elsie finds the overseer on her Louisiana plantation flogging a Black woman; but, when she strongly objects, her father intervenes on the overseer's behalf: "He is a New Englander," says Mr. Dinsmore, "used to seeing every one about him working with steady, persevering industry, and the indolent, dawdling ways of the blacks, which we take as a matter of course, are exceedingly trying to him.'"[112] A house slave takes the same position, explaining to Elsie that "some ob de lazy blood" needed to be beaten out of the woman. Elsie agrees to retain the overseer, but cautions him:

"Some amount of patience with the natural slowness of the negro is a necessary trait in the character of an overseer who wishes to remain in my employ."[113]

It is ironic that, while Finley is by no means an apologist for KKK-type organizations, her works promote the myth of Black inferiority—the tenet used by such organizations as their reason for existence.[114]

Conclusion

Literary forms such as the plantation story, the imperialist novel, and the social protest novel were not new inventions. However, these forms were significantly revitalized in the postbellum era. A belief in race hierarchies persisted, causing white supremacist themes to resurface. But these themes were expressed in new subgenres: in local color fiction, regional satires, and the imperialist adventure tale. Moreover, these literary expansions were to some degree targeted at the young. For example, plantation stories existed before the Civil War, especially in the adult novels geared to refute Harriet Beecher Stowe's *Uncle Tom's Cabin*. But after the war, this kind of narrative evolved for all age levels and in thematic directions that would help reconcile the North and South.

Similarly, novels with imperialistic implications existed for both children and adults before the war, but they provided only a mild foreshadowing of what the imperialist novel would become after the 1880s. Children's novelists would utilize the entire planet in illustrating the glory of European American conquests and in creating an opportunity for jingoistic boasting.

With respect to social protest, here was a mode of writing for children that had thrived in the hands of such a renowned writer as Hans Christian Andersen in the 1840s and after. But when Mark Twain blended elements of "blackface" minstrelsy with social satire, the practice of mocking Black personality received new legitimacy in mainstream culture. Few critics have yet disentangled the ironic treatment of Blacks, which can be found everywhere in Twain's works, from the white supremacist values also found there.

In short, many of the actively expanding literary forms accommodated white supremacist content to an unprecedented degree. It would not be until the twentieth century that a well-crystallized Black aesthetic would emerge to act as a counterforce. In fact, there are still too few applications of the Black aesthetic to adequately counter mainstream notions about what constitutes a classic reading experience for the young. There is not yet general acceptance of the truism that classic quality cannot be claimed for a work that sets one group of children against another. The elevation of such a work to classic status is, in essence, a political maneuver.

Notes

1. Joel Chandler Harris, *Aaron in the Wildwoods* (Boston: Houghton, Mifflin and Co., 1897), 153.
2. R. Bruce Bickley Jr., *Joel Chandler Harris* (Boston: Twayne Publishers, 1978), 36.
3. John Herbert Nelson, *The Negro Character in American Literature* (College Park, MD: McGrath Publishing Co., 1968; originally published in Lawrence: University of Kansas, Humanities Studies, vol. 4, no. 1, 1926).
4. Walter Blair, *Native American Humor (1800–1900)* (New York: American Book Co., 1937), 144.
5. Thomas H. Nelson, "In Memory of Uncle Remus," *Southern Literary History* 2 (February 1940): 77–83.
6. Louis D. Rubin Jr., "Uncle Remus and the Ubiquitous Rabbit," *Southern Review* (October 1974): 784–804.
7. Bickley, 36.
8. Joel Chandler Harris, *The Story of Aaron (So Named) the Son of Ben Ali Told by His Friends and Acquaintances* (Boston: Houghton, Mifflin and Co., 1896), 5.
9. Harris, *Aaron in the Wildwoods*, p. 48.
10. Ibid., 97.
11. Ibid., 88.
12. Ibid., 232–233.
13. Harris, *The Story of Aaron*, 30, 23.
14. Ibid., 16.
15. Ibid., 131.
16. Joel Chandler Harris, *Wally Wanderoon and His Story-Telling Machine* (New York: McClure, Phillips and Co., 1903), 8.
17. Ibid.
18. Harris, *The Story of Aaron*, 155.
19. Ibid., 51.
20. Harris, *Aaron in the Wildwoods*, 98.
21. Ibid., 166.
22. Ibid., 258.
23. Ibid., 153–154.
24. Joel Chandler Harris, *Plantation Pageants* (Boston: Houghton, Mifflin and Co., 1899), 7.
25. Ibid., 6.
26. Ibid., 7.
27. Ibid., 6, 8.
28. Ibid.
29. Ibid., 9.
30. Ibid., 8, 10.
31. Harris, *The Story of Aaron*, 194.
32. Joel Chandler Harris, *Uncle Remus: His Songs and His Sayings*, edited with an introduction by Robert Hemenway (New York: Penguin Books, 1982; originally published by D. Appleton and Co., 1880), 185.
33. Ibid., 24.
34. Joel Chandler Harris, *Uncle Remus and His Friends: Old Plantation Stories, Songs, and Ballads with Sketches of Negro Character* (Boston: Houghton, Mifflin and Co., 1892), 222–223.
35. Thomas Nelson Page, *The Novels, Stories, Sketches, and Poems of Thomas Nelson Page*, The Plantation Edition, vol. 11 (New York: Charles Scribner's Sons, 1906–1912), xi.
36. Theodore L. Gross, *Thomas Nelson Page* (New York: Twayne Publishers, 1967), 7.
37. Thomas Nelson Page, *Two Little Confederates* (New York: Charles Scribner's Sons, 1888), 138.

38. Ibid., 50.
39. Ibid., 152.
40. Thomas Nelson Page, "Jack and Jake" in *The Novels, Stories, Sketches and Poems of Thomas Nelson Page,* The Plantation Edition, vol. 11 (New York: Charles Scribner's Sons, 1908, p. 96; originally published in *Harper's Young People* 12 (October 13, 20, 27, 1891).
41. Ibid.
42. Ibid., 317.
43. Ibid.
44. Ibid., 296.
45. Gross, 49.
46. Louise-Clarke Pyrnelle, *Diddie, Dumps, and Tot, or Plantation Child-Life* (New York: Harper and Brothers Publishers, 1882), 38–39.
47. Ibid., 63.
48. Ibid., 127.
49. Ibid., 203–205.
50. Ibid., 175.
51. William Taylor Adams [Oliver Optic, pseud.], *Brother Against Brother, or The War on the Border* (Boston: Lee & Shepard Publishers, 1894), 25.
52. Ibid., 25–26, 58.
53. Ibid., 45, 49.
54. Ibid., 247.
55. Ibid., 255.
56. Ibid., 67.
57. Ibid., 65.
58. Ibid., 160–161.
59. Ibid., 317.
60. Ibid., 159.
61. Ibid.
62. Ibid., 194.
63. Ibid., 383.
64. Ibid., 334.
65. Ibid., 358.
66. Ibid., 334.
67. Ibid., 331, 245.
68. William Taylor Adams [Oliver Optic, pseud.], *Fighting Joe; or, The Fortunes of a Staff Officer: A Story of the Great Rebellion* (Boston: Lee and Shepard, 1865), 25, 294.
69. G.A. Henty, *By Sheer Pluck: A Tale of the Ashanti War* (New York: A. O. Burt, Publisher, 1890; originally published in 1884), 119–120.
70. Ibid., 129
71. Ibid., 213.
72. Ibid., 173.
73. Ibid., 174–175.
74. Ibid., 117–118.
75. Ibid., 259.
76. Ibid.
77. Guy Arnold, *Held Fast for England: G. A. Henty, Imperialist Boys' Writer* (London: Hamish Hamilton, 1980), 79–80.
78. Edward Stratemeyer, *A Tour of the Zero Club, or Adventures Amid Ice and Snow* (Philadelphia: David McKay, Publisher, 1902; originally published in *Good News,* 1894–1895, under "Harvey Hicks" pseud.), 70.
79. Ibid., 88.
80. Ibid., 100.
81. Ibid., 142.

82. Ibid., 129.
83. Ibid., 13.
84. Ibid., 176.
85. Ibid., 13.
86. Ibid., 88.
87. Edward Stratemeyer, *The Young Auctioneer, or The Polishing of a Rolling Stone* (Boston: Lothrop, Lee and Shepard Co., 1903; originally published by W. L. Allison Co., 1897), 222.
88. Ibid., 238.
89. John T. Dizer Jr., *Tom Swift & Company: "Boys' Books" by Stratemeyer and Others* (Jefferson, NC: McFarland and Co., 1982), 130.
90. Paul C. Deane, "The Persistence of Uncle Tom: An Examination of the Image of the Negro in Children's Fiction Series," *Journal of Negro Education* 37:2 (Spring 1968): 140.
91. Leo Marx, "Mr. Eliot, Mr. Trilling, and Huckleberry Finn" *American Scholar* 22:4 (Autumn 1953): 433.
92. Clemens, Samuel L. [Mark Twain]. *The Annotated Huckleberry Finn [Adventures of Huckleberry Finn]*, intro., notes, and bibliography by Michael Patrick Hearn. (New York: Clarkson N. Potter, Inc., Publishers, 1981; originally published in London by Chatto and Windus, 1884 and in New York by Charles L. Webster and Co., 1885), 109, 111.
93. Ibid., 111.
94. Ibid.
95. Ibid.
96. Ibid.
97. For a detailed examination of Mark Twain vis-à-vis minstrelsy, see Fredrick Woodard and Donnarae MacCann's "Huckleberry Finn and the Traditions of Blackface Minstrelsy" in *The Black American in Books for Children: Readings in Racism*, 2nd ed., ed. Donnarae MacCann and Gloria Woodard, (Metuchen, NJ: Scarecrow Press, 1985).
98. See Daniel Hoffman's *Form and Fable in American Fiction* (New York: Oxford University Press, 1965), 337–338, 341–342.
99. Ralph Ellison. "Change the Joke and Slip the Yoke," *Partisan Review* 25:2 (Spring 1958): 215–222.
100. For a thoughtful study of Mark Twain's images of women, see Nancy Walker's "Reformers and Young Maidens: Women and Virtue in Huckleberry Finn," in *One Hundred Years of 'Huckleberry Finn': The Boy, His Book, and American Culture*, ed. Robert Sattelmeyer and J. Donald Crowley (Columbia: University of Missouri Press, 1985).
101. Samuel Langhorne Clemens [Mark Twain]. *The Works of Mark Twain: The Adventures of Tom Sawyer, Tom Sawyer Abroad, Tom Sawyer, Detective*, ed. John C. Gerber, et al. (Berkeley: University of California Press, 1980), 284.
102. Albert E. Stone Jr., *The Innocent Eye: Childhood in Mark Twain's Imagination* (New Haven: Yale University Press, 1961), 185.
103. Kenneth L. Lynn, *Mark Twain and Southwestern Humor* (Westport, CT: Greenwood Press, 1972), 245.
104. Martha Finley, *Elsie's Motherhood* (New York: Dodd, Mead and Co., 1876), 61.
105. Ibid., 6.
106. Ibid., 63.
107. Ibid., 64.
108. Ibid., 73–74, 64, 65.
109. Ibid., 64.
110. Ibid., 145, 1515.
111. Martha Finley. *Elsie's Womanhood* (New York: Dodd, Mead and Co., 1875), 69.

112. Ibid., 53.
113. Ibid., 56, 59.
114. The circulation of the Black inferiority myth through Finley's works was enormous. According to Edward H. Dodd, an estimated 5 million copies were sold over a 70-year period. See *The First Hundred Years: A History of the House of Dodd Mead, 1839–1939* (New York: Dodd, Mead and Co. 1939), 15.

Chapter Five
The Social/Political Context

From a White Southern perspective, the Southern invasion of the North with the pen was a notable success. In order to defeat the political Reconstruction program of the radical abolitionists, a national mindset was required that would associate Blacks with the immaturity of children, and at the same time, reconcile Northern and Southern White adults. Blacks needed to be viewed in mainstream circles as incapable of adult pursuits (e.g., economic advancement, education, the exercise of the franchise, the responsibility of jury duty). Northern and Southern Whites, on the other hand, needed to be seen as congenial partners in planning and advancing the national agenda. In specific terms, this meant that even books for children would be contrived to illustrate the folly of legislative action in such fields as economic opportunity, educational reform, and electoral reform. Furthermore, protection of jury duty rights for Blacks would appear foolhardy, whereas imperialistic adventures (coupled with the "white man's burden" notion) would seem entirely reasonable.

Reconstruction and post-Reconstruction are highly complex eras and the subject of many careful, scholarly books. I am not attempting to examine this postbellum epoch in depth, but am confining my coverage to historical changes linked to elementary tenets of the American creed. This creed was being instilled in White children—that is, youngsters were learning that people have a voice in government, that everyone is entitled to a jury of one's peers, that education enhances the quality and prospects of life, that upward economic mobility is an achievable goal, that America's world role includes the active promotion of these principles. On all counts, however, the

White child was to be led to understand that the creed was inapplicable to people of color, and the Black child was to be socialized to acquiesce in his or her exclusion.

As noted above, Southern writers in the 1880s took the initiative in producing children's literature about interracial relations. Some of these writers did not attempt to conceal their sociopolitical intentions. Thomas Nelson Page said, in his comments about the dearth of antebellum Southern literature: "It was for a lack of literature . . . that in the supreme moment of her existence [the South] found herself arraigned at the bar of the world without an advocate and without a defence."[1] Page and others would make sure that the propaganda battle was not lost a second time.

It is not surprising that a lawyer such as Page would have concerns about Southern political weaknesses. But it is not so easy to explain the North's complete capitulation to the Southern viewpoint. It will be argued here, as in preceding sections of this study, that prewar cultural similarities in the White North and South made reunification on an anti-Black platform relatively simple. Even the mildest congressional measures to ensure the well-being of ex-slaves went down in defeat. There was a solid intellectual base in the North and South that the war and Reconstruction did not disturb. In a word, that unity can be summed up in the proposition that Blacks were intrinsically inferior. Such a myth, as seen in children's books in the postbellum period, is not significantly unlike its counterpart in the antebellum books.

The immediate postwar years did not result in an extensive body of children's literature about interracial relations, although war stories contained peripheral Black characters, as did Martha Finley's popular "Elsie Dinsmore" books. But a group of authors became nationally prominent after Reconstruction—authors who would place Blacks in major fictional roles and who would abide by a formula for success voiced by Joel Chandler Harris: "Whatever in our literature is distinctly Southern must . . . be distinctly American."[2] In short, the Southern writer would now take care to avoid antagonizing the Northern reader.

Historian Paul Buck has pointed out in his study of reunion that Black characters were used to advance a white philosophy of race relations, and in many respects, this did not make the postbellum stories essentially different from those written by such an antislavery writer as Harriet Beecher Stowe.[3] Only the specific propagandistic thrust of the plotline differed. The overall character of the national postwar literature was summed up by the liberal Northern judge and novelist Albion W. Tourgee when he said, "Our literature has become not only Southern in type but distinctly Confederate in sympathy."[4]

The political tie-ins of the postbellum children's books will be treated below in relation to problems of economic supply, education, the franchise, the judicial system, and imperialist expansion. But first we need to see the general outlines of the "New South."

The "New South"

It is ironic that even in the midst of the heartrending Civil War, the Southern and Northern perceptions of a proper status for Blacks did not widely differ. On the Southern side, the war would not alter that perception. During a journalistic assignment in the South following the war, John Townsend Trowbridge interviewed hundreds of Confederates and wrote the following summation of the prevailing attitude. He quotes a typical interviewee:

"We can't feel towards [the Negroes] as you do; I suppose we ought to, but it isn't possible. They've always been our owned servants; we've been used to having them mind us without a word of objection, and we can't bear anything else from them now. I was always kind to my slaves. I never whipped but two boys in my life, and one of them I whipped three weeks ago."
"When he was a free man?" I said.
"Yes, for I tell you that makes no difference in our feeling towards them."[5]

On the Northern side, while the majority probably opposed the outright resubjugation of ex-slaves, the Northerners' most prominent leader—President Lincoln—did not envision an early shift to an integrated America. He delayed and avoided emancipation, and then finally urged several gradual methods of emancipating slaves, one of which would have delayed full, nationwide manumission until 1900. The evidence compiled in James McPherson's *The Struggle for Equality* substantiates a radical abolitionist's terse critique of Lincoln vis-à-vis the Black community; Stephen Foster said, "He cannot even contemplate emancipation without colonization."[6] As Lincoln worked on a variety of plans that would have extended official, mandatory stewardship over Blacks, so prominent Southerners wistfully outlined interracial relations after the war as a paternalistic relationship with Whites in charge.

Henry W. Grady, an editor and part owner of the *Atlanta Constitution*, spelled out the essentials of this position to the business community of the North in 1886. He had already set forth the main points of his "New South" doctrine in the *Atlanta Daily Herald* in 1874, points that had also been articulated by Benjamin H. Hill and other prominent Southerners in the late 1860s and 1870s.[7] Historian Rayford W. Logan has described Henry Grady's "New South" speech—an oration that distorted and falsified interracial relations, but one that elite Northerners seemed only too ready to hear. Grady claimed that Blacks in the South were the most prosperous laboring population in existence and that they felt entirely sympathetic toward the landowning class. He maintained that ex-slaves shared in the South's school funds and enjoyed the full protection of the laws. Since Blacks, he said, had the faithful friendship of Southern Whites, they needed nothing from the legislature other than the provision for personal liberty and enfranchisement; the rest could be left to conscience and common sense. Furthermore, the slavery issue should be treated as permanently settled in the South, and henceforth the race problem should be exclusively in Southern hands. Grady emphasized the seeming reasonableness of these points by relating how slaves had protected "Massa" in wartime.[8]

Such a "New South" projected an image of a recanting South in that its leaders professed a great desire to imitate its conquerors. In regard to business, trade, and urbanization, the old Confederacy was ready to "out-Yankee the Yankee," as Henry Watterson of the *Louisville Courier-Journal* stated in 1877.[9] Southern business enterprises were attracting Northern capital, professional people were emulating the new work ethic, a middle class was evolving with its foundations in trade and manufacturing. Henry Grady's influence is indicated in the increasing circulation of his newspaper; the *Constitution* out-sold every other paper in the country in 1888.[10] Richard H. Edmonds, founder of the *Manufacturers' Record* in Baltimore in 1882, summed up the prevailing ethos: "The South has learned that 'time is money.'"[11]

This imitation of Northern industriousness may have been flattering to the North, but something was needed to salve the hurts of the demoralized and prostrate South. To that end, a potent and ironic myth began to take shape: namely a legendary "Old South" was conceived that exaggerated the very aristocratic elements that antebellum Northerners had been ready to fight to the death. Moreover, the Northern response now reversed itself. Paul Buck describes the new Northern sympathies: a plantation slave culture "which in its life was anathema to the North, could in its death be honored."[12] Even such staunch abolitionists as John Greenleaf Whittier and Thomas Wentworth Higginson were drawn into the new Southern romanticism.

"Yankeeism took to its heart the Lost Cause," writes C. Vann Woodward in *Origins of the New South, 1877–1913.*[13] But as the Lost Cause of the Confederacy was refurbished in White Northern as well as White Southern hearts, the actual prospects of Southern Blacks plummeted. Woodward comments that "one of the most significant inventions of the New South was the 'Old South'—a new idea in the eighties, and a legend of incalculable potentialities."[14] If one can call a host of new hardships for the Black population "potentialities," then Woodward is right in dubbing the legendary Old South a significant concept. It proved efficient in building an intellectual base for Black peonage, educational deprivation, exclusion from political and legal processes, and more.

When the "Old" and "New" came together and were translated into fictional terms in children's literature, a new generation was primed to share and acquiesce in regressive post-Reconstruction legislation. Anti-Black attitudes would penetrate the culture to such depths as to embrace youth culture. In such a milieu, it was not likely that Congress would support economic development, including Black emigration from the South; nor would the Blair educational bill and the Lodge electoral bill meet with success. Judicial reform, especially the right of Blacks to serve on juries, received some legal backing from the Supreme Court, but the Court also provided the means by which its liberal ruling could be successfully circumvented.

The "Black Exodus"

After federal troops were withdrawn from the South in 1877, living conditions for Blacks deteriorated to the point where emigration was viewed by many as the only real option. The attempts of ex-slaves to resettle in Kansas and elsewhere in 1879 has since been dubbed the "Black Exodus." Such a sign of desperation or despondency hardly corresponded with Henry Grady's representation of Southern Blacks as the world's most prosperous laboring population—a group enjoying educational opportunities and the full protection of the laws. When the Senate instituted a committee to investigate the Black migration, they predictably heard conflicting testimony. Senator Benjamin H. Hill of Georgia insisted, "The colored people of the Southern States are perfectly contented with their situation exactly in proportion to the length of time they have been under the government of what are known as the white people of that country. . . ."[15] On the other hand, Senator John J. Engalls of Kansas said that all the Black people he spoke to gave the same reason for their emigration—namely, to obtain "Protection of . . . political and civil rights and a fair day's wage for an honest day's work."[16]

James McPherson's analysis of economic conditions for Blacks during the war years and Reconstruction indicates that Ingalls's report was largely correct. "The South was not 'reconstructed' economically," says McPherson, "and consequently the other measures of reconstruction rested upon an unstable foundation."[17] However, the widely circulated books for the young gave support to Hill's position in that they depicted the contentment of both slaves and ex-slaves within the plantation framework. Issues pertaining to employment and land distribution were entirely misrepresented or concealed.

One of the most promising land redistribution projects occurred in 1862 after Union forces had captured the South Carolina Sea Islands and their eight thousand abandoned slaves. Lincoln was persuaded to allow the Blacks temporary possessory titles to the plantations, with Northern superintendents and teachers instructing them in the fundamentals of reading, writing, and self-employment. However, this action was a war measure: General Sherman was unable to feed and shelter the thousands of destitute slaves in captured territories. And subsequently abolitionists were not able to extend the life of the Sea Islands experiment when a long-term land policy began to evolve. Northern capitalists wanted to purchase the Confederate plantations for their own advantage, and Northerners joined Southerners in claiming that Blacks were too indolent to manage their own lands. Horace Greeley coined the slogan: "People who want farms work for them. The only class we know that takes other people's property because they want it is largely represented in Sing Sing."[18] This same attitude was voiced in the *New York Times* and in other centers of power—an attitude that utterly contradicted one of the principal rationales of the war: that is, that Blacks had been robbed of *their property* by being treated *as property* and had earned the land or some comparable remuneration for their long years of toil. Since the fruit of slave labor had been plainly stolen from slaves, a normal application of property law would have mandated either restitution or payment of damages for the loss. But only a small group of radical abolitionists took this position.[19] Turning logic on its head, the mainstream groups began to insist that ex-slaves were abusers of the work ethic.

Henceforth, all land distribution measures promoted by abolitionists were a failure. By 1900, three-fourths of the Blacks on farms were tenant farmers and were subjected to the primarily fraudulent crop-lien system. Under this arrangement, farm supplies and implements had to be obtained from rural merchants, many of whom either tampered with the records or used a credit mark-up that ensured that tenant farmers would be perpetually in debt.[20] The Freedmen's Bureau, backed by the presence of federal troops, had been some insurance against such abuses, but it was terminated in 1869. Moreover, the Freedmen's Bureau itself had helped organize the insidious contract labor system under which the freedmen and freedwomen were bound to work for a specific time and planter. For ex-slaves, a semifeudal system was designed from the outset instead of the kind of land distribution plans that brought assistance to many European American immigrants in the American West.

In 1879, Senator William Windom of Minnesota proposed legislation that would encourage and assist Black migration from the South to the western territories. But the Senate's committee of investigation concluded that the rights of Blacks in the South had not been curtailed and that no government assistance was warranted.[21] Meanwhile, more than 40,000 Blacks left Mississippi, Louisiana,

Alabama, and Georgia for Kansas, Nebraska, Iowa, and Oklahoma, as well as Liberia and Mexico. Economic deprivation and/or race bias awaited them in most of these locales.[22]

In contrast to all this anguish, children's literature presented such an Edenic picture of Blacks in rural settings that Black migration efforts must have appeared to young White readers and to their book-buying parents as an instance of pure irrationality. The plantation myth offered images of an economy in which the needs of Blacks were always met. According to the fiction of the times, a governmental assistance program would result in the utter ruin of Black character, not to mention the needless squandering of the nation's resources.

Writers for children went to almost any lengths to instill the idea that plantation life was humane and desirable. Louise-Clarke Pyrnelle in *Diddie, Dumps, and Tot, or Plantation Child-Life* (1882) presents the victims of slave-trading as generally content. Their itinerant camp life resembles a Sunday picnic.

The speculator's camp was situated on the bank of the creek, and a very bright scene it presented as Major Waldron and his party came up to it. At a little distance from the main encampment was the speculator's tent, and the tents for the negroes were dotted here and there among the trees. Some of the women were sitting at the creek, others were cooking, and some were sitting in front of their tents sewing; numbers of little negroes were playing about, and, altogether, the "speculator's camp" was not the horrible thing that one might suppose. . . .
The negroes were well clothed, well fed, and the great majority of them looked exceedingly happy. They came across one group of boys and girls dancing and singing. An old man, in another group, had collected a number of eager listeners around him, and was recounting some marvelous tale; but occasionally there would be a sad face and a tearful eye. . . .[23]

The one tearful slave in this camp, it turns out, is a woman dying from consumption and worrying about who will be available to care for her young son. Such "devotion to her baby was unusual in a slave," comments the author.

As mentioned above, Joel Chandler Harris saw slavery on the

plantation as a great "university" for the Black population. He writes in *Aaron in the Wildwoods* (1897) about an abolitionist schoolteacher who understands after the war how wonderful slavery really was. This teacher learns,

That in the beginning, the slaves who were brought here were redeemed from a slavery in their own country worse than the bondage of death; that though they came here as savages, they were brought in close and stimulating contact with Christian civilization, and so lifted up that in two centuries they were able to bear the promotion to citizenship which awaited them; and that, although this end was reached in the midst of confusion and doubt, tumult and bloodshed, it was given to human intelligence to perceive in slavery, as well as in the freedom of the slaves, the hand of an All-wise Providence, and to behold in their bondage here the scheme of a vast university in which they were prepared to enjoy the full benefits of all the blessings which have been conferred on them. . . .[24]

George A. Henty, the popular British writer, treats American slavery as a basically superior social security system. Henty uses an ex-slave as his mouthpiece:

Me trabel a good deal, and me think dat no working people in de world are so merry and happy as de slabe in a plantation wid a good massa and missy. Dey not work so hard as de white man. Dey have plenty to eat and drink, dey hab deir gardens and deir fowls. When dey are sick dey are taken care ob, when dey are ole dey are looked after and habe noting to do. . . . De slabe hab no care and he bery happy. . . . Me tell you dat de life on a plantation a thousand times happier dan de life of a black man in his own country.[25]

Henty does admit that slavery in America had two drawbacks: a master would "leabe all to overseers, and dese bery often bad, cruel men;" and a master would sell "De husban' . . . to Alabama, de wife to Carolina, de children scattered through de States. Dis too bad, sar'. . . ."[26]

Books that describe the postwar plantation—for example, Martha Finley's *Elsie's Motherhood* (1876)—do not significantly alter the trappings of the plantation culture other than to eliminate the selling of spouses and children. Farm worker wages are mentioned, but they appear to be utterly irrelevant. Finley writes:

The Ion [plantation] negroes were paid liberal wages, and yet [were] kind and generously cared for as in the old days of slavery; even more so, for now Elsie might lawfully carry out her desire to educate and elevate them to a higher standard of intelligence and morality.[27]

Elsie Dinsmore Travilla, the protagonist, provides her farm workers with a schoolhouse and teacher, but Finley, the author, implies by her characterization of Blacks that they are uneducable.

Stories embracing the plantation myth are replete with such contradictions. Since the economic, educational, political, and judicial systems were interrelated, to alter one would bring about change in the others; and any sweeping change is what an author such as Finley is unwilling to support. It is likely that the crop-lien system, for example, could have been overthrown by an educated work force with equal access to the courts. But the White community was not open to the idea of equalizing opportunity on any front.

Educational Reform and the Blair Bill

Education has an essential role to play in the preservation or alteration of a culture. As parents and teachers go about the business of socializing the next generation, they evaluate and clarify their own attitudes. Before people engage in the art of teaching, they ordinarily justify the content of their teachings to themselves. If the South were to sustain a culture based on White dominance in the postwar years, it needed to put forth the argument that Black people were the offspring of a lesser god, so to speak. The core of such an argument was that Blacks were uneducable, except on an exceptionally elementary level.

Such a position was broadly disseminated, and it underpinned other aspects of the cultural status quo; that is, the denial of political and judicial rights to Blacks, mandatory racial segregation, and an economic caste system. There was, however, a countermovement.

One of the enterprises initiated by Northern abolitionists during and after the war was the education of Southern Blacks. It can be argued that one reason for the White Southerners' urgency vis-à-vis removal of Union troops was their wish to discourage the continued presence of abolitionist educators. These educators were clearly a barrier to the propagation of the myth that Blacks were intellectually inferior—a myth needed as the basis for the impending disfranchisement of ex-slaves.

Even as the war was coming to an end, there were nine hundred teachers in the South from Northern and Western freedmen aid societies, enough, perhaps, to foil an easy reestablishment of the prewar social structure. Between 1861 and 1865, more than 200,000 ex-slaves received schooling from the antislavery groups. It is estimated that between 1861 and 1893, 30 percent of Black education in the South resulted from some sort of Northern assistance.[28]

The American Missionary Association (dominated by abolitionists) set up schools in every part of the Confederacy as it was overrun by Union forces. Some antislavery leaders (for example, J. Miller McKim) urged that the abolitionist movement be largely transformed into a movement to educate and assist the emancipated Blacks. The "pulling down" stage must now become the "building up" stage, said McKim.[29] Such a proclamation presaged a potentially deep-seated revolution at the core of Southern culture. But although this threatened revolution may have alarmed the leadership group in the South, it was not the threat to the White social structure that it appeared to be since abolitionist educators were opposed by many in the North. The radical antislavery people were not able to muster the votes to sustain a vigorous educational movement on behalf of ex-slaves, and their own Northern neighbors numbered among their antagonists. According to one representative of the conservative Northern press, the abolitionist educators descending upon South Carolina were "a band of Abolition socialists, free lovers, and disorganizers of society generally."[30]

Moreover, there was dissension within the antislavery ranks because some teachers emphasized secular rather than religious education (the American Missionary Association desiring the latter). Also the charge that teachers indulged in paternalistic behavior was leveled at some aid society people. Frederick Douglass noted that the societies were a "necessity of the hour," but that "the negro needs justice more than pity; liberty more than old clothes; rights more than training to enjoy them."[31]

These were well-grounded concerns because the ongoing problem was to achieve full-scale, practical liberation, not just an official edict proclaiming emancipation. After the slaves were legally free, it would still be the White population that would need to be taught rather than the Black—that is, taught to comprehend the bases upon which to build social and political equality. Yet many of the Northern abolitionist teachers in the South faced more implacable critics than those who charged them with patronizing attitudes toward Blacks. Their Confederate antagonists wanted to restore the prewar racial hierarchies, and to them the carpetbagger teacher represented too much liberalism and interference. McPherson notes that many of these teachers were insulted, beaten, and left with their schoolhouses in ashes because they were accused of either communicating ideas of social equality, or, by example, inculcating such ideas.[32] The contentious and vengeful climate in which they worked demonstrated the need for federal programs and backing. But the divided abolitionist movement was not in a position to organize congressional support.

An example is the failed effort of New Hampshire Senator Henry William Blair, who introduced a series of education bills in Congress in an attempt to keep educational opportunity alive. His plan for federal aid was designed to reduce illiteracy in all states over an eight-year period, with allotments based on the number of illiterates in a state (above the age of ten) in relation to the number in the United States at large. The bill included an antidiscrimination provision, mandating governors to show that educational opportunities were equal for Blacks and European Americans, and a special sum of two million dollars was to be set aside for the construction of school buildings. Blair maintained that educational opportunity had not significantly increased over a twenty-five-year period, and that it had probably declined.[33]

Prior to 1890, these proposals were overturned by the House. Blair's 1890 bill was defeated in both the House and Senate. Opponents of the bill used a number of well-crystallized arguments: that local efforts to support education would be undermined, that inquiries into discriminatory practices violated states' rights, that the bill opened the way for federal interference in textbook selection, teacher behavior, and the separation of races.[34] Since nearly as many members of the Republican (the antislavery) party as the Democratic party voted against the bill in the Senate (seventeen and twenty, respectively), it seems clear that such a socially progressive measure was unacceptable to both the North and the South.[35]

This antieducation solidarity is seen in the widespread acceptance of children's books that encouraged the myth of Black ineptitude. Authors sometimes conveyed that idea by means of jumbled speech. It was not always dialect, per se, but dialect in combination with the misuse of simple words—a confusion in speech that went beyond what one would find even in a child's language. In Martha Finley's *Elsie's Motherhood*, there are at least five different dialects plus baby talk; but none of the characters with these speech patterns make the kind of errors attributed to the Blacks. For example, when the protagonist's household is fending off a Ku Klux Klan attack, one Black servant says he will "expense (boiling lye) out of de windows," and another exclaims: "an dis niggah's to demand de boilin' lye compartment of dis army ob defense."[36] It is doubtful that even a youngster would confuse the words "contents" and "contentions" as a Black character does in the following lines: ". . . when dis niggah says fire, slam de contentions—dat's de bilin' soap, min'—right into dar ugly faces."[37]

Another way that authors hint at Black mental deficiency is by juxtaposing an adult Black character with White children and by demonstrating that the latter have more competence. Mark Twain uses this method in *Tom Sawyer Abroad* when he depicts Huck and Tom as thoroughly rational in an emergency, whereas the ex-slave, Jim, panics. Jim learns to operate the mechanism of a hot-air balloon, but in a moment of stress (the arrival of a lion on the ground below) his flustered reaction contrasts with the children's equanimity.

Jim lost his head, straight off—he always done it whenever he got excited and scared, and so now, 'stead of just easing the ladder up from the ground a little, so the animals couldn't reach it, he turned on a raft of power, and we went whizzing up and was dangling in the sky before he got his wits together and seen what a foolish thing he was doing. Then he stopped her, but had clean forgot what to do next. . . .[38]

In *Two Little Confederates*, Thomas Nelson Page portrays an elderly Black slave boasting to two young White boys about his man-
hood while he makes a fool of himself and becomes the brunt of
their jokes. An unshakably loyal slave, Uncle Balla, locks a captive
Union soldier in the plantation hen house. As he secures the door
with a nail and a piece of string, he talks to himself in a manner that
will duly impress the young bystanders:

"Willy jes' gwi' let you get 'way, but a man *got you now, wha'ar' been
handlin' horses an' know how to hole 'em in the stalls. I bound' he'll have
to butt like a ram to get out dis log hen-house,"* he said, finally, as he
finished tying the last knot in his string. . . . *"Ef he gits out that hen-
house I'll give you ev'y chicken I got. But he ain'* gwine *git out. A man's
done fasten him up dyah."*[39]

The next morning Uncle Balla is seen circling the hen house with a
"comical look of mystification and chagrin" while members of the
household are convulsed with laughter. Both captive and chickens
have escaped through the roof, but Uncle Balla insists that another
soldier has "come back and tooken out the one he had locked up."
He becomes the target of derision as Willy inquires from time to
time whether Uncle Balla has "fastened his horses well."

In these scenes and similar ones, the Black characters are not
treated as people who have made a mistake. They are characterized
as hopelessly immature, as lacking the kind of reasoning power and
facility with language that would give them some success as learners.
Such characterizations added a sense of validity to what the Southern editorial writers were printing about Black education. Said the
Paducah (Kentucky) *Herald:* "To talk about educating this drudge is
to talk without thinking."[40] To such journalists, a logical extrapola-
tion would include the idea that to enfranchise "this drudge" would
be "to talk without thinking."

Electoral Reform and the Lodge Bill

The disfranchisement of Blacks in the South appears at first puzzling, given the way universal male suffrage was built into the
postbellum legal structure. Readmittance of Confederate states into
the Union hinged upon the guarantee of Black male voting rights.

The Fifteenth Amendment of the Constitution, ratified in 1870, was a further assurance that this right was inviolable. Nonetheless, by the late 1870s, American presidents (including Hayes, Arthur, and Garfield) were saying publicly that a lack of literacy in the Black population was justifiable grounds for denying ex-slaves the right to vote.

This reversal of one of the most basic tenets in any democracy placed American Blacks in a no-win dilemma. The presidents listed above gave meager support to the idea of federal aid to education; and without the franchise, it was impossible to legislate the appropriations required in support of an adequate school system. It would appear, as Rayford Logan theorizes, that Northerners as well as Southerners did not want to see the Black population become a real political force.[41] Logan notes that Senator Windom of Minnesota made a perceptive observation when he said in 1890 that "the black man does not excite antagonism because he is black, but because he is a *citizen*, and as such may control an election."[42] The fate of the Lodge Bill lends validity to this observation.

The proposal for federal supervision of federal elections was introduced in 1890 by Henry Cabot Lodge when he was a Representative from Massachusetts. It provided for federal supervisors who could be petitioned to pass judgment on voter qualifications, and who were also empowered to receive ballots from those voters who were unjustly turned away by local election officials.[43] Lodge offered statistics to prove the wholesale disfranchisement of Blacks in such states as Georgia, Mississippi, and South Carolina. He persuasively argued that the conflict over the right to vote was an extension of the conflict over slavery. He said, "If we fail as a people to deal with this question rightly, we shall pay for it just as we paid the debt of slavery of which all this is a part."[44]

The bill passed in the House by a margin of 155 to 149, but was killed in the Senate (after much delay) when eight Republicans voted with the majority. Arguments against the reform were frequently sweeping in their allusions to white supremacy. According to Senator Pasco of Florida: "The Anglo-Saxon will be true to his history. In every quarter of the world where he has been placed side by side with people of other races he has ruled."[45] Moreover, the South, Senator James Z. George of Mississippi warned, would simply not comply if a reform bill should be passed: ". . . it will never come to pass in Mississippi, in Florida, in South Carolina, or any other State of the South, that the neck of the white race shall be under the foot of the negro, or the Mongolian, or of any created being."[46]

Against such vehement Southern antagonists, the supporters of the Lodge Bill appear too ambivalent to offer much hope for the bill's passage. For example, Senator Hiscock of New York agreed with his opponents that Blacks were inferior to Anglo-Saxons, but then presented the argument that Anglo-Saxons were a fair-minded people and needed to act accordingly.[47] This self-congratulatory claim on Hiscock's part proved meaningless. Votes for the Lodge Bill were not forthcoming, and Mississippi, South Carolina, and Louisiana took action in the 1890s that "legalized" Black disfranchisement. Reconstruction's constitutional guarantees were, in the end, completely dismantled.

The interlocking nature of the disfranchisement and education issues is suggested in Louise-Clarke Pyrnelle's *Diddie, Dumps, and Tot, or Plantation Child-Life.* The narrator's resentful comments about a Black Reconstructionist legislator are juxtaposed with an ex-slave's incoherent prattle about schooling. First Pyrnelle describes the legislator as an ungrateful upstart:

Aunt Sukey's Jim . . . is a politician. He has been in Legislature, and spends his time in making long and exciting speeches to the loyal leaguers against the Southern whites, all unmindful of his happy childhood, and of the kind and generous master who strove in every way to render his bondage (for which that master was in no way to blame) a light and happy one.[48]

Aunt Nancy is the emancipated slave who is "not progressing very rapidly" as a scholar:

Yer see, honey, dat man wat larnt me dem readin's, he wuz sich er onstedfus' man, an' gittin' drunk, an' botin' an' sich, tell I furgittin' wat he larnt me; but day's er colored gemman fum de Norf wat's tuck him up er pay-school ober hyear in de 'catermy, an' ef'n I kin git him fur ter take out'n his pay in dat furmifuge wat I makes, I 'low ter go ter him er time

er two, caze he's er membah ob de Zion Chu'ch, an' er mighty stedfus'
man, an' dat wat he learns me den I'll stay larnt.[49]

Perhaps the strongest hint that Black voting would lead to certain chaos comes to the reader from Uncle Snake-bit Bob, who "does
not meddle with politics." Pyrnelle lets him explain:

I don't cas' my suffrins fur de Dimercracks, nur yet fur de 'Pulbicans. I
can't go 'ginst my color by voin' de Dimercrack papers; an' ez fur dem
'Publicans! Well, ole Bob he done hyear wat de Book say 'boutn publicans
an' sinners, an' dat's ernuff fur him. He's er gittin' uperds in years now;
pretty soon he'll hatter shove off fur dat 'eb'nly sho'; an wen de Lord sen'
atter him, he don't want dat angel ter cotch him in no kinwunshuns
'long wid 'publicans an' sinners.[50]

The narrator assures us that Uncle Bob's store-keeping and odd-jobs
allow him to do "just as well as if he were in Congress."[51]

Joel Chandler Harris's *Uncle Remus: His Songs and His Sayings*
includes frequent use of the theme of moral laxness in Blacks, and in
this way suggests their unreadiness for self-government. Like Pyrnelle,
he adds insult to injury by making a Black character his principal
mouthpiece. Pegleg Charley tells Uncle Remus that he is "preparin'
fer to shake worldliness," and Remus gives him encouragement:

Ef you got 'lijjun, you better hole on to it 'twell de las' day in de mornin'.
Hit's mighty good fer yer kyar' 'roun' wid you in de day time an' likewise
in de night time. Hit'll pay you mo' dan politics.[52]

A few lines later it seems that Uncle Remus views the fleecing of
naive churchgoers as an expected mode of behavior:

"How long is you bin in de chu'ch, son?"
"Mighty near a week," replied Charley.
"Well, lemme tell you dis, now, 'fo' you go enny fudder. You ain't bin in
dar long nuff fer ter go 'roun' takin up conterbutions. Wait ontwell you
gits sorter seasoned like, an' den I'll hunt 'round' in my cloze an' see if I
can't run out a thrip er two fer you. But don't you levy taxes too early."[53]

Similarly, in another saying Uncle Remus implies that honest dealings are a temperamental impossibility in Blacks. There is no apparent irony intended when Remus exclaims: "De nigger w'at k'n trapes 'round wid pies and not git in no alley-way an' sample um, den I'm bleedzd ter say dat nigger outniggers me an' my fambly."[54]

Harris persistently impresses upon his readers the futility of educating for citizenship a group that allegedly revels in thievery of one sort or another. As for formal education along other lines, he treats it as hazardous to the work ethic—a proposition that would hardly be applied to young White scholars. In the following lines, Remus preaches about education, work, and uppityness:

"W'at a nigger gwineter l'arn outen books? I kin take a bar'l stave an' fling mo' sense inter a nigger in one minnit dan all de schoolhouses betwixt dis en de State er Midgigan. . . . Wid one bar'l stave I kin fa'rly lif' de vail er ignunce."
"Then you don't believe in education?"
"Hits de ruination er dis country. Look at my gal. De ole 'oman sont 'er ter school las' year, an' now we dassent hardly ax 'er fer ter kyar de washin' home. She done got beyant 'er bizness. . . . Put a spellin'-book in a nigger's han's, en right den en dar' you loozes a plow-hand. I done had de spe'unce un it."[55]

Educational deficiencies in Blacks undergird the related political theme—namely, that it would be a high risk, indeed, to allow this group entry into the political system. Children's books repeatedly imply that ex-slave enfranchisement would be like letting a (mental) infant play with fire. For similar reasons, Blacks could not be viewed as reliable participants on juries.

Equal Protection Clause Nullified

Given the frequent references to childishness in Blacks, it was not surprising that jury duty for African Americans was viewed in the White mainstream as a form of social irresponsibility. The problem for those in power, then, was to find a way to subvert the guarantee of the Fifth Amendment of the Constitution that no citizen could be "deprived of life, liberty, or property, without due process of law," and the reiteration of this principle in the Fourteenth Amendment.

This nullification of the judicial process as it constitutionally applied to Blacks was accomplished in the concluding decade of the nineteenth century.

Immediately following the Civil War, military courts were the means of ensuring due process for ex-slave litigants in the South. Although the Supreme Court in the 1870s began nullifying many of the Reconstruction Acts on the grounds that they usurped states' rights, the Court did sustain the equal protection clause of the Fourteenth Amendment in relation to jury duty. In 1880 the Court overturned the West Virginia laws that excluded Blacks from grand and petit juries. In a case in Virginia the same year, the Court ruled that state agents were bound by the Fourteenth Amendment and that a county judge could not legally exclude Blacks from jury service. Similarly, a Delaware law that restricted jury duty to White persons was overruled.[56]

Unfortunately, there was a loophole offered by one ruling that made the de facto exclusion of Blacks from juries relatively simple to achieve. An 1880 Supreme Court decision held that the Fourteenth Amendment's equal protection clause was not violated if it could not be demonstrated that Black exclusion was based solely on factors of race or color.[57] In the years that followed, it became more and more difficult to offer evidence of race discrimination in jury selection that the courts would accept. For example, a county in Mississippi with seven thousand Blacks, fifteen hundred Caucasians, and records that showed zero number of Blacks summoned for jury duty was nonetheless exonerated on the grounds that no clear proof of race discrimination was available.[58]

It is suggested by Howard N. Meyer, attorney and Fourteenth Amendment expert, that barriers to impartial jury selection clearly violated the intent of the amendment. He cites testimony by one of the drafters, Congressman John A. Bingham of Ohio, about the amendment's scope. In his support for anti–Ku Klux Klan legislation in 1871, Bingham described the conditions that the Fourteenth Amendment was designed to correct. He said that before the Fourteenth Amendment went into effect,

the States did deny to citizens the equal protection of the laws, they did deny the rights of citizens under the Constitution. . . . they denied trial

by jury and he [the wronged citizen] had no remedy. They took property
without compensation and he had no remedy. . . . Who dare say, now
that the Constitution has been amended, that the nation cannot by law
provide against all such abuses and denials of right as these in States and
by States, or combinations of persons?"[59]

The Supreme Court was apparently determined to stay on a
course of government decentralization and, while it doubtless had
motives besides the resubjugation of Blacks, it is hard to interpret
the actions of the post-Reconstruction Court without noting its fa-
cilitation of White rule. Perhaps the most fundamental of all the
constitutional violations of this period was the nullification of the
judicial system vis-à-vis Blacks. A social structure that provides no
legal redress of grievances is one that creates a no-hope cultural milieu for the targeted group.

For the mainstream to move this far from the principles of democracy, an intellectual base had to be established that extended
even into youth culture. Books for children constituted at least a
part of that base by repeatedly putting forth the impression that
Blacks had an inborn incapacity to handle language. A courtroom
was a place where a comprehension of word meanings (or the lack
thereof) could make all the difference.

Moreover, children's books constantly alluded to the Black population as consisting of inveterate thieves. The likelihood of bribes
being accepted by Black jurors was an easily deduced conclusion,
given the general run of narratives about alleged Black kleptomania.

Looking first at Black language in relation to the deteriorating
system of legal protection, we should note at the outset that generally a fictional character's speech patterns bring us about as close as
we can come to the character's thought patterns. In this chapter we
have already seen Martha Finley's use of Black speech to suggest
Black uneducability. Linguistic errors by her population of African
Americans are those that would not be expected from her population of child readers. It will suffice here to show the extremes to
which authors go as they point to mental and verbal incompetence.
In Pyrnelle's *Diddie, Dumps, and Tot,* Black characters turn "situated" into "swotuated," "circumstances" in to "konkumstances," and
"consequences" into "kinsequonces." It is hard to decipher some terms

(for example, "sackremenchus") even within the context of their sentence and paragraph.[60] Louis J. Budd in his essay "Joel Chandler Harris and the Genteeling of Native American Humor" refers to stereotyping in Harris's works and to the way Harris supplies humor through an improvised vocabulary. Budd asks, "Did any black actually say 'surgeon er de armies' for 'sergeant at arms'?"[61] Clearly there would be havoc in a court trial if participants were to mix up such phrases, or such words as "instruct" and "obstruck" (as characters do in *Diddie, Dumps, and Tot*). Such mistakes, combined with an exaggerated phonetic spelling system for the speech of Black characters, provided a thinly disguised method of suggesting a verbal (and mental) distance between Black and European American characters. Folklorist Harold Courlander emphasizes this point when he notes that the rendering of Negro speech bordered on the bizarre, and was an irrational way to suggest an ethnic contrast. He writes:

The speech of whites normally was represented in traditional orthography, even though some of them pronounced various words much the same as did the blacks.[62]

Courlander views this practice as clearly a form of conscious abuse.

The kleptomania theme has already been mentioned with reference to Uncle Remus. One of its more famous manifestations is found in the "moral" code worked out by the slave, Jim, in Mark Twain's *Adventures of Huckleberry Finn*—a code cleverly formed to salve the conscience of the culprits. Huck and Jim need some means of foraging for food as they drift down the river, and Jim's rationalizations combined with Huck's pilfering skills solve the problem.

Mornings, before daylight, I slipped into cornfields and borrowed a watermelon, or a mushmelon, or a punkin, or some new corn, or things of that kind. Pap always said it warn't no harm to borrow things, if you was meaning to pay them back, sometime; but the widow said it warn't anything but a soft name for stealing, and no decent body would do it. Jim said he reckoned the widow was partly right and pap was partly right; so the best way would be for us to pick out two or three things from the list and say we wouldn't borrow them any more—then he reckoned it wouldn't be no harm to borrow the others. So we talked it over all one

night, drifting along down the river, trying to make up our minds whether
to drop the watermelons, or the cantelopes, or the mushmelons, or what.
But towards daylight we got it all settled satisfactory, and concluded to
drop crabapples and p'simmons. We warn't feeling just right before that,
but it was all comfortable now. I was glad the way it came out, too,
because crabapples ain't ever good, and the p'simmons wouldn't be ripe
for two or three months yet.[63]

At this point in the novel, the reader is well aware that Huck is
a physically abused child and must literally fend for himself. Also
Jim, as a runaway slave, must understandably live by a renegade's
rules. But Twain does not show us the conditions within the slave
culture that have led to Jim's deviousness. On the contrary, during
the last fifth of the novel, Jim makes no real effort to escape from
slavery. He is victimized by his child friends more than by his owner,
who ultimately frees him on her own initiative. It can be argued that
Jim's arguments on behalf of stealing are not offered within the context of slavery, but represent the notions held by whites about alleged Black thievery during the 1880s.

It is not surprising that such treatments of Black character were
contemporaneous with exclusions of Blacks from jury duty, from
the witness box, and from the political process. Nor is it surprising
that images of Blacks as overgrown children, or as so dimwitted as to
require caretakers, would ultimately be fastened on people of color
on a world scale.

The "White Man's Burden" in the "Waste Places of the Earth"

The phrase popularized by Rudyard Kipling, "white man's burden,"
contained two of the basic rationalizations used by European American imperialists as they spread their spheres of influence in the world.
The phrase masks the colonizer's self-interests by implying that colonial domination is a burdensome act undertaken on behalf of the
needy. Moreover, this self-sacrifice can be assumed only by a "white
man" because only Whites are viewed as "civilized," as in a position
to uplift others. The non-Anglo-Saxon regions were dubbed "dark
continents" or "waste places." Even the once-liberal Henry Cabot
Lodge (who had argued for electoral reform) stated with obvious

approval: "The great nations of the world are rapidly absorbing the waste places of the earth."[64]

It is this white chauvinism that unified both the imperialist and anti-imperialist factions in the late nineteenth century. There was a prevailing belief in a master race, a trend that has been interpreted by historian Christopher Lasch as evidence that Northern liberals in the 1890s had "retreated from the implications of their emancipation of the Negro. . . ."[65] In other words, even the nation's most liberal wing was asserting that the "negritos" of the Philippines and the Blacks and Creoles of Cuba and elsewhere were unfit for self-government. This was a marked departure from the rationale behind the Fifteenth Amendment, namely, that Blacks as well as other groups warranted full participation in their government.

Experts on American imperialism differ widely as they analyze this contradiction in anti-imperialist thought. But as yet they have not incorporated children's literature into their studies, a field of inquiry that adds additional support to Lasch's hypothesis. Before turning to a specific example of imperialist propaganda for the young, it is necessary to consider briefly the debate on American expansionism.

Historian Daniel B. Schirmer views some of the underlying causes of expansionism as ironic. For example, while the rapid growth of American industry turned the United States into a world power, this growth simultaneously made the American economy more vulnerable to the serious negative effects of an economic slump.[66] Foreign markets offered some relief to a glutted home market, a type of cure that was being vigorously applied by European nations in such regions as Latin America, Africa, and Asia.

Another paradox is discernible in the way American imperialist aims were moved briskly forward under the banner of anti-imperialism. A case in point is the Spanish-American War and the method used by the United States to absolve itself. Americans burned with indignation over the cruel treatment inflicted upon Cubans as they rebelled against Spanish rule—an upheaval sparked by the worldwide economic depression of 1893. But at the same time, the United States was ready to supplant Spain as the colonial ruler in most of the territories where the United States stepped in militarily as the "liberator."[67] Such contradictory behavior is explained, says Schirmer, by two competing traditions in American history. First, there is the anti-imperialist tradition stemming from America's own struggle for liberation and self-determination in 1776. Second, there is the imperialist tradition as demonstrated in the near-extermination of American Indians, the appropriation of Mexican territory in the Southwest, and the proclamation of American hegemony in the Western Hemisphere (the declaration embodied in the Monroe Doctrine of 1823).

By the end of the nineteenth century, the Monroe Doctrine was being stretched to encompass the Pacific Ocean as well as the land masses of the continent. Foreign markets, insisted the industrialist William F. Draper, required the protective oversight of a strong navy in many far-flung bases. "With these bases, a properly organized fleet . . . will hold the Pacific as an American ocean, dominated by American commercial enterprise for all time."[68] The American position vis-à-vis Latin America was clear when Secretary of State Richard Olney sent the following warning to Great Britain in 1895. Its colony British Guiana was embroiled in a boundary dispute with Venezuela.

Today the United States is practically sovereign on this continent, and its fiat is law upon the subjects to which it confines its interposition. Why? . . . It is because, in addition to all other grounds, its infinite resource combined with its isolated position render it master of the situation and practically invulnerable as against any or all other powers.[69]

As for the new territorial holdings in the Pacific, Senator Lodge said about the recently occupied Philippines in 1899: "We have full power and are absolutely free to do with these islands as we please."[70]

Such unabashed muscle-flexing at the center of the U.S. government occurred repeatedly. And concurrently, the white supremacy theme was expressed by diverse social groups. The *Textile Record* spoke for the strong cotton textile industry centered in New England:

Supremacy in the world appears to be the destiny of the race to which we belong . . . the most competent governor of inferior races. . . . The clear path of duty for us appears to be to bring to the people of the Spanish islands in the Pacific and the Atlantic an opportunity to rise from mis-

ery and hopelessness to a promise of just government and commercial success.[71]

Referring to the issue of self-determination for the indigenous peoples of Hawaii, Senator George Frisbie Hoar said, "It would be as reasonable to take the vote of children in an orphan asylum or an idiot school."[72] Senator John W. Daniels's label for the Filipinos was "a mess of Asian pottage," while educator David Starr Jordan made mention of the Philippines when he explained that it lies "in the heart of the torrid zone, 'Nature's asylum for degenerates.'"[73] The New York Mugwump leader, Carl Schurz, predicted an exacerbated internal American race problem should the United States "take in Spanish-Americans, with all the mixtures of Indian and Negro blood, and Malays and other unspeakable Asiatics . . . and all of them animated with the instincts, impulses and passions bred by the tropical sun."[74]

Corporation magnate Andrew Carnegie voiced the conviction that "to that race [the Anglo-Saxon] primarily belongs in a preponderring degree the future of mankind, because it has proved its title to its guardianship."[75] The Episcopal Bishop of New York, Henry Codman Potter, was ambivalent about expansionist policies, but not about his own ethnocentric perspective. "At present," he said, "[the Filipinos] are no more fit to lead themselves, or organize a government, than a parcel of children."[76] Given the abundant pronouncements of this sort, historian James P. Shenton concludes that "the expropriation of colonial property had as its ultimate justification not economic necessity but the belief in the colored man's inferiority and incompetence."[77]

Christopher Lasch has traced white supremacist thinking in the writings of both imperialists and anti-imperialists. The latter group feared militarism and especially the influence of a large standing army, a force that would be necessary to quell rebellions among the colonials and that would eventually undermine democracy at home.[78] But democracy was a phenomenon viewed as suitable for civilizations only, and neither imperialists nor anti-imperialists, according to Lasch, were willing to call tropical zone nations fit for self-government.

Pseudo-Darwinism was, in large measure, the underpinning for these elaborate rationalizations for wars of conquest. But the animosity expressed by soldiers in the field may have been induced by something less abstract—for example, by boys' books that treated Blacks as highly expendable. A collection of American soldiers' letters from the battlefields in the Philippines was published by the Anti-Imperialist League in 1899. One correspondent referred to filling "the blacks full of lead before finding out whether they are friends or enemies"; another said, "Our fighting blood was up, and we all wanted to kill 'niggers'. . . ."[79] The characterizations of people of color in imperialist children's novels usually included the brute beast stereotype—an image that was so fearsome that the Anglo-Saxon liquidation of the "brutes" was treated by authors as entirely reasonable.

George A. Henty's *By Sheer Pluck: A Tale of the Ashanti War* (1884) is an example of how African cultures were depicted as incredibly sadistic. The popularity of such portraiture is indicated by this British author's widespread and ongoing influence. In addition to being read throughout the British empire, his works were pirated by approximately fifty American publishing houses between 1885 and 1920. His bibliographer, Robert Dartt, estimates sales of one hundred fifty thousand copies a year in Henty's peak years, and an overall total sales of about twenty-five million. Moreover, forty titles had come back into print by 1964 (their copyrights having expired) and a Henty Society was organized in Great Britain in 1977.[80]

By Sheer Pluck contains a horrific picture of alleged cultural practices in Coomassie, the Ashanti nation's capital city. The schoolboy protagonist, Frank Hargate, is there during the British invasion of 1873–1874, along with some German missionaries who are being held captive. Frank and the Germans converse about Ashanti customs:

"You noticed," one of them said, "the great tree in the market-place under which the king sat. That is the great fetish tree. A great many victims are sacrificed in the palace itself, but the wholesale slaughters take place there. The high brushwood comes up to within twenty yards of it, and if you turn in there you will see thousands of dead bodies or their remains putrefying together."

"I thought I smelt a horribly offensive smell as I was talking to the king,"

*Frank said, shuddering. "What monsters these people must be! Who would
have thought that all that show of gold and silver and silks and bright
colors covered such horrible barbarism!"[81]*

A description of ritual tortures follows (a fate experienced by no
less than 3,000 persons annually, according to Henty):

*[The man being taken to sacrifice] was preceded by men beating
drums. . . . A sharp thin knife was passed through his cheeks, to which
his lips were noozed like the figure 8. One ear was cut off and carried
before him, the other hung to his head by a small piece of skin. There
were several gashes in his back, and a knife was thrust under each shoulder blade. He was led by a cord passed through a hole bored in his nose.
Frank ran horror-stricken back into the house, and sat for awhile with
his hand over his eyes as if to shut out the ghastly spectacle.[82]*

It is hard to believe that the circulation of nineteenth-century
boys' books (and their lurid scenes of alleged torture) was a phenomenon completely unrelated to the victory of American imperialists over anti-imperialists. The brute stereotype was represented in
adult literature by such a novelist as Thomas Dixon (e.g., in *The
Leopard's Spots* and *The Clansman*), but the overall impact of the
Dixon books may have been less than the impact of imperialists
boys' books, given the latter's extraordinary sales records. Furthermore, Henty was read by people of great influence, including oil
tycoon J. Paul Getty and British Prime Minister Harold Macmillan.
Hugh Walpole assessed the novels as offering a largely authentic treatment of history; he said, "I fancy that all the children of my day who
gloried in Henty were the Realists. . . ."[83] Henty's bibliographer, Eric
Quayle, says he was viewed as a "historian":

*The debt the late-Victorian and Edwardian educationalists owed to G. A.
Henty as a popular historian was often acknowledged in later years. . . .[84]*

Expansionist propaganda in children's books was by no means a
negligible facet of the white supremacy myth's development.

Conclusion

The failure of the radical abolitionists' quest for equal rights in the North is an important behind-the-scenes facet of the story of postbellum children's literature. This is not to put blame on the North for the many Southern, white supremacist literary works for the young. But to understand this literature's nationwide popularity as well as its literary counterpart in Northern publishing establishments, attention needs to be given to the cracks in abolitionist-inspired idealism. It is not surprising that the South would continue its struggle to maintain a White-dominated social structure. But the North's early capitulation in that struggle points to an array of contradictions within American culture at large.

Despite the disunities within abolitionist ranks, abolitionist writings do offer the reader a resounding declaration of principles that could have guided an evolving multiracial nation. Frederick Douglass, the former slave and leading Black abolitionist, told an audience as early as 1862:

Let the American people, who have thus far only kept the colored race staggering between partial philanthropy and cruel force, be induced to try what virtue there is in justice.[85]

Douglass's suggestion, however, had little hope of fulfillment. In the post-Reconstruction era, the North joined forces with the South to create a long-standing underclass, and the rhetoric of racism reached an increasingly higher pitch. Historians have tried to explain why this was so. For example, some have advanced the theory that trends affecting the mainstream in the two regions exacerbated a sense of guilt. That unpleasant emotion, in turn, found relief in the scapegoating of Blacks.

In the North, the trend that gained increasing momentum was summed up in the following terse statement from the *Nation* in 1877: "The nation will have nothing more to do with [the Negro]."[86] Memories of the war, notes historian Larry Kincaid, were fading, antislavery advocates were willing to let the Reconstruction Amendments suffice as protection for Blacks, and a new generation was preoccupied with problems of rapid urban and corporate expansion.[87]

In the South, the underlying causes of guilt were somewhat different. There the problem was to reestablish White hegemony over the region, and without the controlling devices of slavery, that meant the use of increasingly harsher methods of repression and intimidation. To a Christian conscience, writes Kincaid, "in order to justify the barbarity of the assault, the barbarity of the victims had to be painted in more and more lurid hues. The more inhumanely white Southerners behaved, the more they had to believe in the inhumanity of black Southerners."[88]

Historian George Fredrickson makes an analysis similar to Kincaid's with respect to the brute stereotype. He comments that many purveyors of that stereotype probably felt "genuine fears and hatreds," but "what white extremists may have confronted in the image of the black brute was not so much a Negro as a projection of unacknowledged guilt feelings derived from their own brutality towards blacks."[89]

Moreover, there had been a predisposition toward treating Blacks as a permanent underclass in the antebellum period, as Susan B. Anthony implied when she lamented racial discrimination in the North in a speech in 1861. She noted that Northerners hated tales of slaveowner cruelty, "And yet, what better do we? While the cruel slave-driver lacerates the black man's mortal body, we, of the North, flay the spirit."[90]

The radical fringe of the abolitionist group did make some headway in desegregating Northern schools and outlawing segregated public transportation, as James McPherson spells out in detail in *The Struggle for Equality*.[91] But the story of that progress is misread if we believe it bespeaks a predominant liberal force in postbellum culture. Anthony's pessimistic assessment is substantiated by the record of defeats in Congress for abolitionist programs—plans involving land redistribution, educational opportunity, and a guaranteed franchise.

The psychologically oriented interpretations of Fredrickson, Kincaid, and others as they diagnose post-Reconstruction are essentially hypothetical. But their multifaceted approach is an improvement over the kind of analysis that spotlights only a few political leaders. It was not individuals at the center of power who purchased twenty-five million copies of the George Henty books to give to children and libraries, or five million copies of Finley's "Elsie Dinsmore" novels. It was not for a specialized or elite readership that 145 American editions of *Adventures of Huckleberry Finn* were published prior to 1977.[92] Those Reconstruction and post-Reconstruction artifacts have had a broad base of support.

Postbellum writers for children did not advance the equality theme of radical abolitionism. That theme continued to be conspicuously absent from children's books about Blacks for nearly a century. Following the Civil War, it was a white supremacist mythology that was widely and vigorously circulated.

Notes

1. Paul H. Buck, *The Road to Reunion, 1865–1900* (Boston: Little, Brown and Company, 1937), 198.
2. Ibid., 220.
3. Ibid., 210.
4. Albion W. Tourgee, "The South As a Field for Fiction," *Forum* 6 (December, 1888): 405.
5. John Townsend Trowbridge, *My Own Story: With Recollections of Noted Persons* (Boston: Houghton, Mifflin and Company, 1903), 290–291.
6. James W. McPherson, *The Struggle for Equality: Abolitionists and the Negro in the Civil War and Reconstruction* (Princeton: Princeton University Press, 1964), 103.
7. Rayford W. Logan, *The Betrayal of the Negro: From Rutherford B. Hayes to Woodrow Wilson* (New York: Collier Books, new enlarged ed. 1965), 180–181.
8. Ibid., 181.
9. C. Vann Woodward, *Origins of the New South, 1877–1913* (Baton Rouge: Louisiana State University Press and The Littlefield Fund for Southern History of the University of Texas, 1951, 1971), 151.
10. Ibid., 145–153.
11. Ibid., 153.
12. Buck, 208.
13. Woodward, 55.
14. Ibid., 154–155.
15. Logan, 138.
16. Ibid., 140.
17. McPherson, 416.
18. Ibid., 412.
19. Ibid., 251.
20. Logan, 131.
21. Ibid., 140.
22. Ibid., 140–146.
23. Louise-Clarke Pyrnelle, *Diddie, Dumps, and Tot, or Plantation Child-Life* (New York: Harper and Brothers, 1882), 97–98.
24. Joel Chandler Harris, *Aaron in the Wildwoods* (Boston: Houghton, Mifflin and Company, 1897), 153.
25. G.A. Henty, *By Sheer Pluck* (New York: A.L. Burt, Publisher, 1890; originally published in 1884), 189.
26. Ibid., 190.

27. Martha Finley, *Elsie's Motherhood* (New York: Dodd, Mead and Company, 1876) p. 28.

28. McPherson, 171, 407.

29. Ibid., 161.

30. Ibid., 164.

31. Ibid., 397.

32. Ibid., 395.

33. Logan, 67.

34. Ibid., 69.

35. Ibid., 70.

36. Finley, 204, 215.

37. Ibid., 220.

38. Mark Twain, *The Works of Mark Twain: The Adventures of Tom Sawyer, Tom Sawyer Abroad, Tom Sawyer, Detective,* ed. John C. Gerber, et al. (Berkeley: University of California Press, 1980), 305.

39. Thomas Nelson Page, *Two Little Confederates* (New York: Charles Scribner's Sons, 1888), 27–28.

40. McPherson, 395.

41. Logan, 19.

42. Ibid., 137.

43. Ibid., 70–71.

44. Ibid., 71–72.

45. Ibid., 78.

46. Ibid., 77–78.

47. Ibid., 79.

48. Pyrnelle, 237–238.

49. Ibid., 239.

50. Ibid., 238.

51. Ibid., 238–239.

52. Joel Chandler Harris, *Uncle Remus: His Songs and His Sayings,* ed. with an Introduction by Robert Hemenway (New York: Penguin Books, 1982; originally published in 1880), 214–215.

53. Ibid., 215.

54. Ibid., 196.

55. Ibid., 216.

56. Logan, 111–112.

57. Ibid., 112.

58. Ibid., 122.

59. Howard N. Meyer, *The Amendment That Refused to Die,* rev. ed. (Boston: Beacon Press, 1978), 66.

60. Pyrnelle, 139, 158, 159, 29.

61. Louis J. Budd, "Joel Chandler Harris and the Genteeling of Native American Humor," in *Critical Essays on Joel Chandler Harris,* ed. R. Bruce Bickley Jr. (Boston: G.K. Hall & Co., 1981), 203.

62. Harold Courlander, *A Treasury of Afro-American Folklore* (New York: Crown Publishers, 1976), 258.

63. Samuel Langhorne Clemens [Mark Twain], *Adventures of Huckleberry Finn: An Authoritative Text, Backgrounds and Sources, Criticism,* 2nd ed., ed. Sculley Bradley, et al. (New York: W.W. Norton, 1977; originally published in London by Chatto and Windus, 1884 and in New York by Charles L. Webster and Co., 1885), 56.

64. Daniel B. Schirmer, *Republic or Empire: American Resistance to the Philippine War* (Cambridge: Schenkman Publishing Company, 1972), 36.

65. Christopher Lasch, "The Anti-Imperialists, the Philippines, and the Inequality of Man," *Journal of Southern History* 24:3 (August 1958): 319.

66. Schirmer, 21.

67. Ibid., 45.
68. Ibid., 30.
69. Richard B. Morris, ed., *Encyclopedia of American History* (New York: Harper and Brothers, 1953), 286.
70. Schirmer, 236.
71. Ibid., 87.
72. Ibid., 86.
73. Ibid., 328.
74. James P. Shenton, "Imperialism and Racism," in *Essays in American Historiography: Papers Presented in Honor of Allan Nevins*, ed. Donald Sheehan and Harold C. Syrett (New York: Columbia University Press, 1960), 238.
75. Ibid., 239.
76. Ibid., 241.
77. Ibid., 233.
78. Lasch, 322.
79. Schirmer, 142.
80. Guy Arnold, *Held Fast for England: G.A. Henty, Imperialist Boys' Writer* (London: Hamish Hamilton, 1980), 17, 18.
81. Henty, 247.
82. Ibid., 248.
83. Arnold, 177, 176.
84. Ibid., 19.
85. McPherson, 187–188.
86. Buck, 283.
87. Larry Kincaid, "Two Steps Forward, One Step Back: Racial Attitudes During the Civil War and Reconstruction," in *The Great Fear: Race in the Mind of America*, ed. Gary B. Nash and Richard Weiss (New York: Holt, Rinehart and Winston, 1970), 67.
88. Ibid., 66
89. George M. Fredrickson, *The Black Image in the White Mind: The Debate on Afro-American Character and Destiny, 1817–1914* (New York: Harper Torchbooks, 1972), 282.
90. McPherson, 225.
91. Ibid., 221.
92. Robert M. Rodney, ed., *Mark Twain International: A Bibliography and Interpretation of His Worldwide Popularity* (Westport, CT: Greenwood Press, 1981), 264.

Chapter Six
Literary Lives

Racially biased literature poured from the pens of postbellum writers whether they were primarily specialists in the sciences, humanities, or arts. Historian I. A. Newby has noted that the nation experienced an unprecedented inundation of anti-Negro literature between the years 1890 and 1920.[1] Writers for children veered between ambivalence and open hostility, writing for an audience that was perceived as exclusively White. It was understood that Black children could not be expected to enter the realm of the reading public. Such a presumption is clearly tied to a set of political expectations.

There can be little doubt that the Civil War was at the center of life and politics for most postbellum children's writers. Moreover, it is significant that this particular conflict was not about a simple boundary dispute or some other typical form of rivalry; it was about the way an entire section of the human race was to be defined. Thus bitterness about the war became (on the Southern side) bitterness about people, and even emancipationist zeal on the Northern side could not rise above postwar biases bred of nonacquaintance with Black identity and culture. In this chapter, biographical details shed light upon why Blacks were excluded as an audience, yet included as fictional characters in works by postbellum authors. But the "Great Rebellion" itself is the central fact to keep in mind.

We will consider first the group of writers that directed their works primarily toward youngsters. Within this group, William T. Adams and Louise-Clarke Pyrnelle were professional teachers, at least for a time. Edward Stratemeyer and Martha Finley wrote children's books as a business venture (although Finley also spent two years teaching). From these teachers and entrepreneurs, popular modes of thought could be expected. They joined other mainstream communicators in attempting to redefine the status and role Blacks might have in postbellum American life.

Of the remaining four, George Henty, Joel Chandler Harris, and Mark Twain were professional journalists. Thomas Nelson Page began his career as a lawyer, but also served a short stint as a teacher. Henty held strong views about England's imperial role, and spent twenty years representing the Tory viewpoint as a member of the British press. Harris, Page, and Twain tried to have some impact upon serious public issues in the United States, including the problem of post–Civil War reunification.

What we know of the lives of these writers includes information about their political orientation. We can see a specific cultural base from which each one moved into the field of children's literature.

Teachers and Entrepreneurs: Adams, Pyrnelle, Finley, Stratemeyer

William T. Adams (1822–1897) was an educator who believed in freely incorporating entertainment in his instructional methods. By mid-life he had become an entertainer exclusively—that is, a full-time writer of adventurous novels and short stories. But while he amused his readers, he still took care to instill in them his moral and patriotic ideals. Such a career parallels that of the antebellum series author, Jacob Abbott. However, in Adams's day, a higher level of excitement in a formulaic children's story was acceptable in many circles. Thus Adams could combine in his career the serious concerns of a professional educator and the techniques of popular literature. He could even participate actively in the dime-novel industry.

These two aspects of Adams's professionalism are suggested by reviews of his Civil War novels in the *Philadelphia Inquirer* and the *Portland Press*. The *Inquirer* noted about the novel *The Sailor Boy* and its sequels: "The works are prepared with care, and the hero is a pious as well as a brave man." The *Portland Press* stressed the breathtaking adventures in *The Soldier Boy* and concluded with the comment that this "Soldier Boy" series "will thrill the hearts of youthful readers with patriotic fire."[2] Adams was praised by some of his contemporaries for his deep understanding of young people and his willingness to please them on their own terms. Others among his peers saw his suspenseful stories as a form of pandering to the child's escapist reading tastes.

The controversy seems to have centered on the quantity of excitement in an Adams novel, not on the author's general attitudes. In relation to his overall social and political positions, he appears to be typical of Northern, genteel liberals and their ambivalence toward anything culturally or racially different. The clues pointing in this direction are found within Adams's child-related literary activities, for those activities were his chief occupation for more than half a century.

Besides writing 126 novels and more than 1,000 short stories, Adams edited several magazines for the young, including *Oliver Optic's Magazine: (Our Boys and Girls)* beginning in 1867. The content of this weekly indicates the editor's Unionist leanings, his tendency to place blame for the war on the South. In a magazine sample from the first six months of 1869, Civil War articles appeared intermittently by an author who signed himself Millinocket. This author emphasized the martyrdom of Union soldiers and the horrors of the war. He sometimes mentioned the bravery of Black Union infantrymen.[3] The Confederate general, Robert E. Lee, is referred to as "the rebel chieftain," the "stern Lee . . . with his fierce columns."[4]

Another regular feature in the magazine was an essay or poem placed under the column heading "Oratory." This column was by no means exclusively political in subject matter, but Charles Sumner's speeches were used several times and carried to the reader a Northern political perspective. The following excerpt is from Sumner's "The United Republic."

All hail to the Republic! Redeemed and regenerated, one and indivisible. Nullification and secession are already like the extinct monsters of a former geological period—to be seen only in the museum of history. With their extinction must disappear that captious, litigious, and disturbing spirit engendered by state rights. . . . Interlaced, interlocked, and harmonized, [the states] will be congenial parts of the mighty whole; while

*liberty and equality will be the recognized birthright of all, and no local
pretension can interfere against the universal law.*[5]

To balance such serious messages, Adams included short, whim-
sical stories by Willy Wisp. But here Sumner's ringing words about
equality were contradicted, for Willy Wisp treated African peoples
derisively. In his "The Basket-Makers of Bongoloo," Blacks are depicted as inferiors, and Jack, the New England hero, must use all his
wits to escape marriage to the African king's daughter Ko Chee Wassee
Wan Loo.[6] The mocking tone of Willy Wisp was also at odds with
the attitude of Millinocket, who sometimes referred to Black participants in the war as courageous men. Millinocket pointed to a
degree of equality between Black and Caucasian fighting units.

This postwar ambivalence is not surprising in Adams's editorial
work. He has been called "the Homer of Civil War juvenile literature,"[7] but the war novels have been studied only in relation to their
antislavery political content, not their paradoxical ambivalence toward Blacks. Adams did not stay clear of racial stereotyping, but,
like Harriet Beecher Stowe, he brought a considerable passion to his
efforts to encourage a democratic idealism. He proclaimed as his
motto: "First God, then country, then friends."[8]

Adams descended from the same ancestral line as Governor
Samuel Adams and Presidents John Adams and John Quincy Adams.
Perhaps it was this auspicious lineage that caused him to attach many
pseudonyms to his writings and on no occasion use the name Adams.
His father, Laban Adams, was the proprietor of a Boston inn, Adams
House, and he educated William T. in the public and private schools
in the Boston area. Adams was a high achiever in school, especially
in composition, and began his career as a writer at the age of nineteen. His career as a teacher began in his twentieth year. For two
decades he worked as a schoolmaster and a headmaster in the Boston school system,[9] and was simultaneously active in Sunday school
work. In 1869 he served one term in the Massachusetts legislature
(declining renomination).

Eventually Adams found his school duties to be a drain on the
time he needed for writing. He left the school system in 1865 and
embarked on many trips abroad as a stimulus to his novel writing.
In 1867, he helped launch the fabulous career of Horatio Alger Jr.

by serializing Alger's *Ragged Dick; Or, Street Life in New York* in his magazine the *Student and Schoolmate.*[10]

Adams's career offers a good example of how a Northern professional with antislavery leanings would be inclined to treat Blacks first as pure abstractions, and later as pure stereotypes. The prewar rhetoric of equality that sometimes surfaced in his work did not last long under the pressure of postbellum white supremacist propaganda. However, his readers did not apparently object; Adams was one of the nation's most widely read authors by the time of his death at the age of seventy-four.

He had achieved this popularity despite an open battle over the quality of his works at the American Library Association's annual conference in 1879. Abolitionist Thomas Wentworth Higginson had defended him, agreeing with Adams's dictum that it was not sound to "keep young minds always on the high-pressure system of education."[11] Others followed the lead of Louisa May Alcott who had criticized Adams for being preoccupied with the sensational rather than the moral.

Children's books were the center of considerable strife during Adams's lifetime, but what was at issue was child-rearing practices in relation to moral rectitude. Cross-cultural authenticity and social justice were not a focus of debate because the myth of white superiority was not generally questioned in mainstream circles. Biased Black portraiture had an invalid, yet incredibly stubborn social base.

In contrast to William T. Adams, a staunch Unionist, was Louise-Clarke Pyrnelle (1850–1907)—a bitter, dispossessed Secessionist. That is, Pyrnelle's father served in the Confederate Army, and his daughter clearly perceived the Civil War as an outrageous injustice inflicted upon the South. Very little has been written about Louise-Clarke Pyrnelle, but her two novels for children, *Diddie, Dumps, and Tot, or Plantation Child-Life* and *Miss Li'l' Tweetty*, are detailed documents about alleged class and race differences. They reveal viewpoints that were undoubtedly strong convictions in the author.

Pyrnelle was born in 1850 into a distinguished Southern family: her father a prominent Virginian and her mother a member of a leading family in Alabama. Her childhood plantation home and all her father's lands near Uniontown, Alabama, were lost in the war. This did not mean that the family was destitute, for Pyrnelle's father had been a practicing physician as well as a plantation owner. He was able to send his daughter to school in the North following the war, to Professor McKay's Delsarte Academy in New York City and Mrs. Anna Randall Diehl's College of Education on Long Island.[12]

Pyrnelle worked as a governess and as a public schoolteacher in the South prior to her marriage to John R. Pyrnelle of Browns, Alabama, in 1880. It was not a profession that enjoyed much status in the pre–Civil War South—a fact reflected in *Diddie, Dumps, and Tot* when Mammy explains about the family tutor:

She ain't no rich white folks . . .
Caze efn she wuz, she wouldn't be teachin' school for a livin', an' den
ergin, efn she's so mighty rich, whar's her niggers?[13]

Working for a living was not a prospect that Pyrnelle would have been led to anticipate before the war, and the loss of the family fortune must have been traumatic. This loss was the result of a war over slavery, and Pyrnelle did not believe that slavery was a *problem* to either masters or slaves. Her primary motivation in writing her first novel was to clarify that point. She wrote in the preface:

I know not whether [slavery] was right or wrong but it was the law of the land, . . . and, born under that law a slave-holder, and the descendant of slave-holders, raised in the heart of the cotton section, surrounded by negroes from my earliest infancy, "I KNOW whereof I do speak"; and it is to tell of the pleasant and happy relations that existed between master and slave that I write this story of Diddie, Dumps, and Tot.[14]

Pyrnelle develops her narrative as a way to express a somewhat paternalistic relationship, and then concludes with a grim chapter about the lives of her protagonists after the war. The depth of the author's angry feelings come across clearly as she relates the wartime death of the father, the insanity of the mother, the death of Diddie's husband in battle, and the deprived life of Dumps. She attaches to Dumps the thankless job of being a teacher:

And Dumps? Well, the merry, lighthearted little girl is an "old maid" now; and if Mammy could see her, she would think she was "steady" enough at last.

Somebody, you know, must attend to the wants and comforts of the gray-haired woman in the asylum; and Diddie had her boy to support and educate, so Dumps teaches school and takes care of her mother. . . .[15]

Only the youngest, Tot, escapes the devastation of the war; she dies in early childhood.

The sharp contrast between the despondency of Diddie and Dumps at the end of the tale and their effervescence in childhood—their spontaneity, ingenuity, and expressiveness—provides a glimpse of Pyrnelle's overall viewpoint as she penned the lines of her novel in her early thirties.

She would not write again until the close of her life. By then, Susan E. Miller suggests, the passing of time and the considerable public approval and recognition she had received probably lessened the wartime bitterness.[16] In any case, *Miss Li'l' Tweetty* contained the same class and race distinctions as the earlier book, but no references to the war. It was a less complex mixture of plantation folkways and political rationalizations.

Martha Finley (1828–1909) was an expatriate of the North who expressed her affinity for both the Southern and Northern regions by making her most famous heroine, Elsie Dinsmore, a staunch Southern Republican. She was also expressing White attitudes in both regions when she characterized the Blacks in her novels as servile. Yet she deserves more credit than is typically bestowed upon her for an early and unstinting attack upon the Ku Klux Klan. It is possible to interpret Finley as a concerned and hardworking citizen, rather than a neurotic woman who wrote about the plantation as a fairy tale realm in which to escape. But the latter interpretation has been the predominant one.

Finley was ambivalent about Blacks in the same way that William T. Adams was ambivalent, but she came to that political and social perspective by a route that was quintessentially female, as defined by nineteenth-century beliefs. The details of her life suggest that she suffered many of the typical economic, physical, and emotional stresses experienced by women in the 1800s. Finley's mother died when she was very young, and during Martha's growing-up years she lived with her father, her stepmother, and a household of fourteen children. Her father was a doctor who sent Martha to private schools in Philadelphia and in South Bend. She served as a teacher for two years before commencing a career (at the age of twenty-six) as an anonymous writer of Sunday school publications. By this time both parents were dead and Finley was forced into what appears to be an almost lifelong struggle to preserve her self-respect and economic independence. She was the "poor relation" in the households of an aunt, sister, and stepbrother—the latter giving assistance when Finley suffered from a back ailment and was entirely dependent upon her family financially. She seems to have strived diligently, on both a practical and spiritual plane, to extricate herself from this demoralizing position. She is reported to have directed her prayers toward "something which would yield her an income."[17] It is estimated that she wrote about one hundred books in all, often using the name Farquharson when she did not write anonymously. Her family objected to having the Finley name made conspicuous.[18]

The twenty-eight-volume "Elsie" series made Finley her fortune, and she was able to build a home of her own in Maryland in her fifty-first year.[19] Despite frail health, she lived eighty-one years. Although her alter ego Elsie Dinsmore has been called "a nauseous little prig,"[20] there was also a sturdy and rebellious side to this character. As Finley's prodigious literary output demonstrates, there must have been something sturdy in Finley herself. She pulled herself out of pauperism by writing for boys, girls, adults, and Sunday schools. Her first "Elsie" book outsold every other juvenile book of its time with the exception of Alcott's *Little Women*.[21]

Still, "nauseous" is not too strong as a descriptive label of Elsie.[22] The series is nauseous in its Bible-thumping (but not in the eyes of nineteenth-century readers), and nauseous in its portrayal of violent and masochistic relationships between men and women.[23]

Female submissiveness is an undeviating thematic strain in Finley's work and one of its most negative elements. Yet an undercurrent of rebelliousness persists. This tension characterized the lives of many nineteenth-century women. It was perhaps the presence of the nonconformist element that enabled Finley to come forward as an attacker of the Ku Klux Klan in her novel *Elsie's Motherhood*. And while the Dinsmore-Travilla family do sit out the Civil War in a posh Italian villa in *Elsie's Womanhood,* Finley works into this novel of the war years a dramatic exposé of the Andersonville prison camp.

To criticize Finley is to criticize her era and its effects upon her. But there is also reason to acknowledge her contribution to the intellectual history of her time, a contribution that rests primarily on her 1876 condemnation of the Klan. The publication of the anti-Klan novel coincides with the highly turbulent moment when Reconstruction was coming to an end. I know of no other children's book writer who entered so boldly into the political debate of that era.

However, whether a nineteenth-century mainstream author was an expatriate of the North (like Finley) or an expatriate of a slave-holding state (like Mark Twain), a white supremacist mode of thought was clearly apparent. The anti-Klan commitment of Finley was regrettably offset by an equally firm belief in Black inferiority.

Finally, one more irony needs to be mentioned in the "saga of Elsie Dinsmore"—namely, that while Stanley Kunitz and Howard Haycroft saw Elsie as a prig in the 1930s, librarians of the mid-1940s sometimes banned "Elsie" books because of the heroine's rebellious spirit. The following excerpts from letters to Finley scholar Janet E. Brown reveal something of the professional conservatism of the twentieth century (and paradoxically underscore the very strength of Elsie's characterization to nineteenth-century readers):

The Philadelphia Free Library doesn't allow [Miss Finley's] books on the shelves of either the main library or any of its branches; they stand accused of inviting youth to filial disobedience. [Letter from Professor John C. Mendenhall, University of Pennsylvania.]

My "official attitude" towards Elsie is sufficiently lenient to give her shelf room, though not to catalogue her, and anyone is privileged to read our two books as curiosities, but we neither recommend nor give them to children.[24] [Letter from Dorothy Moorhouse, Librarian, Ludington Memorial Public Library.]

Even though Finley was essentially promoting respect for family life and its harmonies, it was the fictionalization of a family tie that would eventually bring her into disfavor. For "Elsie" (read "Finley") despite her lugubriousness and her complexes, did not completely suppress her fighting spirit. Future feminist scholars will doubtless clarify this aspect of Finley's character, rather than dwell upon the veiled incestuousness in her father-daughter characterizations or the stylistic absurdities that resulted from her evangelical zeal.

Edward Stratemeyer (1862–1930) is judged more as an entrepreneur of children's literature than an author in present day scholarship. He was both. But as a person in business, someone searching for income by writing for children, he soon became known for his close connection with the marketplace, popular culture, and heavy commercialization.

Stratemeyer's books and those of his ghostwriters were not just "popular" in the usual sense. According to historian Peter A. Soderbergh, it was Stratemeyer-inspired fiction that constituted the mass medium of the period 1894–1915.[25] Russel Nye has concluded that between 1905 and 1930 Stratemeyer "had probably been read by more Americans than any other publisher. . . ."[26]

To be so massively available to the public was a task of impossible proportions for a single individual, and thus Stratemeyer hired about twenty ghostwriters, many of them contributing manuscripts that would be published under a single pseudonym. The existence of such ghostwriters had to be concealed. Popularity required not only many laborers, but the maintenance of the illusion that real, identifiable personalities were responsible for the books. Thus the life story of Stratemeyer himself had to be concealed. When Stratemeyer's two daughters succeeded him in controlling his syndicate of writers, they sustained the ghostwriting hoax. As a *Fortune Magazine* journalist reported about his efforts to learn about Stratemeyer:

What, the sisters demand in amazement, would their clients think if they knew that the great gallery of juvenile authors, Roy Rockwood, Victor Appleton, Lester Chadwick, Laura Lee Hope, May Hollis Barton, and so on, was nothing but a waxworks invented by their father? So greatly do they feel the need of maintaining the illusion of these fictitious literati that . . . they have refused to authorize any of the many attempts to write his life history.[27]

To this day, only a few details of Stratemeyer's personal story are repeated in essays and books *about* him. This son of German immigrants was himself a product of popular culture (he avidly read and collected the Horatio Alger and Oliver Optic novels). In the manner of a Horatio Alger hero, he drafted his first story on some brown wrapping paper as he waited on customers in his brother's tobacco shop. This was in 1886. The boys' magazine, *Golden Days*, paid seventy-five dollars for this first effort. He continued writing for magazines and dime-novel publishers while he ran a stationery store in Newark. In 1893 he was asked to edit the boys' weekly, *Good News*.[28]

In 1898 Stratemeyer enjoyed another stroke of good luck when Admiral Dewey and his forces defeated the Spanish fleet in Manila. Stratemeyer had written a boys' book about youngsters on a battleship and had submitted it to Lothrop, Lee, and Shepard. No action was taken until the war news inspired a Lothrop editor to ask Stratemeyer to revise his story, giving it a tie-in with the war. Thus *Under Dewey at Manila; or, The War Fortunes of a Castaway* was published in 1898. The next year, the first of Stratemeyer's "Rover Boys" books was published. His series books poured forth until in 1906 he decided he needed the help of a so-called syndicate of writers.[29]

We are able to know Stratemeyer primarily through his works for children. Peter A. Soderbergh, more than any other scholar, has studied those works in their cultural and historical contexts. Soderbergh gives us some clues as to how Stratemeyer's fiction reflected prevailing public opinion in the field of race relations. In thirty-two books that had a tie-in with the Boer War, the Boxer Rebellion, the Russo-Japanese War, or any one of five American wars, Stratemeyer illustrates Soderbergh's contention that any character who opposed the U.S. military was "satanic, deprived, misguided, recalcitrant, cruel, and unseeing."[30] A Stratemeyer hero in the "Old Glory" series viewed the Spaniards as brutes and the "Moros *insurrectos* of Mindanao [as] bloodthirsty, tricky, 'brownies' who would rather decapitate American soldiers than eat."[31] Stratemeyer's military books have yet to receive a comprehensive review. But it has been determined that his canon tends to be anti-Black, anti-Asian, anti-Native American, anti-Semitic, and anti-Hispanic.

At least two distinct aspects of Stratemeyer's influence on American culture need further scrutiny. First, the juvenile ethic that was forged by Horatio Alger and expanded by Stratemeyer needs closer examination in relation to public policy-making. Soderbergh has noted that Stratemeyer's "importance lies in his ability to expand the [Alger] philosophy and relate it to the exigencies of history: war, industrialization, invention, and changes in taste."[32] To know more of the specifics of Stratemeyer's propaganda would be to provide historians with an important predictive tool, for the distribution of the syndicate publications has been and remains enormous. A survey conducted by the American Library Association in 1926 indicated that 98 percent of a sample of 36,000 children selected a Stratemeyer title as a favorite book. Sales figures following World War II showed an *annual* sales record of six million.[33]

The second issue that warrants the attention of historians and theorists revolves around the ghostwriting practices that Stratemeyer did not invent, but significantly strengthened. It is ironic that one of the sleaziest publishing practices was and is connected with the Alger/ Stratemeyer ethic—a code that demands honesty. In the preface to *Joe the Surveyor,* Stratemeyer told his readers that they should understand "that honesty is not only 'the best policy,' but that it should be the only policy considered."[34] Yet when a persistent inquirer asked for information about one of the Syndicate's bogus authors, May Hollis Barton, Stratemeyer had an assistant fabricate a biography. His writers were required to sign a sworn affidavit that included the promise to never divulge to anyone that they had ever written a Syndicate book.[35]

Aside from the obvious ramifications, especially the hypocrisy of this deceptiveness, there is the issue of responsibility and its diffusion in a corporation. If youth culture is shaped in important ways by unknowns, the culture faces unnecessary risk. The treatment of race relations in fraudulently authored books is a case in point. Racial bias has been able to flourish in such works.

Social Commentators: Page, Harris, Twain, Henty

There have always been a number of children's book authors who did not write for young people exclusively or primarily. Some wrote fiction for all age levels and some ventured into nonfiction. Discoveries can be made about the social and political attitudes of Page,

Harris, Twain, and Henty by examining what they wrote for their peers about controversial public issues, as well as what issues they selected for their children's books.

References to lynching, for example, reveal a general point of view in the nonfiction works of Page, Harris, and Twain. In a chapter on this subject in *The Negro: The Southern Problem* (1904), Thomas Nelson Page (1853–1922) wrote a thirty-two-page rationalization of the practice. He posited the blame upon what he called the "animal instincts" in Blacks that turned them into rapists, and the rhetoric of social equality that encouraged Blacks to seek cohabitation with White women.[36] He blamed the Black population for not exercising restraint upon its members, a restraint that had allegedly been built into the functioning of the community during the age of slavery.[37] Page voiced a number of sweeping generalizations:

. . . the Negro does not generally believe in the virtue of women. It is beyond his experience. He does not generally believe in the existence of actual assault. It is beyond his comprehension. In the next place, his passion, always his controlling force, is now, since the new teaching, for the white women.[38]

According to Page, lynching is the natural horror that stems from a deeper horror—as he puts it, "the ravishing [of women] by an inferior race."[39] Since Southern Whites and the federal government were at odds, it was not unreasonable (so Page argues) for extralegal measures to be taken.[40] He insisted that,

the charge that . . . the innocent are sometimes lynched has little foundation. The rage of a mob is not directed against the innocent, but against the guilty; and its fury would not be satisfied with any other sacrifice than the death of the real criminal. Nor does the criminal merit any consideration, however terrible the punishment.[41]

According to literary scholar Theodore L. Gross, the intense negrophobia of Page is practically unique among serious and responsible authors. He quotes Page's contention that "Four thousand years have not . . . developed the forces of the [Black] intellect," and that "the Negroes *as a race* have never exhibited much capacity to advance; that as a race they are inferior to other races."[42] Page said that he did not believe the Negro was the equal of the White, or ever could be. In his book, *The Old South*, Page speaks of a deadly "peril of contamination" that can be expected from "the overcrowding of an inferior race"—an inevitable Anglo-American "race-degeneration from enforced and constant association with [Blacks]."[43]

The biographical details of Page's life do not adequately explain such a phobia although, like Louise-Clarke Pyrnelle, Page may have been particularly embittered because he did not enjoy the aristocratic life that his background made him feel was his due. His wealthy ancestors had lost much of the family fortune after the War of 1812. Still, Page grew up on a plantation with sixty slaves and was enrolled in Washington College in 1869. This does not sound like a life of dire deprivation; but, according to Gross, Page had to tutor his cousin's children to earn enough to enter law school, and he "hated his poverty."[44] Eventually he became a respected Richmond lawyer and a contributor to many newspapers and magazines. His anthology, *In Ole Virginia, or Marse Chan and Other Stories* (1887), was a notable success, and in 1893 Page retired from the legal profession in favor of a full-time literary career. By this time he had been widowed, had remarried, and lived with his wife and stepchildren in Washington, D.C. In 1913, Woodrow Wilson made him the American ambassador to Italy.

"Page completely identified," writes critic Kimball King, "with the Virginia aristocrat," and he could please the reading public of his time because "he wholeheartedly believed in the plantation myth he portrayed."[45] It was perhaps this inner conviction in Page that made him such a spellbinding storyteller.

The paradox of Thomas Nelson Page is that he was politically invidious and anachronistic (i.e., convinced that a slave society was just short of paradise), but artistically somewhat ahead of his time. On the political side, he equated the Old South with the *only* South; he said "The New South is in my judgment only the Old South with slavery gone and the fire of exaction on its back."[46] On the artistic side, he was an impressionist who bypassed the rigid conventions of the nineteenth-century short-story form, often in the face of objections from his editors and literary advisers. As a stylist, he was too modern for some nineteenth-century tastes—too willing to place his focus on characterization and setting. He was not forward-looking nor original in his immoderate idealization of the Old South, but he had fresh talents, which have been recognized by such a contemporary literary historian as Robert D. Rhode. Rhode has seen in Page's short works a fine utilization of the "historical value of a scene," a "high literary efficiency," a "sense of literary proportion," an evocative handling of detail.[47]

Joel Chandler Harris (1848–1908) spent even more time than Page as a commentator on public issues. As an editorial writer for the *Atlanta Constitution* for more than twenty-five years, he made essays on public affairs his vocational mainstay. Like Page, he was preoccupied with the so-called Negro question in all its aspects, including lynching. Like Page, Harris viewed lynching as the spin-off of an equally terrible crime—as "the natural result of the horror that must fill the bosoms of the best men who are brought sharply face to face with such cruelty and bestiality [as that practiced by Blacks against White women]."[48] Harris wrote in a series of articles in the *Saturday Evening Post* in 1904:

Both the crime and the nature of the reprisals [i.e., lynchings] are nauseating and horrible, but where there is one, the other must be expected. . . .[49]

Underlying the whole issue, according to Harris, was the irresponsible talk about the social and political status of Blacks, a form of Northern agitation that resulted in false ideas in the Black population about their status.[50] And not only was the rhetoric damaging; the government, said Harris, had made the Negro "a citizen and a political power before his time."[51] The blame was not to rest with Blacks, so Harris insisted:

The truth is, the responsibility of the negro was no more than that of a little child who had wandered quite by accident, into the halls of legislation, and remained, pleased at the novelty of the situation, and yet wondering what it was all about. Like a novice learning to play chess, he moved whatever pieces he was told to move, and when no one was observing him closely he moved others for his own amusement.[52]

In addition to Northerners (who were the "political instructors" of the Blacks and caused them to forget their proper "place"),[53] Harris singled out Black preachers as the culprit. As a group, Blacks made "inferior preachers" and it was "negro preachers who have had a taste of politics [who] have been disposed to regard the negro criminals as martyrs to race prejudice."[54] However, Harris saw a glimmer of hope when he saw a report of "a meeting of prominent negroes" and they had "discovered the main source of trouble among the blacks"—namely, the need for "the race to live morally and decently."[55]

Harris's views did not differ radically from those of Page although Harris did acknowledge the possibility of cultural "improvement" for Blacks through education. Also he spoke about race relations in a much more conciliatory tone. He undoubtedly had more one-to-one relationships with slaves during his childhood, and this may have been the cause of some degree of ambivalence. Yet Harris gave expression to the plantation myth consistently.

Harris spent the first thirteen years of his life with his unwed, impoverished mother, who worked as a seamstress in Eatonton, Georgia. At the age of fourteen, he was hired as a printer's devil at the Turnwold plantation. The plantation owner published a weekly newspaper, the *Countryman*, and Harris was his helper from 1862 to 1866. This planter, Joseph Addison Turner, encouraged Harris to read widely and to appreciate humor; he also undoubtedly instilled in the youth his fierce sectionalism.[56]

Harris was allowed to include his own short pieces in the pages of the *Countryman*. It was perhaps this early literary experience that helped him find his calling as a journalist. He worked for several newspapers in Georgia and Louisiana before he joined the *Constitution* staff in 1876.

The model for the Uncle Remus character was already well-established in the pages of the *Constitution* when Harris joined the paper. The columnist Sam W. Small had been using a fictional Atlanta Black as his mouthpiece when he commented upon public events. When Small resigned, Harris took over the production of these dialect sketches, substituting his own invention, Uncle Remus, for Small's Uncle Si. He used his second Remus sketch to lead off the "Sayings" section in *Uncle Remus: His Songs and His Sayings* in 1880.[57]

It was an essay in the December 1877 issue of *Lippincott's Magazine* that alerted Harris to the value of Black folklore and its possible usefulness to his *Constitution* columns. This article by William Owens had included the Tar Baby story. Two years later, Harris published a Black fable, "The Story of Mr. Rabbit and Mr. Fox, as Told by Uncle Remus," in his newspaper, and the public response to this tale and others was highly encouraging. For the next twenty-seven years he collected Black folklore, compiling a total of 180 stories.[58] He solicited tales from his readers, and he also used his nine children as scouts who would lead him to new folk materials.[59]

Although Harris wrote in many modes (essays, short stories, novels, children's tales), his favorable reputation has rested primarily upon his efforts as a compiler of African American folk literature. He was an early and ambitious collector. Yet the extravagant claim made by his principal biographer and bibliographer, R. Bruce Bickley Jr. is hard to validate—namely, that "the folklorists have found in Harris's Uncle Remus tales the most important gathering of Negro folk material in the nineteenth century."[60] To accept such a claim, one would have to overlook some significant nineteenth-century collections. For example, Charles C. Jones compiled a valuable collection of tales: *Negro Myths from the Georgia Coasts: Told in the Vernacular* (1888);[61] Mrs. A.M.H. Christensen edited *Afro-American Folk Lore: Told Round Cabin Fires on the Sea Islands of South Carolina* (1892);[62] Mary Alicia Owen's *Voodoo Tales As Told Among the Negroes of the Southwest: Collected from Original Sources* appeared in 1893;[63] *Louisiana Folk-Tales in French Dialect and English Translation* (1895) was collected and edited by Alcee Fortier.[64] It is these anthologists, unlike Harris, who presented the tales to the public minus the white supremacist baggage of a frame narrative. From any folklorist's perspective, this is an important advantage.

Bickley has summed up Harris's lifelong journalistic career as an example of one Southerner's commitment to the eradication of "social and political sectionalism, literary sectionalism, and racial intolerance."[65] He urges us to think of Harris's latter goal in relation to nineteenth-century definitions of racial intolerance, not twentieth-century interpretations.[66] This is the advice of a staunch Harris apologist. A white supremacist attitude does not lend itself to a range of subtle shadings. The best we can do to "rehabilitate" Harris is to analyze the varied manifestations of ambivalence toward Blacks in his writings, as compared with those manifestations elsewhere. For a view of a more consistent opponent of nineteenth-century racial intolerance in the South, we would do better to study the career of the New Orleans writer, George Washington Cable, although Cable was also a child of his time and unable to stay entirely clear of stereotypic characterization. Cable, however, did not direct his writings toward the child and is outside the range of this study.

Like Page and Harris, Mark Twain (1835–1910) objected to lynching. But he was also like these other eminent Southerners in assuming that Blacks who were lynched were guilty of what the mobs charged them with, even though no trial had been convened, no witnesses called, no testimony heard, no jury assembled to weigh the evidence. This racial bias in Twain belies the assertion by Maxwell Geismar that "the source of everything good in Mark Twain lies in [his] transparently honest, open, and full human vision."[67] Similarly, Twain's assumption of Black guilt is a tendency that is at odds with Frederick J. Antczak's view of Twain. Antczak sees him as someone with an "innocent eye," with a "moral and intellectual rebellion against . . . any dogma that prejudices issues, that decides them before they are ever given a clear-eyed, tough-minded look."[68] It is clear from Twain's essay, "The United States of Lyncherdom," that he *did* decide issues before they were adequately examined.

Twain is clearly indicting lynching as a practice when he comments in 1901 about the lynching of three Blacks in Pierce City, Missouri. But he builds his argument on these grounds: (1) that the White townsfolk "had bitter provocation—indeed—the bitterest of all provocations," and (2) that they should, nonetheless, have restrained the mob. He says the law should be allowed to exercise its prerogative in righting wrongs. He condemns the mob because, as he says,

they took the law into their own hands, when by the terms of their statutes their victim would certainly hang if the law had been allowed to take its course. . . .[69]

On what basis does he predict the outcome of the legal measures he is urging upon the community? He seems to be assuring his readers that a trial would be a strictly pro forma exercise, that they need not have concerned themselves about the possibility of a verdict that contradicted their own hypotheses.

Twain continues his analysis by arguing that a lynching is counterproductive in relation to the ultimate goal of the White community: the protection of White women from Black rapists. He says that a luridly described happening will be such a "much-talked-of-event" that it will be "followed by imitations."[70] Twain's critique of lynching is not essentially different from that of Thomas Nelson Page when Page is promulgating the myth that Black males focus their passion on Caucasian females. Twain expresses this fear in the following terms:

The child should know that one much-talked-of outrage and murder committed by a negro will upset the disturbed intellects of several other negroes and produce a series of the very tragedies the community would so strenuously wish to prevent; that, in a word, the lynchers are themselves the worst enemies of their women.[71]

At this point in his essay, Twain shifts his discussion to the problem of the herd instinct in the human race and a prevailing lack of moral courage. Then he concludes with a satirical thrust at missionaries and their imperialist activities in China. "O kind missionary," he writes, "O compassionate missionary, leave China! come home and convert these Christians [lynchers]!"[72]

To find a strong reformist streak in Twain, one must look beyond his attitudes toward African Americans. There is a progressive element discernible in his satiric indictments of imperialism. He protested American intervention in the Philippines, Belgian cruelty in the Congo, and British opportunism in the African regions being exploited by Cecil Rhodes. Writing for the *North American Review* in 1902, Twain summarized in the following terms the U.S. conquest of the Philippines:

We have bought some islands from a party that did not own them, with real smartness & a good counterfeit of disinterested friendliness, we coaxed

a weak nation into a trap, & closed it upon them; we went back on our
honored guest of the stars & stripes when we had no further use for him,
& chased him into the mountains; we are as indisputably in possession
of a wide-spreading archipelago as if it were our property; we have paci-
fied some thousands of the islanders & buried them; destroyed their fields,
burned their villages & turned their widows & orphans out of doors;
furnished heart-breaking exile to dozens of disagreeable patriots & sub-
jugated the remaining millions by Benevolent Assimilation which is the
pious new name of the musket. . . .[73]

Antczak makes the case that Twain did not have a consistent,
liberal doctrine that always guided him. Instead, Twain "went after"
a variety of self-deceptions in the body politic—for example, fashion, false piety, glossed-over corruption, the land-grabs of empire-
building governments. As a rebel against some aspects of the dominant culture, he was a "democratic educator."[74] But pulling him in
the opposite direction was his quest for public approval. That desire
was not difficult to fulfill when he brought to his audiences a variation of minstrel humor, for "blackface" minstrelsy was among the
most popular art forms of Twain's era.[75] Twain's own affinity for this
form of entertainment is explained in some degree by his own background.

Samuel Langhorne Clemens had Southern, aristocratic roots, a
fact we may sometimes overlook when we associate him with the
Western regional stories for which Mark Twain initially became famous. Not only was his hometown (Hannibal, Missouri) a Southern town in which slavery was legal and commonplace, it was a town
dominated socially by upper-class Virginians.[76] Clemens's father, John
Marshall Clemens, was a Virginian of the slaveholding class. His
mother, Jane Lampton, was a high-born Kentuckian. Despite his
father's law practice, the family suffered various financial setbacks.
When Clemens was in his twelfth year, his father died.

Ten years later (after some experience as a printer's assistant),
Clemens became a Mississippi River pilot, a job he held until the
outbreak of the Civil War closed the river. He then enlisted in the
Confederate Army, but after a short stint as a soldier, moved to Nevada where his older brother had been appointed territorial secretary. In Nevada he failed as a miner, but succeeded as a reporter for

the *Virginia City Enterprise.* Various journalistic jobs followed. In 1866 he combined a career as a humorous lecturer with his career as a writer.

Twain's shift to a New England homebase followed his marriage in 1870 to a wealthy New Yorker, Olivia Langdon. This shift also involved a gradual change from newspaper journalism to a broader career as an author. From this point, his fame as a satirist of the human condition and, in particular, a debunker of social conventions, is well known. He is the subject of an undiminishing flow of critical and biographical studies. His life and character seem emblematic of a peculiarly American dilemma—that is, he could see the world around him quite clearly with what has been called his "vernacular perspective" (i.e., his "horse sense"),[77] but at the same time he was easily duped by the American dream (its false hopes and get-rich-quick enticements). His intermittent lecture tours were, in part, a way to recover from his failed commercial enterprises. Besides losses from his unsuccessful business, the Charles L. Webster Publishing Company, he went into debt with his Paige typesetter investment and his speculation in an alleged superfood called Plasmon.[78]

Students of Twain continue to be fascinated by his fame as a humorist in contrast to his frequent personal misfortunes. His son died in infancy; his much cherished eldest daughter died in her twenty-third year. He was bankrupt by the time he reached his prime.

Students of Twain also puzzle over whether or not he was a progressive influence in the field of race relations—a "desouthernized Southerner," to use William Dean Howells's phrase. In life he was sometimes helpful to individual Blacks. For example, he spoke on behalf of Frederick Douglass, and he helped several Black college students financially. However, in literature he utilized the conventions of "blackface" minstrelsy. He viewed the minstrel mockery of African Americans as a "thoroughly delightful thing,"[79] and he confused the stage Negro's behavior with the realities of Black identity. He describes the minstrel skit as an accurate imitation of life:

. . . a delightful jangle of assertion and contradiction would break out between the two [performers]; the quarrel would gather emphasis, the voices would grow louder and louder and more and more energetic and

vindictive, and the two would rise and approach each other, shaking fists and instruments and threatening bloodshed. Sometimes the quarrel would last five minutes, the two contestants shouting deadly threats in each other's faces with their noses not six inches apart, the house shrieking with laughter all the while at this happy and accurate imitation of the usual and familiar negro quarrel. . . .[80]

Given Twain's lifelong enthusiasm for caricatures of Blacks, it is not surprising that as post-Reconstruction prejudices increased, Twain became receptive to that negative influence. He would end up with a confused, ambivalent statement about lynching, as noted above, despite his intention to combat that lawlessness. And his ties in the South retained a high priority, for he asked that his essay on lynching (originally intended for the *North American Review*) be published posthumously. Otherwise, he explained, "I shouldn't have even half a friend left down there [in the South]."[81]

George A. Henty (1832–1902) has been called "one of the famous correspondents of the Crimea," but that commendation scarcely begins to convey the range of his influence. He was dispatched to nearly every war zone on the globe during his twenty years as a full-time journalist, and even in his last days he made regular trips to his Fleet Street office to keep abreast of the reports coming in on the Reuter's news line.[82] He worked primarily for the *London Standard*, a paper that took the Conservative position on foreign policy issues, yet at the beginning of his career, Henty made a reputation as something of a reformer.

After a sickly childhood in Trumpington and Canterbury, and then a few years at Cambridge, Henty became a soldier and went to the Crimean War front to help organize the incredibly disorganized hospitals. His brother had died of cholera after just two weeks in this war zone, and Henty sent scathing reports about hospital incompetence to the British press.

During his five years in the army, he married, had four children, and became a widower. After his wife's death in 1865, he turned to journalism as his chief career. The first campaign that he covered for the *Standard* was the Austro-Italian War of 1866.[83]

His experiences as a war correspondent supplied him with needed material for writing children's books although this second career was not one to which he readily agreed. In 1871 he was approached by publishers Griffith and Farran with the idea that he write a story for children about his war experiences. According to William Allan, it was only the money that appealed to him; he was often worried about his finances.[84] But he was well-equipped for this task. Already experienced as a writer of adult fiction (his first adult novel was *A Search for a Secret* in 1867), he was also the chief storyteller for his own children. Moreover, as Henty's biographer Guy Arnold explains, confining childhood illnesses had turned Henty into a lover of children's books who was acutely aware of the kind of books he had disliked as a child. Henty commented upon this in his preface to *The Young Buglers (A Tale of the Peninsular War)*:

I remember that, as a boy, I regarded any attempt to mix instruction with amusement as being as objectionable a practice as the administration of powder in jam; but I think that this feeling arose from the fact that in those days books contained a very small share of amusement and a very large share of instruction. I have endeavoured to avoid this. . . .[85]

Henty did not refrain from all sermonizing; instead he sought a better balance between suspenseful adventures and thinly disguised lectures about virtue and public policy issues. His general pedagogical plan was to give "under the guise of historical tales full and accurate accounts of all the leading events of great wars."[86]

Because Henty was the son of a stockbroker and mine owner, it is not very surprising that besides informing his readers about "great wars," he also urged them to oppose labor strikes. In his novel *Facing Death*, he makes his hero a strikebreaker.[87]

In his military tales, Henty also reflects class bias. He claimed that his stories were intended to influence boys to seek a military career—but mainly as officers.[88] In a discussion of Henty in the *Journal of Popular Culture*, Roy Turnbaugh comments upon the casual way in which any obstacle to promotion in the military is handled by Henty: "Boers are beaten and shot, Zulus dispatched, Chinese gunned down with complete aplomb. The only reaction to this immense amount of carnage is delight that the ranks have been thinned for advancement."[89] Turnbaugh quotes from the novel, *For Name and Fame.*

"You are the luckiest young dog I ever heard of. You got your commission within a year of enlisting; and now by an extraordinary fatality your regiment is almost annihilated, and you mount up by death steps to a captain's rank."
"I am fortunate indeed, sir."[90]

When Henty discussed American slavery, he not only supported it, he also said that problems in that system arose only when people abused it. The abusers he thought were masters of plantations who were either uppity tradesmen or unscrupulous Northerners. In *With Lee in Virginia* he tells his readers that slavery is abused by certain kinds of people:

The worst masters were the smallest ones; the man who owned six slaves was far more apt to extort the utmost possible work from them than the planter who owned three or four hundred. And the worst masters of all were those who, having made a little money in trade or speculation in the towns, purchased a dozen slaves, a small piece of land, and tried to set up as gentry.[91]

On the last page of this novel, when Henty brings the hero home after service in the Confederate Army, he reiterates his assessment of the Civil War vis-à-vis the slaves:

The negroes . . . very soon discovered that their lot was a far harder one than it had been before, and that freedom so suddenly given was a curse rather than a blessing to them.[92]

Henty wrote five full-length novels about the United States and six about Africa, but it is the African stories and others about the empire to which his followers most frequently allude. Writing for the *Henty Society Bulletin*, Reverend Hugh Pruen states, "Above all, Henty is the great Imperialist. His writing days coincided with the high-water mark of Jingoism. . . ."[93] Guy Arnold describes Henty as a firm believer in British superiority, in the rightness of the empire, and in the notion that world order was enhanced by the Pax Britannica.[94] This was a viewpoint shared by many nineteenth-century British citizens. And the idea is even carried over into the scholarship of the 1980s; for example Patrick A. Dunae, writing for *Victorian Studies*, apparently concurs with a theme of Henty's novels—namely, that "the subject peoples benefited from Britain's imperial policies."[95] Dunae comments upon Henty's own holdings in several overseas consortiums (Transvaal Gold Mining, for example) and the many economic themes in Henty's works. His conclusion is that "although Henty's British empire was commercially oriented, it was still benevolent towards those it embraced."[96]

On the contrary, historians have conscientiously documented the havoc that ensued from European incursions in Africa. In *Africa and the Victorians*, Ronald Robinson and his coauthors write:

> *What had taken place in Sierra Leone and on the Gold Coast was repeated in the palm belt between Lagos and the Niger country. The time-honoured bases of exchange, of inter-tribal politics, of the relations between producers and middlemen were upset by the presence of the Europeans. . . . Instead of spreading peace, commerce seemed to have encouraged unrest and corroded tribal authority. . . .[97]*

After 1871, the British sent "gunboats on annual punitive sweeps up the [Niger] river"—hardly an act of "benevolence." According to Robinson, the British methodically undermined the authority of African governments, thereby creating a vacuum that the imperialists could then insist upon filling with British-chosen deputies.[98] And the whole process was rationalized as a benign gesture.

Henty "became one of the institutions of late Victorian London."[99] With an estimated sales of twenty-five million volumes, his works defined a civilization. "It would seem," says Guy Arnold, "that Henty's popularity as a medium for teaching history in American junior schools lasted in some instances very nearly down to the present time."[100] In 1900, an American boy on his first trip to England made just three requests: to be shown "Westminster Abbey, the Tower of London, and Mr. Henty and all his books."[101]

Conclusion

The late nineteenth century was undoubtedly a time of wrenching change and intellectual turmoil. Such a conclusion is even suggested in the history of children's fiction. Each of the individuals examined in this chapter is conspicuous for his or her paradoxical life experience. For example, William T. Adams was known as an admirable educator in both secular and Sunday schools; yet as Oliver Optic, the author of ultraexciting tales for the young, he fell into disfavor with many in literary and educational circles.

Similarly, it is hard to think of Louise-Clarke Pyrnelle without pondering certain ironies. She was among the authors most committed to an explicit political goal—namely, the legitimization of the Old South and its sectional interests; yet she was somewhat ahead of her time in creating a credible and appealing profile of the child's mind and the child's world. At the opposite extreme, Martha Finley was surely among the world's worst novelists; yet on occasion, she pioneered as a muckraker. In a very narrow field of political commentary, she was in advance of her literary associates.

The paradox of Edward Stratemeyer was somewhat different. He was nurtured on literary tripe and was ready for the mantle of Oliver Optic or Horatio Alger to fall upon him. But the popular literary tradition he admired was preserved by means of subterfuge and overt lies about his business—especially his concealment of his syndicate of ghostwriters. The ethic that he preached to the young was compromised by a Gilded Age ethic that stretched the profit motive out of all proportion.

Pyrnelle's Southern compatriots—Page, Harris, and Twain—were also complex figures. Page gained a reputation as the ultimate apologist for white supremacy and the plantation myth, yet he is rightfully praised by modern scholars as a literary stylist who expanded the dimensions of the short-story form. Harris became known, unjustifiably, as a faithful delineator of African American character, yet his respect for Black folklore is suggested in his lifelong effort to record traditional Black tales. Twain's place in American history and culture is perhaps the most paradoxical of all. Over the past century he has become one of the idols of the intelligentsia, a writer praised for strong egalitarian credentials; yet his portraits of Black characters cannot be justified. In these delineations he remained a Confederate writer.

Turning to the one Briton in the sample, George Henty, we can see how a reformer in some public spheres nonetheless shared a nineteenth-century assumption that was intrinsically self-deceiving—

namely, that what was good for British commerce was equally good for everyone else, even those exploited in the process. Thus he labored to justify incursions into Africa as good, but tried to demonstrate first that the indigenous peoples were in dire need of redemption. To this end he mixed brute-like Africans and carefully supervised noble savages, both characterizations being in line with British economic self-interest. Understandably, he argued the Confederate position in his references to American slavery.

The potential for a new definition of interracial relations was perhaps in reach at the close of the Civil War. With the exception of Pyrnelle, Page, and Harris, all the writers sampled for the postbellum period expressed, at least at times, a conventional Unionist view of slavery. But the only message that ensued with regard to ex-slaves was that the freedmen and freedwomen constituted either an absurdity or a threat—that they required governance and close regulation by the White population. After the immediate throes of postwar adjustment, such attitudes should have faded out; instead, preoccupation with a new reason to subjugate people of color supplanted the intensity of old fears about this group.

The possibilities for positive change following the Civil War were immense, but the forces of regression prevailed. A time of hope was turned into an age of violence, injustice, deprivation, and despair. Signs of this outcome of the war were already visible in the ambivalent children's literature of the antebellum period. What we see in the postbellum children's books is a skewed image of Black identity that is so extreme that subsequent generations still battle to extricate themselves from its effects.

These literary distortions were a means for reinstituting white cultural hegemony, and we need to give special attention to the complex causes behind their staying power. The tenacity of the white supremacy myth in children's books moves into a whole new phase as the book industry and professions become heavily institutionalized. Instead of seeing a predictable cultural conservatism being passed from one generation to the next, we see in the twentieth century an "engineered" lifespan for books. Thus the attitudes of Harris, Twain, Stratemeyer, and others survive. White superiority as an ideology becomes more tenacious as the cultural impact of schools and libraries increases. These institutions legitimized and widened the circulation of that ideology.

Notes

1. I. A. Newby, *Jim Crow's Defense: Anti-Negro Thought in America, 1900–1930.* (Baton Rouge: Louisiana State University Press, 1965), 7.
2. *Philadelphia Inquirer,* quoted in promotional material about *The Sailor Boy; Portland Press,* quoted in promotional material about *The Soldier Boy.*
3. Millinocket, "Assault on Fort Wagner," *Oliver Optic's Magazine: (Our Boys and Girls)* 5 (January–June 1869): 392; rpt. *Oliver Optic's Companion* (Boston: Lee and Shepard, 1872).
4. Millinocket, "The Brave Little Bugler," *Oliver Optic's Magazine: (Our Boys and Girls)* 5 (January–June 1869): 103.
5. Charles Sumner, "The United Republic," *Oliver Optic's Magazine: (Our Boys and Girls)* 5 (January–June 1869): 44; rpt. *Oliver Optic's Companion* (Boston: Lee and Shepard, 1872).
6. Willie Wisp, "The Basket-Makers of Bongoloo," *Oliver Optic's Magazine: (Our Boys and Girls)* 5 (January–June 1869): 199; rpt. *Oliver Optic's Companion* (Boston: Lee and Shepard, 1872).
7. Sam Pickering, "A Boy's Own War," *New England Quarterly* 48 (September 1975): 371.
8. Dolores Blythe Jones, comp., *An Annotated Catalog-Index to the Series, Nonseries Stories, and Magazine Publications of William Taylor Adams.* (Westport, CT: Greenwood Press, 1985), xvi.
9. Ibid., xiii.
10. Ibid., xiv.
11. Gene Gleason, "Whatever Happened to Oliver Optic?" *Wilson Library Bulletin* 49 (May 1975): 650.
12. *American Writers for Children Before 1900,* vol. 42, *Dictionary of Literary Biography, s.v.* "Louise-Clarke Pyrnelle."
13. Louise-Clarke Pyrnelle, *Diddie, Dumps, and Tot, or Plantation Child-Life* (New York: Harper, 1882), 139.
14. Ibid., v–vi.
15. Ibid., 240.
16. Miller, 311.
17. *American Writers for Children, s.v.* "Martha Finley (Martha Farquharson)."
18. Ibid.
19. Janet E. Brown, "The Saga of Elsie Dinsmore: A study in Nineteenth-Century Sensibility," *University of Buffalo Studies* 17:3 (July 1945): 80.
20. Stanley Kunitz and Howard Haycraft, *American Authors, 1600–1900* (New York: H. W. Wilson, 1938), 272.
21. Smedman, 179.
22. For a fuller statement of Elsie's repulsiveness, see the quotation from Leslie McFarlane's *The Ghost of the Hardy Boys* quoted in Jacqueline Jackson and Philip Kendall, "What Makes a Bad Book Good: Elsie Dinsmore" *Children's Literature* 7 (1978): 66. McFarlane writes: ". . . in the Himalayas of junk turned out by writers of juvenile fiction the Elsie Books stand like Everest as the worst ever written by anybody, and . . . Elsie Dinsmore is without peer the Most Nauseating Heroine of all time."
23. Brown, 123.
24. Ibid., 127.
25. Peter A. Soderbergh, "Edward Stratemeyer and the Juvenile Ethic, 1894–1930," *International Review of History and Political Science* 11:1 (February 1974): 62.
26. Quoted in Soderbergh, 61 (see n. 23).
27. "For It Was Indeed He," (by staff writers of *Fortune Magazine*) *Fortune Magazine* 9 (April 1934); rpt. *Only Connect: Readings on Children's Literature,* ed. Sheila Egoff, et al. (New York: Oxford University Press, 1969), 53.
28. Ken Donelson, "Nancy, Tom and Assorted Friends in the Stratemeyer Syndicate Then and Now," *Children's Literature* 7 (1978): 18.

29. "For It Was Indeed He," 51.
30. Peter A. Soderbergh, "The Dark Mirror: War Ethos In Juvenile Fiction, 1865–1919," *University of Dayton Review* 10:1 (Summer 1973): 16–17.
31. Ibid., 17.
32. Soderbergh, "Edward Stratemeyer," 71.
33. *American Writers for Children*, s.v. "Edward Stratemeyer."
34. Soderbergh, "Edward Stratemeyer," 66.
35. Donelson, 25.
36. Thomas Nelson Page, *The Negro: The Southern Problem* (New York: Charles Scribner's Sons, 1904), 111, 112.
37. Ibid., 111.
38. Ibid., 112.
39. Ibid., 100.
40. Ibid., 95.
41. Ibid., 109.
42. Thomas Nelson Page, *The Old South: Essays Social and Political* (New York: Charles Scribner's Sons, 1892), 320.
43. Ibid., 284.
44. Theodore L. Gross, *Thomas Nelson Page* (New York: Twayne Publishers, Inc., 1967), 19.
45. Thomas Nelson Page, *In Ole Virginia, or Marse Chan and Other Stories*, with an introduction by Kimball King (Chapel Hill: University of North Carolina Press, 1969), xxxv.
46. Jay B. Hubbell, *The South in American Literature, 1607–1900* (Durham, NC: Duke University Press, 1954), 801.
47. Robert D. Rhode, *Setting in the American Short Story of Local Color* (The Hague, Netherlands: Mouton and Company, 1975), 57, 58.
48. Julia Collier Harris, ed., *Joel Chandler Harris, Editor and Essayist: Miscellaneous Literary, Political and Social Writings* (Chapel Hill: University of North Carolina Press, 1931), 144.
49. Ibid.
50. Ibid., 138.
51. Ibid., 135.
52. Ibid.
53. Ibid., 154–155.
54. Ibid., 144.
55. Ibid., 145.
56. R. Bruce Bickley Jr., *Joel Chandler Harris* (Boston: Twayne Publishers, 1978), 19.
57. Ibid., 30, 31.
58. Ibid., 37.
59. Stella Brewer Brookes, *Joel Chandler Harris: Folklorist* (Athens: The University of Georgia Press, 1950), 34.
60. Bickley, 66.
61. Charles C. Jones, *Negro Myths from the Georgia Coast, Told in the Vernacular* (Columbia, SC: The State Co., 1925; originally published in Boston by Houghton Mifflin, 1888).
62. Mrs. A.M.H. Christensen, *Afro-American Folk Lore: Told Round Cabin Fires on the Sea Islands of South Carolina* (New York: Negro University Press, 1969; originally published in Boston by J. G. Cupples Company, 1892).
63. Mary Alicia Owen, ed., *Voodoo Tales As Told Among the Negroes of the Southwest: Collected from Original Sources* (NY: G. P. Putnam's Sons, 1893).
64. Alcee Fortier, ed., *Louisiana Folk-Tales in French Dialect and English Translation* (Boston: Published for the American Folk-Lore Society by Houghton, Mifflin and Co., 1895).
65. Bickley, 34.
66. Ibid., 34–35.

67. Maxwell Geismar, *Mark Twain: An American Prophet* (Boston: Houghton Mifflin Co., 1970), 58.
68. Frederick J. Antczak, *Thought and Character: The Rhetoric of Democratic Education* (Ames: Iowa State University Press, 1985), 145.
69. Maxwell Geismar, ed., *Mark Twain and the Three R's: Race, Religion, Revolution—and Related Matters* (Indianapolis: Bobbs-Merrill, 1973), 34.
70. Ibid., 35.
71. Ibid.
72. Ibid., 50.
73. Ibid., 32–33. Geismar's anthology includes Twain's essay on the Philippines ("The Conquest of the Philippines"), his essay on Belgian atrocities ("King Leopold's Soliloquy on the Belgian Congo"), and a piece on Cecil Rhodes ("Race and Imperialism: Mr. Cecil Rhodes").
74. Antczak, 145.
75. Sociologist Alan W. C. Green has studied the extraordinary appeal of "blackface" minstrelsy with White audiences. He writes that "anyone after the early 1840s who wished to portray a humorous Negro on the stage had to conform to the minstrelsy pattern. . . ." (See "'Jim Crow,' 'Zip Coon': The Northern Origins of Negro Minstrelsy," *Massachusetts Review* 11 [Spring 1970]).
76. Hubbell, 823.
77. Antczak, 141.
78. Ibid., 155.
79. Samuel Langhorne Clemens, *Mark Twain in Eruption: Hitherto Unpublished Pages About Men and Events*, ed. Bernard De Voto (New York: Harper, 1922), 115.
80. Ibid., 113.
81. Justin Kaplan, *Mark Twain and His World* (New York: Simon and Schuster, 1974), 194.
82. William Allan, "G. A. Henty," *Cornhill Magazine* 1802 (Winter 1974–75): 99.
83. Guy Arnold, *Held Fast for England: G. A. Henty, Imperialist Boys' Writer* (London: Hamish Hamilton, 1980), 7.
84. Allan, 85.
85. Arnold. 39.
86. Allan, 86.
87. Arnold, 21.
88. Ibid.
89. Roy Turnbaugh, "Images of Empire: George Alfred Henty and John Buchan," *Journal of Popular Culture* 9:3 (Winter 1975): 736.
90. G. A. Henty, *For Name and Fame; or, Through Afghan Passes* (London: Blackie and Sons, 1886) quoted in Turnbaugh, 736 (see n. 89).
91. G. A. Henty. *With Lee in Virginia: A Story of the American Civil War* (Chicago: The Henneberry Co., 1910; originally published in London by Blackie and Sons, 1890), 5.
92. Ibid., 384.
93. Arnold, 63.
94. Ibid., 65.
95. Patrick A. Dunae, "Boys' Literature and the Idea of Empire, 1870–1914," *Victorian Studies* 24:1 (Autumn 1980): 110.
96. Ibid.
97. Roland Robinson and John Gallagher, with Alice Denny, *Africa and the Victorians: The Climax of Imperialism in the Dark Continent* (New York: St. Martin's Press, 1961), 39.
98. Ibid., 51.
99. Allan, 71.
100. Arnold, 19.
101. Allan, 71.

Chapter Seven
Postwar Institutions

The rise of children's literature institutions in the late nineteenth century was to prove a mixed blessing. Undoubtedly the availability of educational facilities, however meager, made a difference in many individual lives. On the other hand, those facilities came increasingly under the aegis of the local government, and, since the government at all levels was distancing itself more and more from abolitionist influences, schools and libraries for children could be expected to reflect that trend.

As described earlier, Congress turned down a bill that would have improved education for Blacks (the Blair Bill). At state and township levels increases in the tax base for education were often voted down on the ground that improved opportunities for Blacks were undesirable. The courts upheld actions at the local level to segregate the schools. In a general sense, then, the post–Civil War educational institutions were the outcome of largely conservative public policies.

Two preliminary points need to be kept in mind as we consider the school, the library, and the periodical press in the late 1800s: (1) the library followed the school in its overall intellectual dimensions, and (2) the children's library started on a course that would eventually make it the major children's book market and, therefore, a considerable influence upon book content. Behind these developments were the gradual scaling down of Sunday school libraries as organizations important to the secular as well as religious community, and the emergence of philanthropic activities with an educational focus. But as libraries and schools developed, the potential for improving interracial relations through these influential, grassroots organizations remained unfulfilled.

Literary and other educational opportunities for the former slave child were conspicuously lacking in the postbellum era. When the keynote for Black education became, in effect, "spend nothing unless absolutely necessary," there was little hope that appropriations would be made for libraries. Moreover, when the mainstream population's goal was to train Blacks for menial work, there was little rationale for building up institutions that tended to foster intellectual activity and opposition to the white supremacy myth.

The maintenance of that myth is perhaps best understood through a study of the schools that embraced it, for the school is one of the most direct institutional expressions of the mainstream population. This point has been suggested in Horace Mann Bond's comment about civil rights and the schools:

There is no index to shifting trends of racial relations more reliable than the agitation regarding separate schools, for the training of the child, dear to the hearts of parents of both races, has always been one of the first of social relations to find its way into legislation and litigation.[1]

Schools and Schoolbooks

The Northern and Southern regions initiated different kinds of programs in relation to education and racial coexistence, but assumptions of race hierarchy characterized the programs of both sections. Initially most Northern states passed progressive legislation, especially laws that mandated school desegregation. Massachusetts, under persistent pressure from radical abolitionists, passed a desegregation law before the Civil War in 1857. It required that school committees admit children to schools irrespective of a child's "race, creed, or previous condition of servitude." Failure to comply could subject a municipality to a suit for damages by the injured parties.[2] Connecticut prohibited separate schools in 1868, New Jersey and Pennsylvania in 1881, Ohio in 1887, and New York in 1900.[3] Not all states moved in this direction. For instance, efforts to desegregate schools never fully succeeded in Indiana and Illinois in the nineteenth century.[4] Moreover, despite a generally progressive legislative record in the North, ways were found in most states to circumvent the law.

Southerners, on the other hand, managed state revenues so as to minimize educational opportunity for Blacks. However, they allowed Northern philanthropic groups to actively support industrial education programs geared for Black students. Unfortunately, the charities that earmarked funds for Black education were administered primarily by White citizens, and, according to H. Leon Prather Sr., these administrators "promoted and kept alive substandard Negro education."[5]

Looking at the Northern schools in some detail, we need to separate the private school period and the public school period. Before Horace Mann, Henry Barnard, and others waged the fight for free public education in the mid-1800s, "public school" was synonymous with "pauper school" in the public mind. Black parents and White parents alike wanted private schools for their children.[6] The mutual benefit associations organized by Blacks often focused their attention on providing educational facilities, and the schools were private in accordance with the prevailing custom. But after a public educational system came to be viewed as a forward-looking idea, even as essential to the national interest, the public school movement concentrated first on free schools for Whites, then on separate schools for Blacks and Whites, and finally on the prohibition of separate schools since racial segregation came to be viewed as a violation of democratic principles.[7]

Prior to the Civil War, the trend toward desegregation in the North was sometimes thwarted by the courts, as when the Massachusetts Supreme Count (in *Roberts v. the City of Boston*) ruled in 1849 in accordance with a separate but equal philosophy. (This idea would be reaffirmed in the *Plessy v. Ferguson* case in 1896.) Mob violence also inhibited desegregation. Race riots in New York, Ohio, and Indiana included attacks on Black educational facilities.[8]

As noted earlier, even though many Northern states gradually outlawed segregated education after 1865, a variety of means were used to nullify the law. In Pennsylvania, school district boundary lines were gerrymandered to ensure separation.[9] In some school buildings in New Jersey, separate classrooms were designated as exclusively for Blacks or Whites, and tall fences were erected to separate the races in the playground areas.[10] The amount of alleged White blood in a student was sometimes the determining factor with regard to admittance in a segregated or mixed school, as in Ohio.[11] And in Indiana, Blacks could be admitted to a White school, only if no White patron of the school objected.[12]

In adjudicating the test cases that came before the courts on this issue, judges were sometimes perfectly candid in expressing the white supremacist convictions that undergirded their rulings. For example, a court decision in Indiana included the following rationale for maintaining the exclusion of Blacks from a White school:

This [exclusion] has not been done because they do not need any education, nor because their wealth was such as to render aid undesirable, but because black children were deemed unfit associates to white, as school companions.[13]

Given such an attitude in the courts, it is not surprising that some individual teachers in mixed schools lost "no opportunity to browbeat their Negro students" and to encourage their White students to heckle and malign Black classmates.[14]

In the South, there was no such hypocritical gap between professed democratic ideals and their application to the classroom. Instead, public perceptions of Black education incorporated the idea of racial hierarchies. Thomas P. Bailey expressed it this way: "In educational policy let the Negro have the crumbs that fall from the white man's table. . . . Let there be such education of the Negro as will best fit him to serve the white man."[15] At the turn of the century, a North Carolina sawmill owner was quoted in a Report of the Bureau of Labor and Printing as follows: "The uneducated negro [is] the best we have for drudgery."[16]

In addition to this explicit treatment of Blacks as inferiors, the history of the South indicates a special connection between Black education and the tactics to disfranchise Blacks. In many districts African Americans had the numerical strength to create a truly viable educational system provided they could mobilize themselves politically. But that mobilization was thwarted by the creation of literacy tests as a prerequisite for voting. This maneuver did not always stem, apparently, from a fear of educated Blacks per se. In North

Carolina in the 1890s, White voters feared the Fusion ticket—a political coalition that joined Black Republicans and dissatisfied White Democrats in the Populist Movement. According to H. Leon Prather, North Carolina led the rest of the South in a campaign to defuse Populism, reassert the political monopoly of the old planter class, and ensure the continuance of that monopoly by manipulating the voting laws in relation to education.[17]

North Carolina prepared to avert the alleged threat of "Black Rule" by a suffrage amendment that would disfranchise Blacks, but not European Americans, on the basis of illiteracy. The plan (passed in the 1900 election) included the provision that only literate citizens would be allowed to vote after 1908. To ensure that Blacks did not gain the necessary education, the conservative Democratic Party passed laws to make key educational posts political appointments. This enabled the party to maintain control of all public schools.[18]

Northern philanthropic foundations assisted school development in the South and did not exclude Black schools in their programs. This produced North/South cooperation and had the appearance of progressive change. However, using North Carolina as a case study, Prather makes a strong argument that the political, social, and educational changes in the region need to be understood in their interrelationships, and that this broader perspective reveals school developments that were decidedly less than progressive.[19] His analysis suggests that the New South's political agenda hinged upon holding Black educational advancement in check. For example, White electoral control and new systems of forced labor (as in the crop lien system) could be justified if inadequate Black schooling produced an impression of innate African American dimwittedness.

In *Managers of Virtue, Public School Leadership in America, 1820– 1980*, David Tyack and Elisabeth Hansot make some related observations. While they credit the General Education Board (financed by the Rockefellers) and the Slater, Rosenwald, and Jeannes Funds with initiating educational improvements, they view this philanthropic activity at the turn of the century as also a means of thwarting unionization in the South.[20] Teacher training facilities, master teacher programs, and county training schools were developed, but the overall patterns of change indicate that the conservatism of Southern political leaders and Northern foundation agents made them compatible working partners. They shared the mainstream's social ideology, which was designed to adjust Blacks to their economic and political subordination.[21] Thus the Southern public education movement improved educational opportunity for Whites, while controlling education for Blacks to sustain a caste of unorganized laborers and a segregated social structure.

Education historian James D. Anderson describes this system as one in which education operated on two tracks: (1) schooling for democratic citizenship and (2) schooling for second-class citizenship. The contradictions in this arrangement were embraced by the White leadership in North and South, creating within American democracy the paradoxical acceptance of classes of oppressed people. And since democracy rested upon the premise that citizenship and universal education were inextricably linked, schools operated as a primary agent in sustaining the contradiction. There has been, notes Anderson, "an essential relationship between education and the politics of oppression."[22]

Novelist Richard Wright indicated in one of his early books *12,000,000 Black Voices,* that such a system was still suspect in the Black community in the early twentieth century:

Deep down we distrust the schools that the Lords of the Land build for us, and we do not really feel that they are ours. In many states they edit the textbooks that our children study, for the most part deleting all references to government, citizenship, voting, and civil rights. . . .[23]

In contrast to what the "Lords of the Land" provided, there was a grassroots educational tradition in the Black community that aided in revolutionizing the learning opportunities of the ex-slaves. Literacy was seen as a powerful symbol of liberation, a tangible indicator of being beyond the reach of slavery. Free Blacks in the pre–Civil War North had persevered in creating schools or gaining admittance for their children in public schools.[24] During Reconstruction, universal education was a major goal of the emancipated people. The Black church Sabbath schools served as the nucleus for this movement, with as many as two hundred thousand Black children enrolled in 1885.[25]

This self-help within the Black community needs to be viewed, however, in relation to the obstacles the Black family faced—for example, the attempts made after the Civil War to re-enslave Blacks, and Black children in particular. There is every indication that education had a high priority in the African American community, but the immediate need after Emancipation was to protect Black children from involuntary apprenticeship schemes. Rebecca J. Scott has analyzed some of the Freedmen's Bureau records in North Carolina with regard to indenture contracts that were put into effect following the war. Those contracts often trapped Black youths in a new form of bondage. Former slave owners invoked the old indenture laws that had been utilized before the war as a means of controlling free Black children.

When the war ended and families that had been split apart tried to reunite, parents found that their children, as Scott reports, were "'lawfully bound' as orphans to a former master."[26] Freedmen's Bureau officials had a lot of discretion in adjudicating the contested claims of masters and parents, and they were often unwilling to rescind an indenture contract. Because slaves had no legalized marriages, their children were dubbed bastards and made subject to the old indenture rules.[27] These rules required that apprentices be fed, clothed, housed, given suitable employment, and taught to read, write, and cipher. Bureau officials often sided with the White employers who argued that they were better able to educate the young Blacks than were their poverty-stricken parents. Government agents, like the masters, ignored the fact that the educational requirements were not being honored.[28] The pressure on the Bureau was to dispose of as many charges as possible, and the indenture system provided a convenient means to that end, while it also relieved the pressure of the plantation labor shortage. Although some Bureau agents did cancel contracts in some contested cases, parental rights were often sacrificed in favor of even fraudulently devised indenture contracts.[29]

Given such power of so-called masters over ex-slaves and given the unwillingness of Bureau agents to protect the rights of the Black family even during Reconstruction, it is not surprising that Black education was one of the concerns of Black churches. It was also likely that the disparity between opportunities in public institutions for Black and European American students would widen over time.

Statistics for a Black belt county in Alabama are indicative of that trend. In 1876–1877, expenditures for teachers' salaries were $2,136 for Whites and $6,055 for Blacks. The school population consisted of 2,403 Whites and 7,357 Blacks. But in 1927–1928, despite a decrease in the white population and an increase in the Black population, salaries of White teachers amounted to $64,622, whereas the amount expended on Black teachers was only $5,090.[30]

In the South as a whole, White teachers received 62.4 percent of school expenditures for teaching 60 percent of the population, while Black teachers taught 40 percent of the school population, but received only 12 percent of school expenditures.[31]

The possibility of closing that kind of gap through the efforts of small, private organizations (for example, the Society of Friends) was unrealistic. Yet the Quaker initiative warrants some mention here because the education of Blacks always had been an integral part of the Quakers' century-long opposition to slavery.

From at least 1774, when Quaker policy in North Carolina was to free Quaker-held slaves, the minutes of the Yearly Meeting of the Friends show a continuous concern for Black schooling.[32] Quakers persuaded some slaveowners to allow slaves to attend a school supposedly designed to teach Bible reading. But the actual curriculum included instruction in some "useful employment in life," in the kind of learning that would "fit [Blacks] for business," and in reading, writing, and ciphering.[33]

After 1831, however, Quaker schools were closed in compliance with the law enacted that year in North Carolina making all slave education illegal. The Friends groups unsuccessfully petitioned the legislature on this issue, but then lapsed into silence in order to "not be drawn into controversy."[34]

After the war, the Quakers resumed the education of Blacks. By 1869 the Quakers were operating thirty-one schools in North Carolina with 5,515 pupils.[35] There were problems, however. Most of these schools were "first day" (Sunday) rather than weekday schools, and the school term was only three to five months. The Quakers could not supply all the facilities that the ex-slaves needed. Children often walked long distances in order to reach a schoolhouse. Despite these shortcomings, the assistant superintendent of the Freedmen's Bureau, J. W. Hood, praised the Friends' schools for offering a secular curriculum that did not attempt to indoctrinate students with the beliefs of the Quaker denomination.[36]

But in spite of the progressive actions suggested by Friends' documents, a recent analysis of Quaker history vis-à-vis abolitionism treats this religious group as an instrument of "gradualist, segregationist, and paternalistic policies."[37] Even in the late eighteenth century, according to Jean R. Sonderlund, Quakers engaged in the invidious practice of "supervising the binding out of children and the drawing up of contracts between Blacks and their employers."[38] Sonderlund comments upon the price the Black community had to pay in exchange for Society "aid." She writes:

In accepting monetary help, freed men and women discovered, as do recipients of public assistance today, that they lost independence in making decisions concerning their own families. And beyond financial matters, the Friends also expected the blacks to conform to white Christian (perhaps Quaker) standards of morality, attend special Friends meetings held for blacks (but conducted by whites), and send their children to special schools set up for blacks (but again controlled by white Quakers). Blacks benefited from the Friends' system of mutual aid and endured, with varying degrees of patience, their paternalistic concern.[39]

Sonderlund's analysis reveals the gradualist attitude toward Black social progress that can be discovered even in a group with the best intentions.

The American Missionary Association's school for Blacks and Indians in Virginia, Hampton Institute, offers another example. Hampton officials, according to a study by David Wallace Adams, viewed Blacks as lower than Whites on a so-called scale of being. The history of that school, says Adams, presents a further illustration of the "paradoxical use of education as an instrument for both social control and social mobility."[40] Founded in 1868 and directed by a Northerner, Samuel Chapman Armstrong, Hampton set about creating a corps of conservative Black teachers. But the school's agenda was ambitious. According to James Anderson, Armstrong identified Hampton as a means of supporting "new forms of external control over blacks, including disfranchisement, segregation, and civil inequality."[41] Armstrong's call for "industrial education" for ex-slaves was merely a tactic for relegating the Black laborer to the lowest menial jobs. At a more insidious level, the curriculum was a weapon against Black self-esteem and self-respect—a strategy for reinforcing the concept of racial hierarchies.

In North Carolina near the turn of the century, Methodist and Baptist colleges were rivals of the state colleges for educational pre-eminence, and leaders within these denominations backed the white supremacist Democratic Party officials in exchange for promises to hold down state appropriations to the state schools. This behind-the-scenes collusion resulted in the pledge by church officials to "throw their influence toward victory for white supremacy."[42]

White-controlled church groups, although deeply involved in Southern education, did not achieve the kind of intellectual and cultural breakthrough that would point them in the direction of social equality rather than social control.

Textbooks also played an important role in this effort to maintain a racial hierarchy. Following the Civil War, the textbook industry remained centered in the North, which was attempting a balancing act between de jure desegregation and de facto segregation in its public schools. In such contradictory circumstances, textbook publishers followed a predictable course: they were all but silent about the activities and welfare of the ex-slaves. In her summary of the content of schoolbooks for the Reconstruction period, Ruth Miller Elson writes:

In the treatment of Reconstruction, [the Negro] appears as a mere pawn in arguments between the President and Congress, an incidental figure of contention. The real problems of Reconstruction were constitutional ones. This seems to be a valid reflection of the way the Negro was treated by political parties at the time; certainly it reflects with some accuracy the role assigned the Negro in the historiography of Reconstruction. The Negro, having been granted freedom, disappears from the schoolbooks.[43]

The few exceptions to this invisibility included references to Booker T. Washington as a self-made man, working in the spirit of American individualism and accepting guidance from his "betters."[44] Also some texts indicated that Blacks could be expected to rise slowly in terms of status and participation as citizens if they would humbly accept paternal White leadership. Elson quotes the following as a typical statement:

The negro race have, by themselves, made only the first steps in civiliza-
tion and the great mass are still in the savage state. Where they have been
brought up under the influence of cultured nations, however, they have
shown themselves capable of a high degree of progress.[45]

Furthermore, Elson continues, the post–Civil War textbook writer often complimented Southern Whites as among the chief uplifters of ex-slaves:

The systematic training bestowed upon [the Negro] during his period of
servitude, and his contact with higher intelligence have given to the
negro an impulse to civilization that neither his inherent inclinations
nor his native environment would of themselves bestow."[46]

Elson concludes that a child reared on such textbooks "would be unlikely to see the Negro as a participant in and a contributor to American culture."[47]

There were also textbooks that overtly supported the Confed-eracy. Ideals of the secessionist states were praised in such general works of history as W. M. McDonald and J. S. Blackburn's *The South-ern History of the United States*, published in 1869. According to textbook historian Charles Carpenter, this book "was in its last pages wholly a Confederate text."[48] When such a Southern interpretation was lacking, teachers in the South instituted the practice of pinning book pages together so they could not be easily read. But such cen-sorship was not needed on a grand scale because "Northern, South-ern, and Confederate books [were with some exceptions] identical in their discussions of the Negro and his racial characteristics."[49]

Another aspect of the white supremacy message appeared in books justifying imperialist actions on the part of the United States government. The antagonists of Americans in colonialist conflicts were viewed as the "passive races." Expansionist policies were pre-sented as a spin-off of an overall Anglo-Saxon "mission"; as one text-book put it, "It is clearly their mission [the Germanic Aryans' mis-

sion] to bring the blessings of their culture to the indolent or bar-
barian nations of the passive races. . . ."[50]

Cubans and Filipinos were among the peoples depicted as benefiting from the guiding hand of American interventionists. In 1869,
long before the outbreak of the Spanish-American War, a general
contrast between peoples of English and Spanish roots was presented
to child readers in the United States:

The people of the Spanish colonies became idle, ignorant and corrupt;
and their descendants retain that character to this day. But the English
were an industrious people, who loved liberty, and humanity, and earned
success by energetic toil in the fields and on the sea.[51]

In a work published in 1900, *Young People's History of the War*
with Spain, a Filipino nationalist leader is treated as making "trouble
for the Americans," although he had been actually waging a nearly
successful war of liberation against Spanish rule. According to the
author of *Young Peoples' History,* General Aguinaldo wanted to be a
dictator, and "entirely ignored the efforts of the U.S. to give his
people a good government."[52] Thus, Filipino revolutionaries were
suddenly turned into enemies against the United States rather than
allies against Spain. Their leader, Aguinaldo, was dubbed a schemer
and insurrectionist, an instigator of a "rebellion against the authority of the United States, who owned the islands by right of conquest
and purchase."[53]

A study of textbook descriptions of American wars led Arthur
M. Schlesinger to suggest that schools and schoolbooks, omnipres-
ent in American culture, might be a cause of war. Schlesinger writes:

[Education] may consciously be used by special groups or by the govern-
ment for chauvinistic propaganda; more often perhaps it represents a
gradual accretion of national traditions, popular hopes, and hates. In
either case, it occupies a central position with reference to all other provo-
cations to war, for insofar as it embodies dangerous nationalistic preju-
dices, it is the means of disseminating them constantly to all the people.[54]

In just such a manner, schools and schoolbooks disseminated
the white supremacy myth. Although that myth had been challenged

by abolitionists at the time of the Civil War, it continued to gain
strength as the nineteenth century drew to a close. In spreading that
myth, libraries played a role, as did the burgeoning periodical
industry.

Libraries

Library service for children did not develop until late in the nineteenth century. Professionals did not organize a Children's Library
Association to serve the under-fourteen age group until 1887. The
first separate room for children in a public library did not appear
until 1890 in Brookline, Massachusetts. But even before public libraries for children were established, lists of preferred children's books
were in circulation. As early as 1865, the American Unitarian Association had compiled a list of good books for the young.[55] Professional dialogues about what constituted a "best book" increased after the American Library Association was formed in 1876. Then, in
1882, Caroline M. Hewins, a librarian who worked with children at
the Hartford Public Library in Connecticut, produced the first of
her influential lists. These would appear intermittently until 1915,
the year of her last revision. In preparing her "Books for the Young,"
Hewins compared her choices with titles recommended by librarians in the Quincy, Buffalo, and Indianapolis libraries, as well as
with those titles preferred in the school libraries throughout Connecticut.[56]

Fictional works about Blacks on the Hewins list included Stowe's
Uncle Tom's Cabin, Trowbridge's *Cudjo's Cave*, Marryat's *The Mission*, and Harris's *Uncle Remus*. Hewins's list as a whole was heavily
weighted on the side of nonfiction, with twenty-five books about
Africa and at least a half-dozen histories of the Civil War.[57]

Frederick Marryat's *The Mission, or Scenes in Africa* (1845) shows
that contradictions were not a problem for the best-book compilers,
so long as an antislavery theme surfaced at some point. As an Englishman, Marryat sends this message while predictably directing
his wrath at the Dutch. He writes:

*[The Boers'] cruelty to the Hottentots and other natives arises from the
prejudices of education: they have . . . treated them as slaves, and do not
consider them as fellow-creatures. . . . [N]othing demoralizes so much,*

or so hardens the heart of man, as slavery existing and sanctioned by law.[58]

But Marryat is himself a notable offender when it comes to "prejudices of education." Whenever he has occasion to describe Blacks, he demeans them. Even Omrah, the African singled out for Christian conversion and a so-called move up the "scale of creation"— even Omrah is beastly, ludicrous, and servile. "Omrah's face," we are told, "was very much like a monkey's and his gestures and manners completely so. . . ."[59] Marryat's Africans are either innocent beasts or despicable humans, the latter supplying the story with familiar stereotypes: they will not exert themselves in any form of labor, but will go to great trouble to find a way to get drunk; they are insubordinate if beyond the reach of the police; they are noted for excessive sensuality; their religious leaders are murderers and frauds. Given this attitude, it is not surprising that Marryat's White hero prays: "Gracious Lord, I thank thee [that my cousin has perished rather than been married to an African]."[60]

Among the purely "informational" works on Hewins's list, Paul Du Chaillu's *Stories of Gorilla Country* and *Lost in the Jungle* were probably the most prominent. Du Chaillu's books were referred to as fine examples of books for the young at the American Library Association's annual conference in 1882,[61] and retained enough popularity with professionals to be included in Jacob Blanck's bibliography of best-loved American children's books published in 1938.[62]

Except for the fact that *Stories of the Gorilla Country* was not cast as a work of fiction, it was very similar to Frederick Marryat's *The Mission.* The text is about equally divided between ridicule of Africans and accounts of animal hunts. The narration is punctuated with such comments as, "What funny people they were," "What a queer way of dressing they had," "Most ugly they looked!";[63] and there is the conventional comic scene in which a village chief tries to generously bestow a native bride upon the White explorer. The European uses all his wits in making his refusal because (Du Chaillu writes), "I did not want to tell him that I would not, for all the world, marry one of his people."[64]

There is, however, occasional ambivalence expressed toward Africans. For instance, the author firmly renounces the European slave trade and exclaims, "I actually felt ashamed of being a white man! Happily, . . . the slave-trade will soon belong to the past."[65]

Beyond the circulation of the best-book lists, we know little about library activity in the 1880s and 1890s that pertained to attitudes about Blacks.[66] Children's libraries were just starting, and the record of library service to the young refers to Black Americans only in a few peripheral ways.

Studies that do exist about early librarianship point to it as a largely White-oriented social service, conceived as a means of keeping unemployed factory workers out of saloons. That libraries developed in the North for purposes of social control can hardly be doubted. The first annual report of the directors of the Chicago Public Library noted that without the counsel of books, the working masses "are easily led aside into the haunts of vice and folly, wasting time in places of ill reputation, contracting habits of crime and ignorance such as disgrace our modern civilization."[67] The records of early public libraries are replete with such statements about the moral vulnerability of White factory workers. Black Americans were not a significant factory constituency and, therefore, not the targeted group in early library development.

Similarly, it was undoubtedly the White child whom early librarians had in mind. While it was admitted that the machine operator might still prefer his or her drink, "yet, [the laborer's] children will use the library, if he does not."[68] More important, children themselves were part of the labor force in the nineteenth century, and, since working children had to forego schooling, the public library was advertised as a substitute for school. Sidney Ditzion has paraphrased a library pamphlet from the 1890s: state aid for libraries was requested because "the library would help regain some ground lost in the battle of life at that time when necessity compelled one to transfer from the schoolroom to the factory."[69]

The connection between Black children and public libraries in the North (aside from the fact that the racist "best books" impacted upon the Blacks) can be defined as a general educational opportunity. Particularly in those schools that were racially integrated, Black and European American children would have had similar access to the rotating collections of books that public libraries placed in the schools.

In the South, just as its public school movement lagged behind that of the North, so public libraries had a slow start. And when libraries in the South did get underway, they imitated the segregated system of Southern schools. Both African American and White women's groups initiated library development in the South, turning club houses into small libraries, and rotating book collections (usually about twenty-five books) among churches and schools.[70] In 1899 the Alabama Association of Women's Clubs was organized by Black women to perform such services in the state's Black community.[71] But a more enduring form of Black library service began in 1903 when a Memphis public library contracted with a Black school to provide books for the Black citizenry. Prior to 1920, Black libraries developed slowly and were largely confined to urban areas.[72]

Periodicals

With respect to periodicals, the pattern that was evident in the abolitionist period was repeated in the postbellum era. That is, many Northern journals for adults ran sympathetic articles about the South, and magazines for children had connections with leading juvenile fiction writers of the times. The new elements in the late 1800s were the rise of Southern journals and the rapid increase in Black American periodicals.

A concerted reconciliation effort began in the *Nation* with a series entitled "The South As It Is." *Lippincott's Magazine* came to be known as a "spokesman for the South," and *Harper's Weekly* published a series of articles to encourage emigration to the South.[73] According to Frank Luther Mott, *Scribner's Monthly* attracted more attention with its series "The Great South" than other periodicals were enjoying because it was splendidly illustrated. In the early 1870s *Harper's Monthly* and the *Atlantic Monthly* issued articles about the New South. By 1881, *Scribner's* could make the claim that the Southern literary school (including such writers as Sidney Lanier, William Gilmore Simms, George Washington Cable, and Thomas Nelson Page) was edging out the New England school:

Attention has recently been called to the large number of southern contributions to the magazine . . . and we are glad to recognize the fact of a

*permanent productive force in literature in the southern states. . . . New
England is no longer king.*[74]

In children's periodical literature, every one of the writers sampled
in this study for the postbellum era was a contributor or an editor
with the exception of Louise-Clarke Pyrnelle. William T. Adams created *Oliver Optic's Magazine*, a periodical for the young. Mark Twain
and Joel Chandler Harris published stories in *St. Nicholas' Magazine*
("Tom Sawyer Abroad" and "Daddy Jake, the Runaway," respectively). Thomas Nelson Page contributed children's stories to *Harper's
Young People* and *St. Nicholas*, and Martha Finley was an early contributor to Sunday school publications. Using different pseudonyms,
Edward Stratemeyer contributed to juvenile magazines, and George
A. Henty edited three different British youth periodicals: *Union-
Jack, Boys' Own Magazine*, and *Camps and Quarters*.

According to Alice M. Jordan, *Our Young Folks* was by far the
most brilliantly edited juvenile magazine published after the Civil
War. John Trowbridge, Lucy Larcom, and Gail Hamilton constituted its editorial triumvirate. Because of business setbacks, this periodical was sold by its parent company, the *Atlantic Monthly*, to
Scribner's after just nine years. In 1873, *Scribner's* created its more
famous and long-lived successor, *St. Nicholas*, a magazine that continued to appear until May, 1943.[75]

The white supremacist bias of *St. Nicholas* has not been mentioned in the studies of children's periodicals with the exception of
one article in the Black press: Elinor Desverney Sinnette's study of a
twentieth-century Black periodical, *The Brownies' Book*, in *Freedomways Magazine*. Sinnette says of *St. Nicholas* that "the impression of
the Afro-American child [it] presented to the white reader is clearly
that this Black creature is not a part of his society but 'something'
apart."[76] She cites the ridicule of young Blacks in cartoons and the
inclusion of offensive stories and jingles. A *St. Nicholas* editor tells
readers they will "split" with laughter over the poem "Ten Little
Niggers" ("Ten little nigger boys went out to dine/One choked his
little self and then/there were nine. . . .")[77] The stories in *St. Nicholas* warrant coverage in some detail since the magazine was consistently racist, yet it has been widely praised in mainstream children's
book circles.

"A Funny Little School," a short story by Ruth McEnery Stuart, is surely among the most derogatory treatments of Black education to find its way into print. It features five Black men who are in their sixties or beyond, a dim-witted Black woman, and a twelve-year-old child who accepts the assignment of teaching the others to read. It would be hard to say which of these characters is the biggest fool. Every scene reads like a "blackface" minstrel skit. The child's grand-father is one of the "scholars" and delivers a monologue about "dat big A, it favors [his long-deceased wife] consider'ble." Another class member is miffed because he suspects unfair treatment when his name is not part of the lesson ("I done tooken notice dat Tom an' Sol been spelt a week ago, an' it's a' outrage dat I ain't been spelt long ago"). The teacher complains about everyone's "ignunce," but every other line suggests that she was an unteachable student herself (she tells her charges that the rule is "No talkin' in school—widout com-mission," she is sometimes "pervoked" or has "onrespect," and she is never sure of the alphabet she is teaching).[78]

Slave/master relationships were often described in *St. Nicholas* narratives by ex-slave characters and implied an unabashed adula-tion of Whites. In Ruth McEnery Stuart's "An Old-Time Christmas Gift," when a slave infant and slaveowner's baby are both born on Christmas, the slave master "gently opened their tiny right hands, and laying them one within the other, closed them for a moment. Then he lifted the white hand and placed it on the black baby's head. This . . . meant obedience on one side and protection on the other."[79]

The subsequent narrative chronicles the lives of the two girls through the Civil War and concludes with a repetition of the White hand on the Black head; this time, however, the ceremony is at the insistence of the newly freed slave. The African American girl will have no part in her own emancipation. She explains to her former owner what the hand-on-head gesture means: "It mean dat I 's yo' little nigger, an' you 's my little mistus—dat what it mean." The slave has vehemently insisted upon a condition of servitude forever. "'As long as we live?' Mimi added. 'Yas, o' co'se, as long as we live,' Yuyu repeated."[80] Here Stuart has written a tract devoted to the exoneration of slavery (war or no war) and the message is voiced through the African American protagonist. Slaves became the chief supporters of their own enslavement, thus alleviating any guilt that members of the former slavocracy might experience.

To make such unlikely sentiments plausible, the character of the African American must be dehumanized. In "An Old-Time Christmas Gift," Yuyu is distinctly set apart from Mimi in a portrayal that highlights superstition, cowardice, and an inability to draw reasonable conclusions. These traits, plus the fact that "Yuyu [was] a terrible fib-teller," allow the author to contrive scenes reminiscent of "blackface" minstrel skits. For example, Yuyu's fear of the dark makes her take a shortcut through the chicken yard, but she is equally terrified by the chickens. Much sport is made of her maneuvers through these dangers: ". . . she always kicked and shouted aloud during the passage, and Mimi, hearing her cries, would say: 'Listen to Yuyu comin' through the chicken-hole!'"[81] Such slapstick episodes are attached to the Black character exclusively, and reinforce the point that Blacks must, for their own safety, be under the surveillance of the White population.

Slavery receives a similar nostalgic boost from Joel Chandler Harris in "Daddy Jake, the Runaway," a story published originally in *St. Nicholas*. Harris indulges in less overt editorializing than Stuart, but creates a similar theme about unshakable slave/slaveowner solidarity. First Harris inserts a direct proslavery message. When fifty-year-old Daddy Jake hits an overseer with a hoe and escapes, Harris comments: "[other slaves] thought it was time for the rest to follow suit, but this proposition was hooted down by the more sensible among them."[82] It seems that "sensible" slaves gave their allegiance solely to the master; in fact, they identify with the master rather than with their own peer group, and to make this plausible, Harris shows slave disapproval extending only to evil slaveowners, not to slavery per se. As one slave puts it in a scene about his devotion to the "marster": "You know how marster is. He think kaze *he* treat his niggers right dat eve'y body else treat der'n des dat a-way."[83] In the end, Jake eagerly returns to the plantation after being assured by master's children that the cruel overseer has been dismissed. Jake was the favorite of the children, an ever available court jester: "he was always ready and anxious to amuse them." Harris assures his readers that the plantation was truly a good home and "there was not one [of the slaves] but would have swapped places with [Jake]."

Avuncular Black males had their counterpart in the mammy figure in *St. Nicholas.* With similar devotion to the plantation owners, Mammy Prissy says, "'T wuz a treat jes' ter lib on de same plantation 'long o' dem."[84] This mammy in Jessie C. Glasier's "Ole Mammy Prissy" describes a flood that separated her from her White owners (especially from the child whom she had nursed) and tells how they are reunited several decades later. In the course of this story she puts down the "free niggah" in favor of people like herself: the loyal house slaves. Of necessity she was forced during her adventures to associate with "low-down, no 'count brack critters," and readers learn from Prissy about the superiority of life in slavery: "Dey cud n't none on um no mo' 'preciate de diff'unce 'twixt a common eb'ry-day free niggah an' an ole fam'ly suvvant w'at had al'ays lived right 'mongst de bery top sort!"[85] Mammy's whole life centers upon her fixation with the "top sort"![86]

Criminality is also attributed to Black personality, as seen in Clara Morris's "My Little 'Jim Crow.'" First we encounter the young protagonist as he travels "a very short distance along the paths of education":

He could count up to six with temperate calmness, but beyond that point his figuring was directed by an absolutely tropical imagination; while his joyous greeting of A, B, C, and D was in marked contrast to his doubtful acknowledgment of E and his absolute non-recognition of F.[87]

After this joke about Jim Crow's feeble success as a scholar, the narrative presents the child's mother, who is a thief as well as a cook, and abuses her small son to the point where the White mistress of the house must protect him. Moreover, Jim Crow's sister is so threatening that the benevolent employer exclaims: "Time and again I had to fling the shield of my authority above little Jim Crow's head to save him from the vengeful wrath of his buff and sullen sister."[88] The "buff" sister (implicitly associated with miscegenation) is the primary villain, but in the end "too much liquor and a narrowly averted conflagration caused the dismissal of them all."[89]

St. Nicholas gives convincing proof that "yankeeism," as C. Vann Woodward notes about the postbellum era, took to its heart the Lost Cause."[90] The stories were no simple put-down, but part of that postbellum ethos that was redefining what the plantation slave culture implied—namely that ex-slaves would again constitute an exploitable labor system for the benefit of White society.[91]

Turning to the postbellum South, we find that at least a score of journals with literary content were issued before 1870.[92] This fact alone suggests a remarkable vitality within the impoverished region, and some of that intellectual energy was directed at White regional self-recovery. For example, the *Southern Bivouac* (a project of the Southern Historical Association) devoted much of its space to war-related materials such as camp humor, war songs, and other "papers on the Civil War." Similarly, *The Land We Love* emphasized the South's story of the war: histories of military campaigns, tales of heroism, and so on.[93] These journals did not address a young audience, but the *Sunny South* was a family weekly with miscellaneous contents.

Black newspapers were not geared to the child audience, but their focus on education involved them indirectly in child development. Also, the wide coverage given to issues of political freedom suggests the utility of Black newspapers as a counteraction to the white supremacy myth. More than eleven hundred newspapers were founded in the Black community between 1865 and 1900.[94] In *The Afro-American Periodical Press, 1838–1909*, Penelope L. Bullock cites numerous examples of journals about education published by such organizations as the African Civilization Society, the African Methodist Episcopal Church, and the many state teachers' associations.[95]

Black women's magazines were published with a clear concern for the care of the young. For example, *Our Women and Children* was founded in 1888 with Ida B. Wells as editor of the home department.[96] *Women's World* was advertised as containing "good stories, with colored men and women as heroes and heroines; . . . special talks for girls; a page for children" and so on. Similar journals were published by women's club federations.[97] The Woman's Era Club of Boston sponsored the *Women's Era*, a publication that supported the establishment of kindergartens, opposed the imprisonment of youngsters for minor offenses, suggested role models in its sketches of eminent women, and contained other features that could be expected to impact upon the lives of children.[98]

Penelope L. Bullock notes that the proliferation of Black journals began after Reconstruction when the prospects for meaningful

citizenship began to deteriorate. The press was one means that could
be used to agitate for social justice and, since 90 percent of the Black
population was still residing in the South in 1900, many issues highlighted in the press were Southern regional issues. But the children's-
book publishing center was the North,[99] and both during Reconstruction and after there was a white supremacist slant in works for
children.

Conclusion

One of the great ironies in American public school history was the
creation of racially segregated schools on one hand, and on the other
hand a curriculum that extolled political freedom. Moreover, the
schools generally encouraged the idea that the United States was the
world's best example of democratic government. The contradiction
in such a line of thought is highlighted by education historian Robert A. Carlson. He writes:

*The white people of the United States considered themselves superior to
the "Tawnies," the "Niggers," the "Chinks," and the "Japs," as they termed
their fellow citizens. Despite all his problems, the lowliest peasant from
Europe . . . was in a better position on first landing in the United States
than a Protestant Negro whose ancestors trod American soil in colonial
times. . . . After the abolition of slavery, Americans banished black people
to a life of segregation.[100]*

It did not matter how Americanized (how culturally homog-
enized) African Americans would become through contact with the
public schools; the non-White groups were persistently rejected as
part of the national community. As Arthur M. Schlesinger suggested,
there was tremendous power within schools to carry out a contradictory policy, because the school could build up layers of prejudice
(not to mention self-rejection) through a slow process of accretion.
The child was a captive audience and subject to long-term incar-
ceration within the school environment.

The power of the public library was somewhat different, but it
had its own means of functioning as a force in the community. The
librarian's job was to sift through the available books, create a canon
or honor list, and circulate the works in that canon as widely as

possible. By examining the actions of librarians in relation to groups targeted as problem groups, we can follow the evolution of strategies of social control. Public library service is largely a twentieth-century phenomenon, but by studying its history we gain glimpses of how the white supremacy myth is repeatedly injected with new life.

As for the periodicals of childhood, they carried their full share of racially biased narratives, but in the twentieth century they slowly began to decline as a major socializing force within the mainstream. Children would be served by an array of cultural gatekeepers—by librarians and school personnel rather than directly through the mails from a publishing establishment. This fact alone is suggestive. It points to a consolidation of institutional power, power that would create new challenges for those seeking to dismantle the intricate white supremacy myth.

Notes

1. Horace Mann Bond, *The Education of the Negro in the American Social Order* (New York: Octagon Books, 1966), 373.
2. Ibid., 375.
3. Ibid., 376, 378–380, 377.
4. Ibid., 381–383.
5. H. Leon Prather Sr., *Resurgent Politics and Educational Progressivism in the New South: North Carolina, 1890–1913* (Cranbury, NJ: Fairleigh Dickinson University Press and Associated University Presses, 1979), 281.
6. Bond, 370.
7. Ibid., 373.
8. Ibid., 372.
9. Ibid., 378.
10. Ibid., 379.
11. Ibid., 380.
12. Ibid., 381.
13. Ibid.
14. Ibid., 386.
15. Prather, 255.
16. Louis R. Harlan, *Separate and Unequal: Public School Campaigns and Racism in the Southern Seaboard States, 1901–1915* (Chapel Hill: University of North Carolina Press, 1958), 102.
17. Prather, 10–11. Prather quotes the following vehement denunciation of Black education from the *Wadesboro [N.C.] Intelligencer*: "Nothing is so surely ruining Negroes of the South as the accursed free schools. . . . [T]hey should be wiped out of existence instead of having their capacity increased."
18. Ibid., 24–25, 174.
19. Ibid., 12.
20. David Tyack and Elisabeth Hansot, *Managers of Virtue: Public School Leadership in America, 1920–1980* (New York: Basic Books, Inc., 1981), 91.
21. James D. Anderson, *The Education of Blacks in the South, 1860–1935* (Chapel Hill: University of North Carolina Press, 1988), 3.
22. Ibid., 12

23. Richard Wright, *12,000,000 Black Voices: A Folk History of the Negro in the United States* (New York: Viking Press, 1941), 64.

24. Tyack, 85.

25. Ibid., 85–86.

26. Rebecca J. Scott, "The Battle Over the Child: Child Apprenticeship and the Freedmen's Bureau in North Carolina," *Growing up in America: Children in Historical Perspective*, ed. N. Ray Hiner and Joseph M. Hawes (Urbana and Chicago: University of Illinois Press, 1985), 194.

27. Ibid.

28. Ibid., 196.

29. Ibid., 201.

30. Horace Mann Bond, *Social and Economic Influences on Public Education of Negroes in Alabama, 1865–1930* (Washington, D.C.: The Associated Publishers, 1939), 162.

31. Prather, 76–77.

32. Zora Klain, "Quaker Contributions to Education in North Carolina: A Thesis in Education" (Ph.D. diss., University of Pennsylvania, 1924), 318.

33. Ibid., 312.

34. Ibid., 313–314.

35. Ibid., 320, 318.

36. Ibid., 320.

37. Jean R. Soderlund, *Quakers and Slavery: A Divided Spirit* (Princeton: Princeton University Press, 1985), 187.

38. Ibid., 184.

39. Ibid.

40. David Wallace Adams, "Education in Hues: Red and Black at Hampton Institute, 1878–1893," *South Atlantic Quarterly* 76:2 (Spring 1977): 176.

41. Anderson, 36.

42. Prather, 139–140.

43. Ruth Miller Elson, *Guardians of Tradition: American Schoolbooks of the Nineteenth Century* (Lincoln: University of Nebraska Press, 1964), 96.

44. Ibid.

45. Ibid., 97.

46. Ibid.

47. Ibid., 98.

48. Charles Carpenter, *History of American Schoolbooks* (Philadelphia: University of Pennsylvania Press, 1963), 209.

49. Elson, 100.

50. Ibid., 298–299.

51. Ibid., 156.

52. Prescott Holmes, *Young Peoples' History of the War with Spain* (Philadelphia: Henry Altemus Co., 1900), 180.

53. Ibid.

54. Arthur Walworth. *School Histories at War: A Study of the Treatment of Our Wars in the Secondary School History Books of the United States and in Those of Its Former Enemies*, with an introduction by Arthur M. Schlesinger (Cambridge: Harvard University Press, 1938), xiii.

55. R. Gordon Kelly, *Mother Was a Lady: Self and Society in Selected American Children's Periodicals, 1865–1890* (Westport, CT: Greenwood Press, 1974), 96.

56. Caroline M. Hewins, *Books for the Young* (New York: P.F. Leypoldt, 1882), 6–7.

57. Since there was little interest in the late 1800s in promoting the library as anything other than an educational institution, professionals tried to build up the percentage of nonfiction titles in their collections. For a detailed account of this trend, see Dee Garrison's *Apostles of Culture: The Public Librarian and American Society, 1876–1920* (New York: Free Press, 1979).

58. Captain [Frederick] Marryat, *The Mission, or Scenes in Africa* (London: 1845; rpt. intro. Tony Harrison, New York: Africana Publishing Corp., 1970), 70.

59. Ibid., 76.

60. Ibid., 305.

61. Miss C. M. Hewins [Caroline Hewins], "Yearly Report on Boys' and Girls' Reading," *Library Journal* 7:7–8 (July–August 1882): 187.

62. Jacob Blanck, *Peter Parley to Penrod: A Bibliographical Description of the Best-Loved American Juvenile Books, 1827–1926* (New York: R. R. Bowker, 1938).

63. Paul Du Chaillu, *Stories of the Gorilla Country* (New York: Harper and Bros., 1869), 21.

64. Ibid., 19.

65. Ibid., 121

66. Besides extolling best books, Caroline Hewins named specific authors she deemed the enemies of youth, dubbing them facetiously "the immortal four": Oliver Optic, Horatio Alger, Harry Castelmon, and Martha Finley. The name Horatio Alger became a symbol associated with nineteenth-century popular fiction, and Alger's ideas about race warrant some mention here. In *Frank's Campaign; or, The Farm and the Camp* (1864), Alger is ambivalent about Pomp, a slave child who has escaped with his mother to the North. Pomp is described as "bright," but his characterization resembles that of a bright animal. He has no memory, no reasoning power that is not on a purely literal level, is said to be "incorrigibly idle," and demands instant gratification of whims. Alger's political opposition to slavery is plain in this novel, but every Black characterization tends to support the idea that Blacks are hopelessly ill-prepared for citizenship.

67. Sidney Ditzion, "Social Reform, Education, and the Library, 1850–1900," *The Library Quarterly* 9:2 (April 1939): 166–167.

68. Ibid., 168.

69. Ibid., 172. For an extensive treatment of libraries as a means of social control in the name of community reform, see Rosemary Ruhig Du Mont's *Reform and Reaction: The Big City Public Library in American Life* (Westport, CT: Greenwood Press, 1977)

70. Kenneth R. Johnson, "The Early Library Movement in Alabama," *Journal of Library History* 6:2 (April 1971): 121, 126.

71. Ibid., 122. Johnson does not provide comparative statistics for Black and white libraries prior to 1911. During that year, the year that a school library support act was passed, Alabama had 468 libraries (83,152 volumes) for Whites, and 47 libraries (3,723 volumes) for Blacks. The gap widened after state support became available: 2,135 libraries for Whites in 1919 and 131 for Blacks.

72. Eliza Atkins Gleason, *The Southern Negro and the Public Library: A Study of the Government and Administration of Public Library Service to Negroes in the South* (Chicago: University of Chicago Press, 1941), 28.

73. Frank Luther Mott, *A History of American Magazines, 1865–1885* (Cambridge: Harvard University Press, 1938), 47–48.

74. Ibid., 48–49.

75. Alice M. Jordan, *From Rollo to Tom Sawyer and Other Papers* (Boston: The Horn Book, Inc., 1948), 124–145.

76. Elinor Desverney Sinnette, "The Brownies' Book: A Pioneer Publication for Children," *Freedomways* 5:1 (Winter 1965): 134.

77. Ibid.

78. Ruth McEnery Stuart. "A Funny Little School," *St. Nicholas,* November 1897, 40–46; rpt. in *The St. Nicholas Anthology,* ed. Henry Steele Commager (New York: Random House, 1948), 371–378.   In his introduction, Commager called Stuart's tale among the "best" of the stories from *St. Nicholas.* His unstinting praise of white supremacist materials for children suggests that the socializing power of the tales was indeed great—greater than Commager's extensive training in history could overcome.

79. Ruth McEnery Stuart, "An Old-Time Christmas Gift," *St. Nicholas*, December 1897, 94.
80. Ibid., 102.
81. Ibid., 99.
82. Joel Chandler Harris, "Daddy Jake, the Runaway," *St. Nicholas*, March–May 1889, 323.
83. Ibid., 431.
84. Jessie C. Glasier, "Ole Mammy Prissy," *St. Nicholas*, October 1887, 916.
85. Ibid., 918.
86. In her comments about the mammy type, bell hooks explains the usefulness of this mythical being to her White creators:

    [The mammy's] greatest virtue was of course her love for white folk whom she willingly and passively served. The mammy image was portrayed with affection by whites because it epitomized the ultimate sexist-racist vision of ideal black womanhood—complete submission to the will of whites.

    This image, says hooks, contained the characteristics that colonizers wished to exploit—namely, the woman who would give all and expect no compensation, someone who loved whites while acknowledging her own inferiority. See hooks's *Ain't I a Woman: Black Women and Feminism* (Boston: South End Press, 1981), 84, 85.
87. Morris, Clara, "My Little 'Jim Crow,'" *St. Nicholas*, December 1898, 151.
88. Ibid., 151.
89. Ibid., 157.
90. Woodward C. Vann, *Origins of the New South, 1877–1913* (Baton Rouge: Louisiana State University Press and The Littlefield Fund for Southern History of the University of Texas, 1951, 1971), 55.
91. Out of dozens of stories with a strong Confederate slant, just two noticeably neoabolitionist stories appeared in *St. Nicholas* in the nineteenth century: the novel by Noah Brooks, "The Fairport Nine," *St. Nicholas*, May-October 1880, and Louise Seymour Houghton's short story, "Bossy Ananias," *St. Nicholas*, June 1879. While white norms are not called into question, the authors do take a stand against overt forms of racial discrimination.
92. Mott, 45.
93. Ibid., 46–47.
94. Sharon Murphy, *In Other Voices: Black, Chicano, and American Indian Press* (Dayton, Ohio: Pflaum/Standard, 1974), 80–81.
95. Penelope L. Bullock, *The Afro-American Periodical Press, 1838–1909* (Baton Rouge: Louisiana State University Press, 1981), 151–159.
96. Ibid., 168.
97. Ibid., 167–169.
98. Ibid., 191–193.
99. Although there were few antebellum novels for children with Southern origins, one did reach best-seller status: F. R. Goulding's *Robert and Harold, or The Young Marooners on the Florida Coast* (1852). In this novel slaves are part of a search party, and while they look for their master's children, they perform the usual gestures: rolling their eyes, secretly swilling rum, fainting with fright over "sperits." Goulding's one accolade to a slave is faint praise: "Ah—black and ugly as she was, that Judy [the cook] was a jewel!"
100. Robert A. Carlson, *The Quest for Conformity: Americanization Through Education* (New York: John Wiley and Sons, 1975), 13.

Chapter Eight
Literary Methods and Conventions

Children's literature of the 1865–1900 period is, in some cases, a literature that is still alive, whereas stories for the young in the antebellum era are now obsolete. To study the art of the earlier period is primarily an antiquarian exercise; but the late nineteenth century represents a new age in the stylistic and structural features of children's books. All the writers in my postbellum sample could be called modern with the exception of Martha Finley. That is, they wrote in a straightforward, sometimes journalistic, style that would not signal to the reader that the works were of an earlier time. Other aspects of content and form send a similar signal. The heavy use of dialect is the principal device that distinguishes some books as antiques, but even that convention is overlooked by present-day readers of Mark Twain's novels. Finley, as noted above, is a throwback to an earlier era because she wrote moralizing tracts interwoven with countless biblical quotations and allusions. Her novels represent the flattest kind of evangelical propaganda.

Twain, Harris, Page, and Pyrnelle were, in varying degrees, literary artists. Even when we look at their works as social documents, we need to examine them as artistic objects because a skillful technique has a direct bearing upon persuasiveness.

Finley, Stratemeyer, Henty, and Adams were not literary artists in the same sense, but they did create what could be called publishing phenomena. The characteristics of the phenomenon had a bearing upon the power of the works. For years librarians and teachers evaluated books by these hack writers as failed works of art and therefore as insignificant. They missed the point about the nature and function of popular culture. The meaning of series books of the nineteenth-century variety is better understood when they are studied as a series, as a family of stories with connections intentionally contrived.[1]

We can divide books in the sample, then, into two general narrative modes: local color fiction and series novels. Books in the first category could become classics; books in the second category could not, generally speaking, get past the library door. Even such a hardworking writer as William T. Adams (Oliver Optic) caused an upheaval in public library circles because librarians argued consistently against series books. (They objected to the implausibilities in popular fiction.) On the other hand, some avid readers of series books—people who were occasionally numbered among the community's leaders—thought it entirely unreasonable that their childhood tastes should be impugned in such a stiff-necked manner. A similar polarization among gatekeepers has continued into our own age.

In the pages that follow both series books and local color fiction are considered and commented upon in relation to the Black aesthetic. Since the books in the sample include major and minor Black characters, the use of a Black aesthetic is not just one of many approaches that is appropriate; it is an essential point of departure.

The concept "Black aesthetic" is as imprecise as its counterpart, the Western, White aesthetic. As used here, the term refers to three basic elements: (1) historical, culture-specific qualities that a narrative must not misrepresent if the work is to have artistic meaning; (2) a pragmatic dimension that means a work does not undermine the quality-of-life issues that seriously impact upon readers; and (3) formal features that nearly all artists and critics (irrespective of ethnicity) view as important, even while these features are admittedly varied. The Black aesthetic is a flexible concept, encompassing as it does the idea of abstract beauty (which is always, to some extent, experimental) and the idea of social responsibility. The social dimension is related to aspects of African art—to the functional, collective, and committed—but is not on that account dogmatic or doctrinaire. When Alice Childress refers to her intention "to move beyond the either/or of 'artistic' and politically imposed limitations," she may be said to affirm, albeit indirectly, the Black aesthetic's complexity.[2]

The series books of popular culture are perhaps the most glaring example of how such complexity can be ignored in both content and form.

The Methods of Series Writers

To review the techniques in either adventure or tear-jerking series books is to examine storytelling methods with intentional mesmeric effects. No injustice is done when Edward Stratemeyer, William T. Adams, George Henty, and Martha Finley are grouped together and treated as a single kind of writer because in each case the aim was the same: "Force the kid to turn the page."[3]

That statement by Albert Svenson, a latter-day member of the Stratemeyer syndicate, sums up the aesthetic of the series book. The writers listed above could be placed in various relationships with techniques that "force the kid," but Svenson describes an approach that all the writers shared when he says, "The trick in writing children's books is to set up danger, mystery, and excitement on page one."[4] In boys' books there was usually an ever-present sense of peril that centered on survival and property. In girls' books (as in those by Finley), the peril centered on various emotions, but only intermittently on survival itself.

The forerunners of such series books were the narratives cranked out by Samuel Goodrich and Jacob Abbott in the antebellum period, but their works had a more clear-cut pedagogic component. In the late nineteenth century, the formulas that stress hyperactivity stand out as an end unto themselves rather than as merely a means of sugarcoating some moralistic or educational "pill." There was, nonetheless, serious subject matter in the series books (sometimes introduced in a preface and even backed up with bibliographic references). But the narrative techniques for grabbing and holding the child's attention were paramount. Svenson has described the Stratemeyer formula in the following terms:

A low death rate but plenty of plot. Verbs of action, and polka-dotted with exclamation points and provocative questions. No use of guns by the hero. No smooching. The main character introduced on page one and a slambang mystery or peril set up.[5]

The superficiality indicated by such an approach does not im-

ply that Stratemeyer and the others were not creating influential
social documents. The white supremacist element was one of many
components that reflected mainstream culture. Stratemeyer gave tribute to the earlier series writers who inspired him, writers who were
spinning out the American dream in story form for children. About
these mentors Stratemeyer said, "I had quite a library, including many
of Optic's and Alger's books. At seven or eight when I was reading
them I said: 'If I could only write books like that I'd be the happiest
person on earth.'"[6]

Stratemeyer did become the heir of Oliver Optic and Horatio
Alger in many respects, but it is doubtful whether Optic would have
even tried to refine his formula to such a point that he would be able
to dash off a two-hundred-page novel in two days, as Stratemeyer
said he could. Eventually it became irrelevant whether Stratemeyer
himself or some ghostwriter produced the Stratemeyer novels because an invariable procedure was followed in any case. There was,
according to Stratemeyer scholar Carol Billman, a three-page outline that contained a list of characters, notes as to their fate, a blow-
by-blow plot outline, and the novel's time elements.[7]

Adams planned incidents of suspense with the same dogged
persistence as Stratemeyer, but surrounded such scenes with more of
the complexities of character, setting, and political conflict. In these
respects his novel, *Brother Against Brother*, bears some resemblance
to Trowbridge's *Cudjo's Cave*, which also centers on the Civil War's
border state conflicts. Adams writes dialogue that is slightly less stilted,
takes care to downplay the melodramatic incidents, and tries to
present his moral positions in dramatic terms rather than as slightly
disguised sermons. However, he sometimes polarizes his characters
excessively as he tries to drive home a point. *Brother Against Brother*
reads like the Cain and Abel myth, with Noah Lyon depicted as a
saint and Titus Lyon portrayed as an alcoholic who neglects his studies, keeps company with the "wrong class of persons," and beats his
wife. Additional vices include slangy speech and dancing!

Another series writer, George Henty, also relied upon a mechanical plot, but he wrote with the assurance of a practicing journalist.
In *By Sheer Pluck* there are repeated scenes of jeopardy and rescue,
each predictably casting some light upon a moral quality that interests Henty. He uses rags-to-riches and stress-in-battle themes as ways

to commend bravery, resourcefulness, perseverance, generosity, thankfulness to God, self-reliance, and racial hierarchies. As artificial as the book appears to a modern critic, the story must have represented for nineteenth-century White children a relief from the heavy-handed preaching found in the books belonging to their parents.

If Martha Finley's books are more tedious than the Henty, Adams, and Stratemeyer books, the reason may reside in their glaring hypocrisy. A white supremacist ideology alongside talk of fair play makes the boys' books incongruous, but in Finley's *Elsie's Womanhood* and *Elsie's Motherhood*, the reader is asked to swallow that ideology in conjunction with phony sentiment and New Testament Christianity. The novels are saturated with a spurious piety.

There is scarcely a moment when a character is not dying, languishing in illness, marrying, groaning over unrequited love, fending off rape, or offending God by violating some social taboo. But in spite of all these predictable traumas, Elsie's characterization gathers momentum. Though excessively deferential to the men in her life, she represented a relatively strong, talented, and independent personality for nineteenth-century readers. If Elsie Dinsmore was a role model, however, that makes her white supremacist attitudes all the more treacherous to the development of the young women who looked to Elsie as someone to emulate. Moreover, even when there is constructive content, the work as a whole comes across as essentially propaganda. Even honesty becomes dishonest when it makes its appeal by capitalizing upon manipulated and misused emotion.

Theories about such formulaic works, as for example in the writings of John G. Cawelti, are in some ways illuminating. Popular culture, says Cawelti, involves collectively generated products.[8] Those products are formulaic in that they are structured as a conventional (in contrast to an invented) system.[9] Characters, settings, lines of action, and metaphoric language can be predicted, and such predetermined elements offer a resynthesis of agreed-upon values. Additionally, they contribute to further group solidarity, encourage vicarious emotional release, and afford escape from frustration.[10] They may even suggest the presence of a collective dream.[11] Everything can be arranged on a continuum, says Cawelti, reaching from the highly familiar to the highly unique. As useful as this kind of analysis may be, it does not explain the sharply defined attacks against Blacks in nineteenth-century fiction.

In a popular story such as Edward Stratemeyer's *Tour of the Zero Club*, the values, solidarity, and escapism served a White readership and followed literary conventions that a White readership would easily grasp. Conversely, this story represents a denial of values, solidarity, and ego release to any typical Black reader. It is hard to envision a creative continuum in which the Black protagonist, Pickles, could be deemed a tenable character by a non-White audience. Instead he is a literary weapon in the service of a political cause. He does not arise mysteriously within a collective dream.

Even within the cultural mainstream, Cawelti's ideas need to be weighed against what we learn from series book writers. Their methods suggest a high degree of calculated manipulation and exploitation of child readers. After-the-fact critiques about "collective dreams" need some adjustment given the realities of publisher motivations, methods, and marketing goals.

Popular literature theories also need to take account of cultural diversity. Popular art, writes Russel Nye, is standardized at the "median level of majority expectation."[12] It depends, he says, upon a law of supply and demand, upon a large, middle-class market whose members have a certain level of disposable income.[13] In return for its dollars, this audience expects the popular artist to reflect its attitudes and concerns. Statistically, Black children are among the most poverty-stricken group in America and could not, by Nye's analysis, generate a series of books.[14] The Stratemeyer syndicate initiated a series about a Black family in 1967, *The Toliver Adventure Series*, but it was terminated after just three volumes.[15] Popular culture theory needs to address both the stereotypic characterization of Blacks and the social implications of excluding Blacks as audience. If popular culture is purely market oriented and exclusionary, popular culture theory need not be. Its practitioners need not remain complacent in the face of antisocial literature for children.

The Local Colorists

Like the series writers, local colorists had traits in common. The general character of local color fiction is well-expressed in Walter Blair's reference to such works as "historical landmarks." Specific locales, in other words, are presented by local colorists with notice-able realistic detail. "Whole communities, as well as individuals, came to life," says Blair.[16] The palpable texture of a place, according to critic Claude M. Simpson, is evoked through the inclusion of "ver-nacular speech, proverbial lore, regional superstitions, and folkways." Moreover, a relationship between physical setting and human psy-chology is suggested by the writer.[17] The results—especially a blend of tenderness, nostalgia, exuberance, humor, and hard realism— marked literary progress in the nineteenth century. For children, a group that had been subjected to heavy sermonizing and sentimen-tality, the local color tradition offered welcome relief. The local color story was written "with no moral determination except that which may be the legitimate outcome of the story itself."[18]

These literary features, in various combinations, are traceable in the works of Louise-Clarke Pyrnelle, Thomas Nelson Page, Joel Chandler Harris, and Mark Twain. But there is an additional feature prominent enough to warrant comment—namely, insightful per-ceptions of childhood. The mannerisms and thoughts of White chil-dren are viewed with the eyes of the realist and presented with un-usual precision. Each of the writers listed above highlights the spirit of childhood in a different way.

Pyrnelle's *Diddie, Dumps, and Tot* has not remained in print into the last half of the twentieth century, but it did last into the 1940s—an instance of exceptional staying power for a nineteenth-century children's novel. To some extent, the book's Black portrai-ture probably accounts for its demise after World War II, yet Pyrnelle's Black characters are not essentially different from those of the other three authors. Pyrnelle blended astute childhood observation with "blackface" minstrelsy, and the humor was conveyed in such a cum-bersome dialect that the public was apparently willing to forego it in the 1950s, as it had already rejected minstrelsy on the stage. A sec-ond dominant quality of the book, its authentic evocation of child-hood, was no longer a rarity in children's books after the Second World War. Thus, the two most prominent features of Pyrnelle's fiction were either no longer desired or no longer unique.

Pyrnelle convincingly captures the naïveté of childhood and the intimacy of the storyteller-listener relationship in her narrational

style. The novel opens with simple directness and a hint of collo-
quial speech:

*They were three little sisters, daughters of a Southern planter, and they
lived in a big white house on a cotton plantation in Mississippi. . . .
Now, you must not think that the little girls had been carried to the font
and baptized with such ridiculous names as Diddie, Dumps, and Tot:
these were only pet names that Mammy had given them. . . .
The little girls were very happy in their plantation home. 'Tis true they
lived 'way out in the country, and had no museums nor toyshops to visit,
no fine parks to walk or ride in, nor did they have a very great variety of
toys. They had some dolls and books, and a baby-house furnished with
little beds and chairs and tables. . . .[19]*

Instead of seeking ways to create humor through incongruity,
the author immerses the reader in the child's psychic world. Incongruous elements, with the exception of the dialect, stem from the
readers' own juxtaposition of the fictional world with their own. In
accordance with the dominant society's view of Blacks in the nineteenth century, the slaves in the narrative are presented as intrinsically part of the childish world.

The sense of credibility stems in part from the evocation of
place—from an extraordinarily astute eye for detail. This gift belongs to local colorists generally. Pyrnelle used the many self-gener-
ated games of her child characters to draw the reader into a graphi-
cally defined environment. Her method had such an effortless quality
that readers who were White and could empathize with the protagonists could easily lose themselves in the author's point of view.

However, if we apply the constituents of the Black aesthetic to
this novel, we see a work with no redeeming qualities. Nearly every
formal dimension—plot, characterization, setting, and style—is contrived to debase Black identity and reinforce a rationale for the continuing subjugation of Blacks.

Perhaps the most insidious tactic by Pyrnelle is her misuse of
Black folktales. Although she sometimes retells an authentic African
American tale, the context of the narrative turns it into pure white
supremacist dogma. For example, she includes a "pourquoi" story
that whimsically chronicles the way that laziness resulted in a per-

manently subservient status for Blacks. The oldest slave on the plantation informs the children:

Ef'n de nigger hadn't ben so sleepy-headed, he'd er ben white, an' his hyar'd er ben straight des like yourn. Yer see, atter de Lord make 'im, den he lont him up 'gins de fence-corner in the sun fur to dry; an' no sooner wuz de Lord's back turnt, an' de sun 'gun ter come out lin'er hot, dan de nigger he 'gun ter nod, an'er little mo'n he wuz fas' ter sleep.[20]

Later on the Lord sent an angel to fetch his newly made people so that he could finish them properly, but the sleeping Blacks did not hear the angel call them.

Well, by'mby de nigger he waked up; but, dar now! he wuz bu'nt Black, an' his hyar wuz all swuv'llt up right kinky. De Lord, seein, he wuz spilte, he didn't 'low fur ter finish 'im, an' wuz des 'bout'n ter thow 'im 'way, wen de white man axt fur 'im.[21]

And thus it was that whites came to own Blacks "plum tell yit."

Since a young slave in the novel is shown to have the same absurd self-perception as the characters in the tale, it is hard to view the story in the same ironic terms in which it exists within Black culture. This young slave is depressed over unrequited love and explains how he believes his unresponsive girlfriend should be killed by "marster." Then he muses about how he would "jump right inter dis creek an' drown myse'f. But I ain't got no right ter be killin' up marster's niggers dat way. . . ."[22]

"I'm wuff er thousan' dollars, an' marster ain't got no thousan' dollars ter was'e in dis creek, long er dat lazy, shif'less, good-fur-niffin' yaller nigger."[23]

Pyrnelle used the devices of art to forge a political weapon. From a historical perspective, there is no authenticity in her treatment of African American personality. And from a pragmatic perspective, Pyrnelle's novel can only mean embarrassment and disenchantment for the Black child who wishes to enjoy the pleasures of literature.

Thomas Nelson Page was more of a spellbinder than Pyrnelle.

His children's novel, *Two Little Confederates,* when reprinted in 1976, was designated a classic. He skillfully blended a sense of childhood, a sense of place, and a deep sense of grief over the loss of the Old South. His range is greater than Pyrnelle's because he weaves together several subplots as a means of underscoring his belief that the Civil War and its aftermath were unspeakably tragic and thoroughly unnecessary. He includes among his lines of action the reconciliation of North and South by both child and adult characters, the friendship of Northern infantrymen and Southern youngsters, the friendship of Black slaves and European American children, the camaraderie between the backwoods folk and the plantation aristocrats, and the marriage of two Southern young people. There is such a palpable gentleness in this vision that the debasement of Black identity is insidiously masked.

As in the Pyrnelle novel, the opening of *Two Little Confederates* offers a child's perspective on life:

The "Two Little Confederates" lived at Oakland. It was not a handsome place, as modern ideas go, but down in Old Virginia, where the standard was different from the later one, it passed in old times as one of the best plantations in all that region. The boys thought it the greatest place in the world, of course excepting Richmond, where they had been one year to the fair, and had seen a man pull fire out of his mouth, and do other wonderful things.[24]

Page then provides a panoramic view of the whole countryside: its "poor white section," railroad depot, Trinity Church, and so on. He explains how different generations built additions to "the greathouse" and finally "a separate building had been erected on the edge of the yard which was called 'The Office,' and was used as such, as well as for a lodging-place by the young men of the family."[25] To move into "The Office" was a kind of initiation rite and the protagonists, Frank and Willy,

. . . looked forward to having [one of the rooms] as their own when they should be old enough to be elevated to the coveted dignity of sleeping in the Office. Hugh already slept here, and gave himself airs in proportion; but Hugh they regarded as a very aged person; not as old, it was true, as

their cousins who came down from college at Christmas, and who, at the
first outbreak of war, all rushed into the army; but each of these was in
the boys' eyes a Methuselah.[26]

The credible portraits of Frank and Willy are in marked contrast to Page's delineation of Blacks—characters described by the
critic and poet, Sterling Brown, as "more ventriloquist's dummies
than people."[27] They are all politically charged stereotypes contrived
to proclaim a race hierarchy. The Black children are cowards compared to Frank and Willy, an old Black "uncle" is a fool compared to
both the children and adults occupying the great-house, and a Black
nursemaid, whose job it is to run after the youngsters, has sympathies that are entirely on the side of the Confederacy.

From the standpoint of the Black aesthetic, there is no way to
elevate Page to the status of classic author given such portraiture. If
literary critics ignore the Black characters, they commit a political
act equivalent to Page's own biased manipulations. If the critic dis-
cusses Page's stereotypic Blacks for what they are, but insists that this
facet of his novel is unimportant, then a new act of white domination has been accomplished. That is, a white priority has been introduced in a manner reminiscent of nineteenth-century forms of cultural imperialism.

The reputation of Joel Chandler Harris has been sustained more
successfully than the literary status of Page. In presenting the culture
of childhood, Harris either evokes it realistically or he romanticizes
it as when he describes the angelic cripple, Little Crotchet, in the
series about Drusilla, Sweetest Susan, and Buster John. It is paradoxical that Harris's six books about that threesome (beginning with
Little Mr. Thimblefinger and ending with *Wally Wanderoon and His
Story-Telling Machine*) are seldom critiqued, while the books about
Uncle Remus, in which Harris is heavily trading upon the reputation of Black folklore, remain a solid part of the canon. At the height
of the revolutionary stirrings of the 1960s, Harris was criticized for
his appropriation of Black art and his misrepresentation of Black
identity in the Uncle Remus volumes. But approving scholars continually reinterpret and revitalize his position in American letters.[28]

From the perspective of a children's literature specialist, Harris
could be viewed as a skillful writer for children were it not for his

white supremacist convictions. His child characters are not as appealing as Page's, but he could write credible animal fantasies, devising animal personalities that function well in the role of narrators. He could frame one story within another and shift the time frame backwards and forwards in a story without creating confusion. He kept his emphasis upon human-interest material rather than isolated historical facts. He preserved for children a wealth of African American and European folklore, and also ventured into the realm of original fairytale creation, always encompassing these materials within a frame story with familiar child characters.

Harris was a vivid scene painter, and he was also ingenious in finding indirect ways to make a statement. For example, in *Plantation Pageants* we learn about General Sherman's protection of the Abercrombie plantation, and readers anticipate the Confederate defeat by surveying the wartime scene with the sensibilities of children and animals.

. . . when, on a misty morning in November, the Federal commander bade the place good-by, and pushed his army southward along the Milledgeville road, he left the plantation in very bad shape, so far as Buster John and Sweetest Susan were concerned. Something was wanting—the place wasn't the same.

There was no gossip among [the] animals that people think are dumb. They had been badly frightened by the hurly-burly that beset them; they might talk about it after a while when the sun shone out, or when the grass came; but meantime the east wind was blowing, and no matter how intelligent an animal may be, he can never tell what that wind will bring when it has begun to blow. . . .[29]

Harris continues with a description of how the animals had been driven off by the foraging troops, and then "driven helter-skelter back again [when the orders were countermanded], with drums beating and bugles blowing, and nobody to explain it all."[30]

Old June, the milch cow, thought she had lost her calf, but after a while she felt it running along by her side, and it was standing under her now, a shivering, shaky, shaggy thing. . . .

Anyhow, they all stood on the sheltered side of the gin-house, and were very quiet, as the steam rose from their backs and the fog issued from their nostrils. They were not in a playful mood. . . .[31]

Focusing exclusively upon Harris's ability to characterize animals and White children, or upon his descriptive powers, it can be argued that he was a better-than-average writer for children. But his handling of Black characterization has all the problems that are built into the plantation myth. Drusilla, the slave companion of Buster John and Sweetest Susan, is always presented in comparative terms as an inferior of the White children. Aaron, Son of Ben Ali, is contrived to suggest a three-way race hierarchy: European American/ Arabic/African American. His characterization resembles that of the tragic mulatto stereotype, and while he is not killed off as are so many mulattoes in fiction, he is dehumanized as an asexual mammy figure. He becomes the ideal family retainer, but with a difference: he is proud of his identity rather than self-deprecating, and he is intellectually independent rather than servile. Other Blacks on the Abercrombie plantation are either minstrel types or the customary devoted servants.

In the Uncle Remus story-cycle, the leading character was used by Harris for multiple purposes and may, for that reason, be seen as more complex. He was used as a mouthpiece for pure anti-Reconstruction propaganda; he was used to symbolize the conciliatory ex-slave who would not hinder North/South reunification; he was used as a minstrel figure.[32] In none of these roles was he an authentic representative of Black identity. However, he was a conveyor of Harris's child-rearing principles and a vehicle for the dissemination of Black folktales. While the characterizations in the frame story were often stereotypic, the tales themselves were presented straightforwardly.

Bernard Wolfe attributes this glimmer of ambivalence to Harris's professionalism. He writes:

Harris all his life was torn between his furtive penchant for fiction and his profession of journalism. It was the would-be novelist in him who created Remus, the "giver" of interracial caresses, but the trained jour-

*nalist in him, having too good an eye and ear, reported the energetic folk
blow in the caress.[33]*

On the other hand, Harris's position as a journalist did not trans-
late into any great reverence for facts, as Darwin T. Turner documents when he describes Harris's distortions of Reconstruction politics.[34] While both Turner and Wolfe give Harris some benefit of the
doubt as a New South writer, they do not qualify their assessment of
him as a white supremacist. Turner notes that the Black/European
American interrelationships do not express the interdependence of
equals, for Harris "believed nineteenth-century Negroes to be intellectually and socially inferior to the nineteenth-century Anglo-
Saxons."[35] To a degree, then, critical analyses have moved beyond
the insistence that Harris "illumined Negro character." He is less
often credited with "clearly . . . [setting] forth the racial relationships of the pre-war South," treating Black characters "with loving
accuracy,"[36] or recording reliably the "negro spirit." John Herbert
Nelson, however, claimed that the temperament of Negroes was
marked by the Blacks' "prying dispositions, their neighborliness, their
company manners, their petty thefts, . . . [their inability to take]
account of the hard logic of consistency."[37] The critical perspective
of Nelson was on a par with Harris' own preconceptions about Black
character.

Uncle Remus is, then, both inconsistent and consistent as a
character. He is sometimes the headscratching "darky" figure, as when
he "dis'member'd" his own name or got "de facks mix up 'mong
deyse'f," or tells the little White boy:

*"De fus' thing when I get ter de house I'm gwinter be weighed fer ter see
how ol' I is. Now, whar wuz I at?"[38]*

But at other times he is confident and self-assertive. For example, he
decides to expose his employer, Miss Sally, as the dupe of a swindler.
This is to be a gesture of retaliation, says the narrator, because Miss
Sally has been teasing Uncle Remus unmercifully. Yet this whole
scene retains a white supremacist slant. Remus's foolishness is at a
different level from Miss Sally's foolishness when she is taken in by a
fast-talking salesman. She lacks judgment because she lacks horti-

cultural expertise (the salesman is peddling phony "ornamental" shrubs). But Remus comes across as an almost mindless person—someone who cannot grasp the full meaning of Miss Sally's cruel jokes. In accordance with the myth that Harris is promoting, Blacks not only lack a normal acumen, they also accept the notion of their own inferiority. When Miss Sally sends him a valentine ("volymtine" says Remus) with the inscription, "He eats, he sleeps, he steals on the sly,/Nigger, big nigger, with a mouthful of pie,"[39] the narrator comments that this verse is appropriate, it fits Remus's character. And the ex-slave is himself oblivious to the affront. The instances of reciprocity between Remus and the White characters seldom suggest a true reciprocity, for Harris always makes it clear that the ex-slave exists on a lower intellectual plane.

Scholarship about Harris has become better balanced in recent years, and critics find it less easy to gloss over his participation in the methods of white domination. Additionally, they do not conclude that his New South activism implied a departure from the racism of the times.

The continuing canonization of *Adventures of Huckleberry Finn,* like the canonization of *Uncle Remus,* is hard to align with a culturally pluralistic perspective. That an author of the nineteenth century is insensitive to issues of cultural diversity as we define them in the twentieth century is not surprising. Moreover, that insensitivity did not prevent Twain from becoming a masterful ironist, satirist, and local colorist—one who could turn scenes into vivid "historical landmarks." Walter Blair notes that like others in the local colorist group, Twain achieved a certain tenderness in his novels.[40] His acerbic community portraits had an appealing counterbalance. But having applauded Twain for such achievements, literary critics are still faced with the untenable, nineteenth-century treatment of Black characters. No fast footwork by theorists will eradicate Twain's white supremacist orientation.

The body of critical writings on Twain's work is voluminous, but relatively little has been said about his ambivalence toward Blacks. Essays by Ralph Ellison, Leo Marx, Donald B. Gibson, and Rhett S. Jones, as well as two essays by Fredrick Woodard and this writer, are unusual in this respect. These essays analyze, in various ways, the scope of Twain's nonironic distortions of Black identity and culture.

Twain is a classic example of how a highly inventive author can embrace a purely conventional nineteenth-century perception of Blacks. It did not follow that a belated antislavery viewpoint would produce in Twain an acceptance of African American/European American equality. Ralph Ellison comments upon several phases of Twain's dehumanization of Blacks when he writes:

It is not at all odd that this black-faced figure of white fun [Jim, the runaway slave] is for Negroes a symbol of everything they rejected in the white man's thinking about race, in themselves and in their own group. . . .

Writing at a time when the blackfaced minstrel left even the abolitionists weary of those problems associated with the Negro, Twain fitted Jim into the outlines of the minstrel tradition, and it is from behind this stereotype mask that we see Jim's dignity and human capacity—and Twain's complexity—emerge. Yet it is his source in this same tradition which creates that ambivalence between his identification as an adult and parent and his "boyish" naïveté, and which by contrast makes Huck, with his street-sparrow sophistication, seem more adult. . . .

Jim's friendship for Huck comes across as that of a boy for another boy rather than as the friendship of an adult for a junior; thus there is implicit in it not only a violation of the manners sanctioned by society for relations between Negroes and whites, there is a violation of our conception of adult maleness.[41]

In his critique of *Huckleberry Finn* for the *American Scholar*, Leo Marx examines other facets of the novel that relate to race relations, especially Twain's compromises with a slave-holding society. Marx reaffirms George Santayana's insight about American humorists—namely, that they had only "half escaped" the genteel tradition. Specifically, Marx calls attention to the way Twain concludes his novel with a scene "fairly bursting with approbation" of Tom Sawyer's family. He continues:

Like Miss Watson, the Phelpses are almost perfect specimens of the dominant culture. They are kind to their friends and relations; they have no taste for violence; they are people capable of devoting themselves to their spectacular dinners while they keep Jim locked in the little hut down by

the ash hopper, with its lone window boarded up. . . . These people,
with their comfortable Sunday-dinner conviviality and the runaway
slave padlocked nearby, are reminiscent of those solid German citizens
we have heard about in our time who tried to maintain a similarly
gemütlich *way of life within virtual earshot of Buchenwald.*[42]

Marx assures us that Twain understood the "shabby morality of such
people," but he nevertheless relied upon them "to provide his happy
ending."[43]

Donald B. Gibson, in his analysis of the novel, speaks of the
numerous critics who ignore Twain's ambivalence toward Jim, a fail-
ing due either to inattentiveness or "too great commitment to particular critical schemes." Gibson urges a look at the book's sociological ramifications, and at Twain's inability to entirely "overcome the
limitations imposed upon his sensibilities by a bigoted early environment." To teach the book in its full complexity, says Gibson,
means that we deal with its author's willingness to "compromise his
morality and his art."[44]

Another treatment of the white supremacy issue is in Rhett S.
Jones's insights about *Huckleberry Finn* and white double-consciousness. Twain demonstrates this double-consciousness by shifting his
perspective back and forth, at one moment viewing Blacks as human beings and at another "regarding them as an inferior folk." Jones
cites, as an example, Huck's willingness to protect Jim from slave
hunters even at the risk of being labeled "a low-down Abolitionist"
and then Huck's indifference to Jim's welfare in other scenes. Jones
writes:

Here is a clear example of white double-consciousness, for Huck indi-
cates he understands the attitude of whites toward fugitive slaves and
then consciously defies it. He does not, however, maintain this defiance,
as he later surrenders his knowledge of Jim's humanity and allows Tom
to play with his friend as though he were a toy.[45]

Twain's moral compromises and connections with the "blackface"
tradition are also explored in essays I coauthored with Fredrick
Woodard.[46] Specific aspects of the novel determined this direction:
(1) the book was designed for a child audience and (2) Twain handled

his themes ironically. This set of observations point to Twain's overall strategy: he devised an attack upon slavery that contained ironies
at the child's level of comprehension. His dehumanizations of Blacks
are primarily the result of minstrel-like characterization, not the result of elementary ironies. For example, in the slave-holding context
of the novel, there are no white supremacist implications in the scene
in which Huck answers the question, "Anybody hu't?" with the reply, "No'm. Killed a nigger." But there *are* such implications in the
head-scratching stage-Negro scenes (Jim says, "Is I me, or who *is* I?
Is I heah, or what *is* I? Now dat's what I wants to know") and in the
intermittent minstrel sketches in which Jim plays a prominent role
(examples were quoted above).

That reverence is bestowed upon a writer who viewed race in
purely hierarchical terms—this is incongruous in a society that as-
pires to be democratic and culturally pluralistic. Yet Twain and his
works are not only widely revered; they are idolized.

Conclusion

A society's conceptions of beauty are among its most enduring features. They do not lend themselves to easy revision, even when history has moved into a new phase and a people's traditional aesthetic
is glaringly inadequate. A multicultural approach to aesthetics is
particularly imperative when intense struggles are underway between
cultural groups. The dominant power is in a position to produce an
array of artistic objects in support of its cause. It has the means for
controlling the gatekeeping and tastemaking institutions and can
indoctrinate its population with self-serving conceptions of beauty.
Artistic strategies, therefore, are essentially abstractions. The themes,
plots, characterizations, settings, language, and narrative viewpoints
are all "statements." Cornel West has summed up the central issue:

*There is indeed an inescapable evaluative dimension to any valid cul-
tural criticism. Yet the literary objects upon which we focus are themselves cultural responses to specific crises in particular historical moments.
Because these crises . . . must themselves be mediated through textual
constructs, the literary objects we examine are never merely literary, and
attempts to see them as such constitute a dehistoricizing and depoliticizing
of literary texts that should be scrutinized for their ideological content,*

role, and function. In this sense, canon formations that invoke the sole criterion of form—be it of the elitist or populist variety—are suspect.[47]

A preoccupation with form, therefore, can be misleading whether a work is notable for its conventions or inventions.

The question needs to be raised: "Is there a targeted group within a work that is being alienated, and if so, for what purpose is that alienation produced if not a political purpose?" It is often said that an artistic work should be appreciated in its own time frame and studied with that historical context in view. However, treatises on the classics often belie that assertion because the historical context is handled selectively. Black history, until recently, has been emphatically absent.

Specialists in the field of children's literature must approach this issue with extra care because children generally lack a sense of history. They come to an author's presentation with few, if any, modifying perspectives. The "beautiful" story can be misleading. Society leaves a mark on artistic objects, and the power rebounding in a symbolic object can shift the direction of a society.

Notes

1. For an excellent study of this subject in relation to early nineteenth-century girls' series books, see Nancy T. Romalov's "Modern, Mobile, and Marginal: American Girls' Series Fiction, 1905–1925" (Ph.D. diss., University of Iowa, 1994).
2. Alice Childress, "A Candle in a Gale Wind," in *Black Women Writers*, ed. Mari Evans (New York: Anchor Press/Doubleday, 1984), 114. For new insights, I am indebted to Sandra Y. Govan's application of the Black aesthetic to an important work of children's literature. See Govan's "Alice Childress' *Rainbow Jordan:* The Black Aesthetic Returns Dressed in Adolescent Fiction." *Children's Literature Association Quarterly* 13:1 (Summer 1988): 70–74.
3. Carol Billman, *The Secret of the Stratemeyer Syndicate: Nancy Drew, The Hardy Boys, and The Million Dollar Fiction Factory* (New York: The Ungar Publishing Co., 1986), 27.
4. Ibid.
5. Ibid., 26.
6. Ibid., 17.
7. Ibid., 25, 26.
8. John G. Cawelti, "The Concept of Formula in the Study of Popular Literature," in *Popular Culture and the Expanding Consciousness*, ed. Ray Browne (New York: John Wiley, 1973), 110.
9. Ibid., 114.
10. Ibid., 117–118.
11. Ibid., 119.
12. Russel Nye, "The Popular Arts and the Popular Audience," in *The Popular Arts in America: A Reader*, ed. William M. Hammel (New York: Harcourt Brace Jovanovich, 1972), 12.

13. Ibid., 8.
14. According to the 1990 census, 44.8% of Black children live below the poverty line (in contrast to 15.9% of White children). The infant mortality rate was 16.5 (per 1,000 births) for Blacks and 8.1 for Whites. Twice as many Blacks have low-weight babies.
15. Billman, 14.
16. Walter Blair, *Native American Humor (1800–1900)* (New York: American Book Co., 1937), 139, 160.
17. Claude M. Simpson, ed., *The Local Colorists: American Short Stories, 1857–1900* (New York: Harper and Brothers, 1960), 1, 13.
18. Bret Harte, "The Rise of the 'Short Story,'" *Cornhill*, n.s. 7:8 (July 1899), quoted in *Native American Humor (1800–1900)* 126–127.
19. Louise-Clarke Pyrnelle, *Diddie, Dumps, and Tot, or Plantation Child-Life* (New York: Harper and Brothers, 1882), 1, 3–4.
20. Ibid., 226.
21. Ibid., 226–227.
22. Ibid., 25–26.
23. Ibid., 26.
24. Thomas Nelson Page, *Two Little Confederates* (New York: Charles Scribner's Sons, 1888), 1.
25. Ibid., 2.
26. Ibid., 2–3.
27. Sterling Brown, "A Century of Negro Portraiture in American Literature," *The Massachusetts Review* 7 (Winter 1966): 77.
28. See Notes in chapter 4, "Children's Fiction: A Sampling."
29. Joel Chandler Harris, *Plantation Pageants* (Boston: Houghton, Mifflin and Co., 1899), 2.
30. Ibid., 3.
31. Ibid.
32. Robert Hemenway, Introduction to *Uncle Remus: His Songs and His Sayings*, by Joel Chandler Harris (New York: Penguin Books, 1982), 20, 24.
33. Bernard Wolfe, "Uncle Remus and the Malevolent Rabbit: 'Takes a Limber-Toe Gemmum fer ter Jump Jim Crow'" in *Critical Essays on Joel Chandler Harris*, ed. R. Bruce Bickley Jr. (Boston: G. K. Hall and Co., 1981), 75.
34. Darwin T. Turner, "Daddy Joel Harris and His Old-Time Darkies," in *Critical Essays on Joel Chandler Harris*, ed. R. Bruce Bickley Jr. (Boston: G. K. Hall and Co., 1981), 127.
35. Ibid., 123.
36. Blair, 144.
37. John Herbert Nelson, *The Negro Character in American Literature* (New York: AMS Press, 1970; originally published in Lawrence: University of Kansas, Humanities Studies 4:1, 1926), 116.
38. Joel Chandler Harris, *Told by Uncle Remus: New Stories of The Old Plantation* (New York: Grosset and Dunlap, 1905), 51–52.
39. Joel Chandler Harris, *Uncle Remus and His Friends: Old Plantation Stories, Songs, and Ballads, with Sketches of Negro Character* (Boston: Houghton, Mifflin and Co., 1892), 229.
40. Blair, 160.
41. Ralph Ellison, "Change the Joke and Slip the Yoke!" *Partisan Review* 25:2 (Spring 1958): 215–216.
42. Leo Marx, "Mr. Eliot, Mr. Trilling, and *Huckleberry Finn*," *American Scholar* 22:4 (Autumn 1953): 432.
43. Ibid., 432–433.
44. Donald B. Gibson, "Mark Twain's Jim in the Classroom," *English Journal* 57:2 (February 1968): 202.

45. Rhett S. Jones, "Nigger and Knowledge: White Double-Consciousness in *Adventures of Huckleberry Finn*," *Mark Twain Journal* 22:2 (Fall 1984): 28, 34.

46. Fredrick Woodard and Donnarae MacCann, "*Huckleberry Finn* and the Traditions of Blackface Minstrelsy," in *The Black American in Books for Children: Readings in Racism*, 2nd ed., ed. Donnarae MacCann and Gloria Woodard (Metuchen, NJ: Scarecrow Press, 1985). Also "Minstrel Shackles and Nineteenth-Century 'Liberality' in *Huckleberry Finn*," in *Satire or Evasion? Black Perspectives on* Huckleberry Finn, ed. James S. Leonard, Thomas A. Tenney, and Thadious M. Davis (Durham and London: Duke University Press, 1992).

47. Cornel West, "Minority Discourse and the Pitfalls of Canon Formation," *Yale Journal of Criticism* 1:1 (Fall 1987): 200.

Chapter Nine
Conclusion
The "Lost Cause" Wins

Modern historians analyze the makeup of an era. Assigning blame for past actions is usually found to be difficult, if not impossible. By emphasizing the complexities, readers are moved in the direction of understanding rather than mere censure. But when we examine history in relation to the education of children, we face a new kind of problem. We are confronted with predetermined and premeditated actions on the part of adults. We cannot, then, so easily dismiss motivational factors. We cannot say that intentional behavior is forever hidden in a web of ambiguous possibilities. When adults introduce specific kinds of experience into the lives of youngsters, they usually do so with forethought, with a purpose that relates to the child's alleged well-being. In American history, the white supremacy myth needs to be examined with this in mind.

The myth of white superiority was introduced into each successive generation's social conditioning, and the very act of passing down white supremacist attitudes to children tells us much about the importance of this myth to the child-raisers. There was little reason for the European American child to doubt his or her racial superiority because the storybooks, periodicals, schools, churches, and government authorities were all sending the same signal. Racial bias reached White children through books, and also by way of the institutions that constantly impinged on their lives. The Black child, on the other hand, was treated in the publishing world as a legitimate target of derision. By making Black children the brunt of racist humor, the mainstream's effort to discourage African American education through segregation, inadequate funding, short school terms, and other measures was given additional impetus.

Since the notion of white preeminence was transmitted to children over such an extended period of time, we must ask what gave that fiction such a hold on white consciousness. What was gained by it? How did mainstream adults relate a belief in white superiority to their children's welfare? Why did the very essence of the Confederate cause gain ground in the postbellum era?

On a philosophical level, mainstream Americans had created a problem for themselves at the outset by insisting that they were a favored nation in the sight of God. Only negative consequences could follow this notion—this myth—that Deity plays favorites and that White settlers in America were selected for a unique moral role in the world. At best this myth led to a paternalistic attitude toward non-Anglo-Saxon groups; at worst it produced the conviction that outsiders were expendable.

A study of the European American abolitionists indicates that some wanted to modify this premise. Quakers generally opposed slavery and drew fire for being mavericks. Traditional religious leaders fashioned the idea of a more social church, one with a benevolent outreach. On the one hand, the new direction resulted in strong antislavery agitation; on the other, it could not dismantle a fundamental assumption of Anglo-Saxon superiority.

This whole exercise in cultural self-delusion never really worked intellectually; and, pragmatically, it sustained white hegemony only at the cost of increasingly repressive measures. It created the strains and relapses that accompany any serious inner contradiction. After a few years of lofty abolitionist rhetoric, the nation returned to the full dimensions of the white supremacy myth. Although the Constitution was amended to guarantee male suffrage and due process of law, people's lives returned to old hierarchic patterns under the piecemeal policies of Reconstruction, and the antidemocratic policies of post-Reconstruction.

The specifics of the myth evolved in different ways in different geographic regions. In the North the shift from rural to urban living generated collective anxieties, and it was easier to invent a simple safety valve than to deal with the turbulent changes. Alexander Saxton sees this widespread dislocation of the antebellum period as an underlying reason for "blackface" minstrelsy and its extensive popularity. So numerous were the tensions projected onto stage Negroes that their performances, says Saxton, "provided a window into the complex culture developing in the new cities."[1] The city as the unfulfilled source of new work, new money, and new social relations was transmuted into the ridiculous Black clown—into a scapegoat for urban failures.

In the South, race and class hierarchies remained in place until abolitionist agitation and regional rivalry over western territories led to war. After the armed conflict, the South reinvented a cheap labor system by means of ex-slave contract labor, convict leases, crop liens, indenture contracts, and obsolete forms of industrial education in place of educational opportunity. The North did not intervene in this process. It seems evident that the North and South did not disagree about designing a status for Blacks that would mean perpetual subservience. Disfranchisement, denial of legal redress, and meager educational opportunity were indispensable to the maintenance of the new labor system and became the norm rather than the exception. H. Leon Prather's analysis of relationships between politics and educational systems in North Carolina illumines a power struggle that had white economic advantage at its very core.[2]

But a description of such tangible reasons for the white supremacy myth may cause us to lose sight of its more ambiguous appeal. "Superiority" does not generally move into the foreground as a cultural ideal per se. It needs legitimization; it subserves other values. For example, nineteenth-century white supremacists frequently argued that European Americans alone could produce constitutional government and maintain public order. Democracy itself, according to this view, was served by a hierarchic social structure; a racialized hierarchy was the only viable path to "liberty without anarchy."

Perhaps we should ask, then, whether or not White parents were attempting to instill in their children an overall political conservatism. Was the exclusion of Blacks from the democratic framework part of a larger pattern? Were nineteenth-century Blacks perceived as too far removed from private property rights and their linkage with liberty and order? Was this a reason to reinforce the image of Black otherness?

Historian Michael Kammen makes a persuasive case when he documents the elevation of order over liberty in American intellectual history. Liberty, Kammen explains, was thought to encourage factionalism. Freedom was seen as all too apparent already on the frontier. Freedom could easily slide into licentiousness. "Ordered liberty," said Fisher Ames in the late 1700s, is preferable to "natural liberty." To champion the latter was to promote "revolution itself."[3] Ames defined "ordered liberty" as the kind of freedom that recognized the sacredness of liberty and property.

A schoolbook used in the 1830s and 1840s defined liberty as "moral liberty" and took account of the property issue. Such moral freedom gave "to all mankind [permission to dispose] of their persons and property in the manner they shall judge most consonant to their own happiness; on condition . . . that they do not abuse this liberty to the injury of other men."[4]

Slavery and abolitionism played a part in the debate about liberty because the rescue of fugitive slaves was said to violate the precept "liberty-with-law." The schoolbook's maxim about "injury to other men" did not count vis-à-vis slaves. In abolitionist children's books, writers sometimes counteracted the slogan "liberty and property" with the slogan "liberty and humanity." And it was slavery as an institution that offended their sense of humanity. After emancipation, there was no strong neoabolitionist force to oppose the Supreme Court's broadening protection of property rights, a trend that lasted until 1934.[5]

Political conservatism was strengthened at the expense of Black American civil rights, and the Progressive Era after 1900 did not significantly alter that conservatism. A few Progressives began to speak about liberty as a precondition for order, but Theodore Roosevelt was not among them, and his expansionist goals set the tone of the debate. In references to the U.S. annexation of the Philippines, Roosevelt used the phrase "orderly liberty," alluding to the blessing Filipinos could expect as Americans accepted the "white man's burden." Ceremonies commemorating the Civil War also gave him an opportunity to link liberty with order. At Gettysburg in 1904 he said,

> *Some wars have meant the triumph of order over anarchy and li-*
> *centiousness masquerading as liberty; . . . but this victorious war of ours*
> *meant the triumph of both liberty and order, the triumph of orderly*
> *liberty. . . .*[6]

Woodrow Wilson made the point about order even clearer in his public pronouncements about Filipino "primitives":

> *In the wrong hands,—in hands unpracticed, undisciplined,—[liberty]*
> *is incompatible with government. Discipline must precede it,—if neces-*
> *sary, the discipline of being under masters.*[7]

Some Progressives were more in the liberal wing of the move-ment than Wilson and came under the influence of German social scientists and their cross-cultural studies. These studies pointed in the direction of universal patterns rather than cultural and racial hierarchies. L. L. Langness describes the new intellectual constructs as defining "'normal' and 'abnormal' [as] relative to the cultural con-text in which they occur"; he notes that "no definite scale exists whereby we can measure behavior. . . ."[8] As this idea attracted sup-port, physical and social scientists in the 1930s began to rethink their advocacy of racism.

But it should be noted that a century earlier (in the 1830s) Lydia Maria Child was a cultural relativist in her story for children, "Lariboo." She described an African woman and included her own commentary:

> *I don't suppose you would have thought her very good-looking, if you*
> *had seen the . . . coral passed through her nose. . . . But . . . I do not*
> *know why it is considered more barbarous to bore the nose for orna-*
> *ments, than to pierce holes through the ears, as our ladies do.*[9]

Child demonstrates that on an intellectual level she could challenge the white supremacy myth. That kind of clear-sightedness evapo-rated after the Civil War, and even in the writings of Child, cultural relativism was sometimes subordinate to minstrel-like humor.

The white supremacy ideology was not only rationalized as an element of orderly government; it was also thought to serve the purpose of entertainment. Stereotypic Black clowns became a standard feature in the theater, in radio, in motion pictures, and in television, as well as in books for children. This is a facet of the white supremacy myth that is difficult to combat even as the twentieth century winds down. No one, it seems, wants to be charged with having a lame sense of humor. The philosopher Ronald de Sousa has, however, posed the question, "When is it wrong to laugh?" His "ethics of mirth" rests upon the proposition that "like belief, laughter is wrong when it is grounded in the deception of self or others."[10]

Sociologist Hugh Dalziel Duncan makes a similar point—that "comedy is ethical because it is rational and rational because it leads to good social relationships."[11] Humor depends upon an assumption of equality and mutuality. Without the idea of equals enjoying comparable dignity and status, humor becomes ridicule. "The social essence of comedy is joy in reason—the shared joy of him who is laughed at, as well as he who laughs."[12] Ridicule, on the other hand, is a weapon, according to Duncan. "It wounds deeply; often, indeed, it kills. . . . Ridicule makes us inferiors. Only equals can laugh and tease together."[13] Children of course are more vulnerable to the pain of ridicule than adults. As already noted, psychiatrists James P. Comer and Alvin F. Poussaint caution Black parents on this point: "You don't want to let some adult 'humorist' take care of his anger and hate feelings at your child's expense."[14]

Similarly, anti-imperialist scholars Chris Tiffin and Alan Lawson highlight effects upon children. They note with irony that "it is when the children . . . internalize their own subjection that the true work of colonial textuality is done."[15] When children internalize the concept of racial hierarchy, then the lifespan of that myth has been extended.

Finally, a word needs to be said about this study as an experiment in method as well as an overview of historical conditions. It takes an interdisciplinary approach: it mixes political, biographical, institutional, and literary history and theory. The value of an expanded historical method is especially apparent in relation to children's literature because this literature is not written by authors addressing their own peer group. Since writers are crossing the generational line, we can know more about why they take this initiative and what they are trying to convey when we study their relationships with their social milieu, with the influential institutions of their day. At the same time we can uncover weaknesses in contemporary book criticism by examining its many historical blind spots. The record of white supremacist thinking is clear enough, but literary critics find ingenious ways to sidestep it. Margery Fisher, for example, is not considering African or African American history when she exonerates George A. Henty. She claims "historical accuracy," nonstereotypic treatment of characters, and a nonracist tenor in his novels.[16] She sees charges of racism as stemming from modern attitudes improperly imposed upon works of the past, but the implication here is that Black history is somehow outside the past, outside time. Africans have never been outside time and racism has never been justifiable except in the minds of Western literary interpreters.[17]

Historical blind spots have also been characteristic in discussions of *St. Nicholas Magazine*. As a truly monolithic instance of white racism, this periodical has no equal, yet it generally receives unqualified praise. Fred Erisman gives this assessment:

[St. Nicholas] *provided American children with the work of the most notable writers of the past and the present. . . . [I]t served . . . as a powerful force in striving to maintain a degree of cultural continuity in American life . . . even as it lived up to [Mary Mapes] Dodge's literary goals, [it] was in every way . . . a literate, principled, conservative, yet open-minded voice of the nineteenth-century elite.*[18]

When Erisman speaks here of "American life" and "American children," he is clearly not considering the Black American child. For African American children, *St. Nicholas* typically offered nothing but an array of degraded portraits. Its stories cannot be called "principled" unless its white supremacist elements are deemed acceptable. Its "cultural continuity" entailed the spread of the white supremacy myth.[19]

Books by Edward Stratemeyer are specifically targeted for praise by John T. Dizer, who writes that Stratemeyer takes a "basically friendly and positive" attitude toward Blacks. He sees "unusually objective and liberal" portrayals, considering the times.[20] Dizer's own overview of the novels (the quotations he includes) contradicts this assessment, but he justifies his conclusions by insisting that "we must be aware of the social attitudes of the day. . . ."[21] He is taking no account of African American social attitudes, even though Stratemeyer made frequent use of the Black population. In his sample of 137 titles authored by Stratemeyer, 92 contained Black characters. Dizer asks: "Why [were] blacks included in boys' books at all? Blacks were a minute portion of the reading population."[22] Blacks were included because they were positioned everywhere in American society within a strict caste system. They were widely represented but held distinctly separate from non-Blacks. They appeared in Stratemeyer's books as ruffians, menial laborers, or clowns—the roles the caste system permitted. Critics misname this phenomenon when they label it liberal, tolerant, and positive, as in Dizer's critique. Certainly the caste system was not liberal, and it is hardly liberal to attempt to justify its symbolic presence in fiction.

Similar apologies for racism are commonplace in children's book criticism. Commendations of *Adventures of Huckleberry Finn* are so numerous as to constitute a veritable industry. A recent example is by culture critic/historian Martin Green. When Green refers to "Twain's racism with regard to the American Indian," and only eight lines later characterizes *Huckleberry Finn* as "gentle and playful," he reveals a glaring gap in his historical consciousness.[23] He applauds Twain for turning his back on "the historical forces" in his own era; he comments that Twain is asking readers for their "affection . . . for the alternatives—the other and the past." "In Twain's case," says Green, "it is the recent American past we visit, the South before the Civil War. . . ."[24] Such nostalgia for "the Lost Cause"—the antebellum slavocracy—is incongruous with Green's indignation about the racism that targets Amerinds. And as noted in a previous chapter, Twain's minstrel antics were anything but playful and gentle. Literary historian Donald Gibson uses the lens of Black history when he writes that Twain "was not always capable of resisting the temptation to create laughter through compromising his morality and his art." "Critics," urges Gibson, should "avoid making the same kinds of compromises Mark Twain made."[25]

In order to serve children equitably, book critics need to take account of the same knowledge that social historians find pertinent. They need to examine the monolithic character of the white supremacy myth. They need to study the frequency and intent of so-cial or antisocial messages. They need to take note of the predictive power of children's literature whenever narrative trends persist from one generation to the next. Such knowledge would serve as a re-straint upon scholars who speak of American children but mean only White children.

In studying the links between history and nineteenth-century literature, connections between political domination and the disinformation process come into focus. The total human experi-ence, notes Asa Hilliard, is denied as the human record is changed on behalf of monocultural privilege. The central issue is not about building esteem or achievement, as important as these are in the childhood years; the issue is about valid scholarship—about the prin-ciple that "there is truth in the whole human experience."[26] The valid rendering of African and African American history in school and library collections has scarcely begun, whereas stereotyping and distortion continue to be commonplace.

Children's literature awaits a program of culturally inclusive, historically valid study, a program that honors entertainment but opposes storytelling as a repressive weapon. The questions remain: In the upcoming century can we expect the arts and institutions to maximize social justice? Or will the record reveal once again that the Confederate cause wins?

Notes

1.   Alexander Saxton, "Blackface Minstrelsy and Jacksonian Ideology," *American Quarterly* 27:1 (March 1975): 4.
2.   H. Leon Prather Sr., *Resurgent Politics and Educational Progressivism in the New South: North Carolina, 1890–1913*, (Cranbury, NJ: Fairleigh Dickinson Uni-versity Press and Associated University Presses, 1979).
3.   Michael Kammen, *Spheres of Liberty: Changing Perceptions of Liberty in Ameri-can Culture* (Madison: University of Wisconsin Press, 1986), 78.
4.   Ibid., 82.
5.   Ibid., 102.
6.   Ibid., 111.
7.   Ibid., 112.
8.   L. L. Langness, *The Study of Culture* (San Francisco: Chandler and Sharp Publish-ers, Inc., 1974), 134–135.
9.   Maria Child, "Lariboo," pt. III of *Flowers for Children* (New York: C.S. Francis and Co., 1854), 156.
10.   Ronald de Sousa, *The Rationality of Emotion* (Cambridge: The M.I.T. Press, 1987), 295.
11.   Hugh Dalziel Duncan, *Communication and Social Order* (New York: The Bedminster Press, 1962), 390.

12. Ibid., 404.

13. Ibid., 404–405.

14. James P. Comer and Alvin F. Poussaint, *Black Child Care* (New York: Pocket Books, 1976), 185.

15. Chris Tiffin and Alan Lawson, *De-Scribing Empire: Post-colonialism and Textuality* (London and New York: Routledge, 1994), 4.

16. Margery Fisher, *The Bright Face of Danger* (London: Hodder and Stoughton, 1986), 352, 353, 355.

17. For an excellent study of George A. Henty's six novels about Africa, plus critiques of imperialistic works by Defoe, Marryat, Kingston, Ballantyne, Haggard, and Kipling, see Mawuena Kossi Logan's "Africa Through Victorian Eyes: George Alfred Henty and the Fiction of Empire" (Ph.D. diss., University of Iowa, 1996). For a study of modern children's novels and picture books about Africa, see Yulisa Amadu Maddy and Donnarae MacCann's *African Images in Juvenile Literature: Commentaries on Neocolonialist Fiction* (Jefferson, NC: McFarland and Company, 1996).

18. Fred Erisman, "St. Nicholas," in *Children's Periodicals of the United States*, ed. R. Gordon Kelly (Westport, CT: Greenwood Press, 1984), 386, 387.

19. For a work that similarly trivializes the mistreatment of Black characterization in *St. Nicholas*, see Mary June Roggenbuck's "St. Nicholas Magazine: A Study of the Impact and Historical Influence of the Editorship of Mary Mapes Dodge" (Ph.D. diss., University of Michigan, 1976).

20. John T. Dizer Jr., *Tom Swift and Company: Boys' Books by Stratemeyer and Others* (Jefferson, NC: McFarland and Co., 1982), 130.

21. Ibid., 108.

22. Ibid., 111, 112.

23. Martin Green, *Seven Types of Adventure Tale* (University Park: The Pennsylvania State University Press, 1991), 151.

24. Ibid.

25. Donald Gibson, "Mark Twain's Jim in the Classroom," *English Journal* 57:2 (February 1968): 202.

26. Asa G. Hilliard III, "Why We Must Pluralize the Curriculum," *Educational Leadership* 49:4 (December 1991/January 1992): 12, 14.

Bibliography

Works for the Young

Abbott, Jacob. *Congo; or, Jasper's Experience in Command.* New York: Harper and Brothers, 1857.

————. "The Three Pines," *Stories of Rainbow and Lucky.* New York: Harper and Brothers, 1860.

Adams, William Taylor [Oliver Optic]. *Brother Against Brother, or The War on the Border.* Boston: Lee and Shepard, 1894.

————. *Fighting Joe; or, The Fortunes of a Staff Officer: A Story of the Great Rebellion.* Boston: Lee and Shepard, 1865.

————. *Hatchie, the Guardian Slave; or, The Heiress of Bellevue.* Boston: B. B. Mussey and Co. and R. B. Fitts and Co., 1853.

Alger, Jr., Horatio. *Frank's Campaign; or, The Farm and the Camp.* Boston: A. K. Loring, 1864.

Brooks, Noah. "The Fairport Nine," *St. Nicholas,* May-October, 1880.

Child, L. Maria. *Fact and Fiction: A Collection of Stories.* New York: C. S. Francis and Co., 1846.

————. "Jumbo and Zairee," *Juvenile Miscellany,* n.s., 5 (January 1831): 291.

————. "Lariboo," in *Flowers for Children,* part 3. New York: C. S. Francis and Co., 1854.

————. "The Little White Lamb and the Little Black Lamb," in *Flowers for Children,* part 2. New York: C. S. Francis and Co., 1854.

Clemens, Samuel Langhorne [Mark Twain]. *Adventures of Huckleberry Finn.* New York: Charles L. Webster and Co., 1885; originally published in London by Chatto and Windus, 1884.

————. *Tom Sawyer Abroad.* New York: Charles L. Webster and Co., 1894; originally published in *St. Nicholas Magazine,* November 1893–April 1894.

Colman, Julia. "Little Lewis: The Story of a Slave Boy," in *The Child's Anti-Slavery Book: Containing a Few Words About American Slave Children, and Stories of Slave-Life.* New York: Carlton and Porter, 1859; rpt. Miami: Mnemosyne Publishing Co., 1969, 21–62.

Du Chaillu, Paul. *Stories of the Gorilla Country.* New York: Harper and Brothers, 1869.

"A Few Words About American Slave Children," in *The Child's Anti-Slavery Book: Containing a Few Words About American Slave Children, and Stories of Slave-Life.* New York: Carlton and Porter, 1859; rpt. Miami: Mnemosyne Publishing Co., 1969, 9–16.

Finley, Martha. *Elsie's Motherhood.* New York: Dodd, Mead and Co., 1876.

————. *Elsie's Womanhood.* New York: Dodd, Mead and Co., 1875.

Follen, Eliza Lee. *May Morning and New Year's Eve.* n.p.: Wittemore, Niles, and Hall, 1857; rpt. Boston: Nichols and Hall, 1870.

Glasier, Jessie C. "Ole Mammy Prissy," *St. Nicholas,* October, 1887.

Goodrich, S. G. [Peter Parley]. *History of Africa.* Louisville, KY: Morton and Griswold, 1850.

————. *The Tales of Peter Parley About Africa.* Boston: Carter, Hendee, and Co., 1833.

Goulding, F. R. *Robert and Harold, or The Young Marooners on the Florida Coast.* Philadelphia: William S. Martien, 1852.

Harris, Joel Chandler. *Aaron in the Wildwoods.* Boston: Houghton, Mifflin and Co., 1897.

————. "Daddy Jake, the Runaway," *St. Nicholas,* March–May 1889.

————. *Plantation Pageants.* Boston: Houghton, Mifflin and Co., 1899.

————. *The Story of Aaron (So Named) the Son of Ben Ali, Told by His Friends and Acquaintances.* Boston: Houghton, Mifflin and Co., 1896.

————. *Told by Uncle Remus: New Stories of the Old Plantation.* New York: Grosset and Dunlap, 1905.

Brookes, Stella Brewer. *Joel Chandler Harris: Folklorist*. Athens: University of Georgia Press, 1950.

Brown, Janet E. "The Saga of Elsie Dinsmore: A Study in Nineteenth-Century Sensibility," *University of Buffalo Studies* 17:3 (July 1945): 75–103.

Brown, Sterling. "A Century of Negro Portraiture in American Literature," *Massachusetts Review* 7 (Winter 1966): 73–96.

Buck, Paul H. *The Road to Reunion, 1865–1900*. Boston: Little, Brown and Company, 1937.

Budd, Louis J. "Joel Chandler Harris and the Genteeling of Native American Humor," in *Critical Essays on Joel Chandler Harris*, ed. R. Bruce Bickley Jr. Boston: G. K. Hall and Co., 1981, 196–209.

Bullock, Penelope L. *The Afro-American Periodical Press, 1838–1909*. Baton Rouge: Louisiana State University Press, 1981.

Bushnell, Horace. *Christian Nurture*. New York: Charles Scribner's Sons, 1861; original title: *Views of Christian Nurture and of Subjects Adjacent Thereto*, 1847.

Carlson, Robert A. *The Quest for Conformity: Americanization Through Education*. New York: John Wiley and Sons, 1975.

Carmichael, Stokely, and Charles V. Hamilton. *Black Power: The Politics of Liberation in America*. New York: Random House, 1967.

Carpenter, Charles. *History of American Schoolbooks*. Philadelphia: University of Pennsylvania Press, 1963.

Cawelti, John G. "The Concept of Formula in the Study of Popular Literature," in *Popular Culture and the Expanding Consciousness*, ed. Ray Browne. New York: John Wiley, 1973, 109–119.

———. "Notes Toward an Aesthetic of Popular Culture," *Journal of Popular Culture* 5:2 (Fall 1971): 255–268.

———. "Recent Trends in the Study of Popular Culture," *American Studies: An International Newsletter* 10:2 (Winter 1971): 23–37.

Chambers, Aidan. "The Reader in the Book," in *The Signal Approach to Children's Books*, ed. Nancy Chambers. Metuchen, NJ: Scarecrow Press, 1980, 250–275.

Child, L. Maria. *An Appeal in Favor of Americans Called Africans*. Boston: Allen and Ticknor, 1833; rpt. New York: Arno Press

———. *Uncle Remus and His Friends: Old Plantation Stories, Songs, and Ballads, with Sketches of Negro Character*. Boston: Houghton, Mifflin and Co., 1892.

———. *Uncle Remus: His Songs and His Sayings*. Edited with an introduction by Robert Hemenway. New York: Penguin Books, 1982; originally published by D. Appleton and Co., 1880.

———. *Wally Wanderoon and His Story-Telling Machine*. New York: McClure, Phillips and Co., 1903.

[Hawthorne, Nathaniel]. *Parley's Universal History on the Basis of Geography*, 1. New York: Nafis and Cornish, 1845.

Henty, G. A. *By Sheer Pluck: A Tale of the Ashanti War*. New York: A. L. Burt, Publisher, 1890; originally published in 1884.

———. *With Lee in Virginia: A Story of the American Civil War*. Chicago: The Henneberry Co., 1910; originally published in London by Blackie and Sons, 1890.

Holmes, Prescott. *Young People's History of the War with Spain*. Philadelphia: Henry Altemus Co., 1900.

Houghton, Louise Seymour. "Bossy Ananias," *St. Nicholas*, June 1879.

Marryat, Captain [Frederick]. *The Mission, or Scenes in Africa*. London: 1845; rpt. with an introduction by Tony Harrison. New York: Africana Publishing Corp., 1970.

"Me Neber Gib It Up!" in *The Child's Anti-Slavery Book: Containing a Few Words About American Slave Children, and Stories of Slave-Life*. New York: Carlton and Porter, 1859; rpt. Miami: Mnemosyne Publishing Co., 1969, 157–158.

Millinocket. "Assault on Fort Wagner," *Oliver Optic's Magazine: (Our Boys and Girls)* 5:129 (June 19, 1869); rpt. *Oliver Optic's Companion*. Boston: Lee and Shepard, 1872.

———. "The Brave Little Bugler," *Oliver Optic's Magazine: (Our Boys and Girls)* 5:111 (February 15, 1869).

Morris, Clara. "My Little 'Jim Crow'," *St. Nicholas*, December 1898.

Page, Thomas Nelson. "Jack and Jake," in *The Novels, Stories, Sketches and Poems of Thomas Nelson Page*. Plantation Edition, vol. 11. New York: Charles Scribner's Sons, 1908; originally published in *Harper's Young People* (October 13, 20, 27, 1891).

———. *Two Little Confederates*. New York: Charles Scribner's Sons, 1888.

Pyrnelle, Louise-Clarke. *Diddie, Dumps, and Tot, or Plantation Child-Life*. New York: Harper and Brothers Publishers, 1882.

Stowe, Harriet Beecher. *Uncle Tom's Cabin; or, Life Among the Lowly*. Boston: John P. Jewett and Co., 1852; rpt. *The Annotated Uncle Tom's Cabin*, ed. Philip Van Doren Stern. New York: Paul S. Eriksson, Inc., 1964.

Stratemeyer, Edward. *A Tour of the Zero Club, or Adventures Amid Ice and Snow*. Philadelphia: David McKay, Publisher, 1902; originally published in *Good News*, 1894–95, under "Harvey Hicks" pseud.

———. *The Young Auctioneer, or The Polishing of a Rolling Stone*. Boston: Lothrop, Lee and Shepard Co., 1903; originally published by W. L. Allison Co., 1897.

Stuart, Ruth McEnery. "A Funny Little School," *St. Nicholas* November 1897: 40–46; rpt. in *The St. Nicholas Anthology* Intro. by Henry Steele Commager, New York: Random House, 1948.

———. "An Old-Time Christmas Gift," *St. Nicholas*, December 1887.

Thompson, Matilda G. "Aunt Judy's Story: A Story from Real Life," in *The Child's Anti-Slavery Book: Containing a Few Words About American Slave Children, and Stories of Slave-Life*. New York: Carlton and Porter, 1859; rpt. Miami: Mnemosyne Publishing Co., 1969, 109–153.

———. "Mark and Hasty; or, Slave-Life in Missouri," in *The Child's Anti-Slavery Book: Containing a Few Words About American Slave Children, and Stories of Slave-Life*. New York: Carlton and Porter, 1859; rpt. Miami: Mnemosyne Publishing Co., 1969, 69–104.

Trowbridge. J. T. *Cudjo's Cave*. Boston: J. E. Tilton and Co., 1864.

Wisp, Willie. "The Basket-Makers of Bongoloo," *Oliver Optic's Magazine (Our Boys and Girls)* 5 (January-June 1869); rpt. *Oliver Optic's Companion*. Boston: Lee and Shepard, 1872.

Other Sources

Abbott, Lyman. *Reminiscences*. Boston: Houghton, Mifflin Co., 1915.

Adams, David Wallace. "Education in Hues: Red and Black at Hampton Institute, 1878–1893," *South Atlantic Quarterly* 76:2 (Spring 1977): 159–176.

Anderson, James D. *The Education of Blacks in the South, 1860–1935*. Chapel Hill: University of North Carolina Press, 1988.

Antczak, Frederick J. *Thought and Character: The Rhetoric of Democratic Education*. Ames: Iowa State University Press, 1985.

Berger, Peter L., and Hansfried Kellner. *Sociology Reinterpreted: An Essay on Method and Vocation*. Garden City, NY: Anchor Press/Doubleday, 1981.

Berger, Peter L., and Thomas Luckmann. *The Social Construction of Reality*. Garden City, NY: Doubleday, 1966.

Berghahn, Marion. *Images of Africa in Black American Literature*. Totowa, NJ: Rowman and Littlefield, 1977.

Bergman, Peter M. *The Chronological History of the Negro in America*. New York: Harper and Row, 1969.

Bickley, R. Bruce Jr. *Joel Chandler Harris*. Boston: Twayne Publishers, 1978.

Billman, Carol. *The Secret of the Stratemeyer Syndicate: Nancy Drew, the Hardy Boys, and the Million Dollar Fiction Factory*. New York: The Ungar Publishing Co., 1986.

Bingham, Jane, and Grayce Scholt. *Fifteen Centuries of Children's Literature: An Annotated Chronology of British and American Works in Historical Context*. Westport, CT: Greenwood Press, 1980.

Blair, Walter. *Native American Humor (1800–1900)*. New York: American Book Co., 1937.

Blanck, Jacob. *Peter Parley to Penrod: A Bibliographical Description of the Best-Loved American Juvenile Books, 1827–1926*. New York: R. R. Bowker Co., 1938; rpt. 1956.

Bond, Horace Mann. *The Education of the Negro in the American Social Order*. New York: Octagon Books, 1966.

———. *Social and Economic Influences on Public Education of Negroes in Alabama, 1865–1930*. Washington, DC: The Associated Publishers, 1939.

Bontemps, Arna. "Ole Sis Goose," in *The American Negro Writer and His Roots*. New York: American Society of African Culture, 1960.

Broderick, Dorothy. *The Image of the Black in Children's Fiction*. New York: R. R. Bowker, 1973.

and the *New York Times,* 1968.

―――. *The Freedman's Book.* Boston: Ticknor and Fields, 1865.

Childress, Alice. "A Candle in a Gale Wind," in *Black Women Writers,* ed. Mari Evans. New York: Anchor Press/Doubleday, 1984, 111–116.

Christensen, A. M. H. *Afro-American Folk Lore: Told Round Cabin Fires on the Sea Islands of South Carolina.* Boston: J. G. Cupples Company, 1892; rpt. New York: Negro University Press, 1969.

Clemens, Samuel L. [Mark Twain]. *The Annotated Huckleberry Finn [Adventures of Huckleberry Finn].* Introduction, notes, and bibliography by Michael Patrick Hearn. New York: Clarkson N. Potter, 1981; orig. published, London: Chatto and Windus, 1884; New York: Charles L. Webster, 1885.

Comer, James P., and Alvin F. Poussaint. *Black Child Care.* New York: Pocket Books, 1976.

Cooley, John R. *Savages and Naturals: Black Portraits by White Writers in Modern American Literature.* Cranbury, NJ: University of Delaware Press, 1982.

Coser, Lewis A., Charles Kadushin, and Walter W. Powell. *Books: The Culture and Commerce of Publishing.* New York: Basic Books, 1982.

Council on Interracial Books for Children. *Human (and Anti-Human) Values in Children's Books.* New York: Box 1263, Ansonia Station, New York, NY 10023, 1976.

Courlander, Harold. *A Treasury of Afro-American Folklore.* New York: Crown Publishers, 1976.

Cowley, Malcolm. "Criticism: A Many-Windowed House," *The Saturday Review* 44 (August 12, 1961): 10–11.

Crandall, John R. "Patriotism and Humanitarian Reform in Children's Literature, 1825–1860," *American Quarterly* 21:1 (Spring 1969): 3–22.

Craven, Avery. *The Coming of the Civil War.* 2nd ed. Chicago: University of Chicago Press, 1957.

Deane, Paul C. "The Persistence of Uncle Tom: An Examination of the Image of the Negro in Children's Fiction Series," *Journal of Negro Education* 37:2 (Spring 1968): 140–145.

Dillon, Merton L. *The Abolitionists: The Growth of a Dissenting Minority.* De Kalb: Northern Illinois University Press, 1974.

Ditzion, Sidney. "Social Reform, Education, and the Library, 1850–1900," *Library Quarterly* 9:2 (April 1939): 156–184.

Dizer Jr., John T. *Tom Swift and Company: "Boys' Books" by Stratemeyer and Others.* Jefferson, NC: McFarland and Co., 1982.

Dodd Jr., Edward H. *The First Hundred Years: A History of the House of Dodd Mead, 1839–1939.* New York: Dodd, Mead and Co., 1939.

Donelson, Ken. "Nancy, Tom and Assorted Friends in the Stratemeyer Syndicate Then and Now," *Children's Literature* 7 (1978): 17–44.

Du Mont, Rosemary Ruhig. *Reform and Reaction: The Big City Public Library in American Life.* Westport, CT: Greenwood Press, 1977.

Dunlop, Donald. "Popular Culture and Methodology," *Journal of Popular Culture* 9 (Fall 1975): 23–31.

Ellison, Ralph. "Change the Joke and Slip the Yoke," *Partisan Review* 25:2 (Spring 1958): 215–222.

Elson, Ruth Miller. *Guardians of Tradition: American Schoolbooks of the Nineteenth Century.* Lincoln: University of Nebraska Press, 1964.

Erisman, Fred. "St. Nicholas," in *Children's Periodicals of the United States.* ed. R. Gordon Kelly. Westport, CT: Greenwood Press, 1984, 377–388.

Fisher, Margery. The *Bright Face of Danger.* London: Hodder and Stoughton, 1986.

Floan, Howard R. *The South in Northern Eyes, 1831–1861.* Austin: University of Texas Press, 1953.

Follen, Eliza Lee, ed. *The Works of Charles Follen, with a Memoir of His Life in Five Volumes.* Vol. 1. Boston: Hilliard, Gray, and Co., 1841.

"'For It Was Indeed He.'" *Fortune Magazine*, April 1934; rpt. *Only Connect: Readings on Children's Literature*, ed. Sheila Egoff, G. T. Stubbs, and L. F. Ashley. New York: Oxford University Press, 1969, 41–61.

Fortier, Alcee, ed. *Louisiana Folk-Tales in French Dialect and English Translation.* Boston: Published for the American Folk-Lore Society by Houghton, Mifflin and Co., 1895.

Fredrickson, George M. *The Black Image in the White Mind: The*

Debate on Afro-American Character and Destiny, 1817–1914.
New York: Harper Torchbooks, 1972.

———. *White Supremacy: A Comparative Study in American and South African History.* New York: Oxford University Press, 1981.

Garrison, Dee. *Apostles of Culture: The Public Librarian and American Society, 1876–1920.* New York: Free Press, 1979.

Gayle, Addison, Jr., ed. *The Black Aesthetic.* New York: Anchor/ Doubleday, 1972.

Geismar, Maxwell. *Mark Twain: An American Prophet.* Boston: Houghton Mifflin Co., 1970.

———, ed. *Mark Twain and the Three R's: Race, Religion, Revolution—and Related Matters.* Indianapolis: Bobbs-Merrill, 1973.

George, Carol V. R. "Widening the Circle: The Black Church and the Abolitionist Crusade, 1830–1860," in *Antislavery Reconsidered: New Perspectives on the Abolitionists,* ed. Lewis Perry and Michael Fellman. Baton Rouge: Louisiana State University Press, 1979, 75–95.

Gibson, Donald G. "Mark Twain's Jim in the Classroom," *English Journal* 57:2 (February 1968): 196–199, 202.

Gleason, Eliza Atkins. *The Southern Negro and the Public Library: A Study of the Government and Administration of Public Library Service to Negroes in the South.* Chicago: University of Chicago Press, 1941.

Gleason, Gene. "Whatever Happened to Oliver Optic?" *Wilson Library Bulletin* 49 (May 1975): 647–650.

Gossett, Thomas F. *Race: The History of an Idea in America.* Dallas: Southern Methodist University Press, 1963.

———. *Uncle Tom's Cabin and American Culture.* Dallas: Southern Methodist University Press, 1985.

Green, Alan W. C. "'Jim Crow,' 'Zip Coon': The Northern Origins of Negro Minstrelsy," *Massachusetts Review* 11 (Spring 1970): 385–397.

Green, Martin. *Seven Types of Adventure Tale.* University Park: Pennsylvania State University Press, 1991.

Green, Roger Lancelyn. "The Golden Age of Children's Books," in *Only Connect: Readings on Children's Literature,* ed. Sheila Egoff, G. T. Stubbs, and L. F. Ashley, 2nd ed. Toronto: Oxford University Press, 1980, 1–16.

Groff, Patrick. "Abolition in High School History Texts: The Latest Versions," *Negro Educational Review* 32:2 (April 1981): 27–37.

———. "The Freedman's Bureau in High School History Texts," *Journal of Negro Education* 51:4 (1982): 425–433.

Gross, Theodore L. *Thomas Nelson Page*. New York: Twayne Publishers, Inc., 1967.

Guy, Arnold. *Held Fast for England: G. A. Henty, Imperialist Boys' Writer*. London: Hamish Hamilton, 1980.

Hale-Benson, Janice E. *Black Children: Their Roots, Culture and Learning Styles*. Rev. ed. Baltimore: John Hopkins University Press, 1986.

Harlan, Louis R. *Separate and Unequal: Public School Campaigns and Racism in the Southern Seaboard States, 1901–1915*. Chapel Hill: University of North Carolina Press, 1958.

Harris, Julia Collier, ed. *Joel Chandler Harris, Editor and Essayist: Miscellaneous Literary, Political, and Social Writings*. Chapel Hill: University of North Carolina Press, 1931.

Harte, Bret. "The Rise of the 'Short Story'," *Cornhill*, n.s., 7:8. (July 1899), quoted in *Native American Humor (1800–1900)*, by Walter Blair. New York: American Book Co., 1937.

Heins, Ethel L. "Da Capo," *Horn Book Magazine* 53:5 (October 1977): 502.

Hemenway, Robert. "Introduction," in *Uncle Remus: His Songs and His Sayings* by Joel Chandler Harris. New York: Penguin Books, 1982.

Hewins, Caroline M. *Books for the Young*. New York: P. F. Leypoldt, 1881.

———. "Yearly Report on Boys' and Girls' Reading," *Library Journal* 7:7–8 (July-August 1882): 182–190.

Hilliard, Asa G., III, "Why We Must Pluralize the Curriculum," *Educational Leadership* 49:4 (December 1991/January 1992): 12–14.

Hoffman, Daniel. *Form and Fable in American Fiction*. New York: Oxford University Press, 1965.

Hofstadter, Richard. *Anti-Intellectualism in American Life*. New York: Vintage Books, 1963.

hooks, bell. *Ain't I a Woman: Black Women and Feminism*. Boston: South End Press, 1981.

Hubbell, Jay B. *The South in American Literature, 1607–1900.* Durham, NC: Duke University Press, 1954.

Hunt, Peter. "Narrative Theory and Children's Literature," *Children's Literature Association Quarterly* 9:4 (Winter 1984–85): 191–194.

Jackson, Jacqueline, and Philip Kendall. "What Makes a Bad Book Good: Elsie Dinsmore," *Children's Literature* 7 (1978): 45–67.

Johnson, Kenneth R. "The Early Library Movement in Alabama," *Journal of Library History* 6:2 (April 1971): 120–132.

Jones, Charles C. *Negro Myths from the Georgia Coast, Told in the Vernacular.* Boston: Houghton, Mifflin and Co., 1888; rpt. Columbia, SC: The State Co., 1925.

Jones, Dolores Blythe, comp. *An Annotated Catalog-Index to the Series, Nonseries Stories, and Magazine Publications of William Taylor Adams.* Westport, CT: Greenwood Press, 1985.

Jones, Rhett S. "Nigger and Knowledge: White Double-Consciousness in *Adventures of Huckleberry Finn*," *Mark Twain Journal* 22:2 (Fall 1984): 28–37.

Jordon, Alice M. *From Rollo to Tom Sawyer and Other Papers.* Boston: The Horn Book, Inc., 1948.

Kammen, Michael. *Spheres of Liberty: Changing Perceptions of Liberty in American Culture.* Madison: University of Wisconsin Press, 1986.

Karcher, Carolyn, L. "Lydia Maria Child and the *Juvenile Miscellany*," in *Research About Nineteenth-Century Children and Books*, ed. Selma K. Richardson. Urbana-Champaign: University of Illinois Graduate School of Library Science, 1980, 67–84.

Kelly, R. Gordon. *Mother Was a Lady: Self and Society in Selected American Children's Periodicals, 1865–1890.* Westport, CT: Greenwood Press, 1974.

Kimball, Gayle. "Harriet Elizabeth Beecher Stowe," in *American Women Writers*, ed. Lina Mainiero. New York: Frederick Ungar, 1982, 175–178.

Kincaid, Larry. "Two Steps Forward, One Step Back; Racial Attitudes During the Civil War and Reconstruction," in *The Great Fear: Race in the Mind of America*, ed. Gary B. Nash and Richard Weiss. New York: Holt, Rinehart and Winston, 1970, 45–70.

Klain, Zora. "Quaker Contributions to Education in North Carolina: A Thesis in Education." Ph. D. diss., University of Pennsylvania, 1924.

Kunitz, Stanley, and Howard Haycraft. *American Authors, 1600–1900*. New York: H. W. Wilson, 1938.

Kuznets, Lois R. "Some Issues Raised by the 'Issues Approach,'" *Children's Literature Association Quarterly* 5:3 (Fall 1980): 19–20.

Ladner, Joyce A., ed. *The Death of White Sociology*. New York: Random House, 1973.

Larrick, Nancy. "The All-White World of Children's Books," *The Saturday Review* 48 (September 11, 1965): 63–65.

Lasch, Christopher. "The Anti-Imperialists, the Philippines, and the Inequality of Man," *Journal of Southern History* 24:3 (August 1958): 319–331.

Logan, Mawuena Kossi. "Africa Through Victorian Eyes: George Alfred Henty and The Fiction of Empire." Ph.D. diss., University of Iowa, 1996.

Logan, Rayford, W. *The Betrayal of the Negro: From Rutherford B. Hayes to Woodrow Wilson*. New enlarged ed. New York: Collier Books, 1965.

Lott, Eric. *Love and Theft; Blackface Minstrelsy and the American Working Class*. New York and Oxford: Oxford University Press, 1993.

Loveland, Anne C. "Evangelism and Immediate Emancipation in American Antislavery Thought," *Journal of Southern History* 32:2 (May 1966): 172–188.

Lutz, Alma. *Crusade for Freedom: Women of the Antislavery Movement*. Boston: Beacon Press, 1968.

Lynn, Kenneth L. *Mark Twain and Southwestern Humor*. Westport, CT: Greenwood Press, 1972.

MacCann, Donnarae, and Gloria Woodard, eds. *The Black American in Books for Children: Readings in Racism*. 2nd ed. Metuchen, NJ: Scarecrow Press, 1985.

MacLeod, Anne Scott. *A Moral Tale: Children's Fiction and American Culture 1820–1860*. Hamden, CT: Archon Books, 1975.

McPherson, James M. *The Struggle for Equality: Abolitionists and the Negro in the Civil War and Reconstruction*. Princeton: Princeton University Press, 1964.

Marryat, Captain Frederick. *A Diary in America with Remarks on its Institutions,* vol. 2. London: Longmans, Orme, Brown, Green, and Longmans, 1939.

Marx, Leo. "Mr. Eliot, Mr. Trilling, and *Huckleberry Finn" American Scholar* 22:4 (Autumn 1953): 423–440.

Meltzer, Milton. *Tongue of Flame: The Life of Lydia Maria Child.* New York: Thomas Y. Crowell Co., 1965.

Meyer, Howard N. *The Amendment That Refused to Die.* Rev. ed., Boston: Beacon Press, 1978.

Miller, Susan E. "Louise-Clarke Pyrnelle," in *Dictionary of Literary Biography,* vol. 42. *American Writers for Children Before 1900,* ed. Glenn E. Estes. Detroit: Gale Research Co., 1985, 308–311.

Moe, Phyllis. "Eliza Lee Cabot Follen," in *American Women Writers,* ed. Lina Mainiero. New York: Frederick Ungar, 1980, 58–60.

Moses, Wilson Jeremiah. *Black Messiahs and Uncle Toms: Social and Literary Manipulations of a Religious Myth.* University Park: The Pennsylvania State University Press, 1982.

Mott, Frank Luther. *A History of American Magazines, 1865–1885.* Cambridge: Harvard University Press, 1938.

Murphy, Sharon. *In Other Voices: Black, Chicano, and American Indian Press.* Dayton, OH: Pflaum/Standard, 1974.

Murrell, Peter S. J. "The Imperial Idea in Children's Literature, 1840–1902." Ph.D. diss., University of Wales, 1975.

Nelson, John Herbert. *The Negro Character in American Literature.* Lawrence: University of Kansas, Humanities Studies 4:1 (1926); rpt. College Park, MD: McGrath Publishing Co., 1968; rpt. New York: AMS Press, 1970.

Newby, I. A. *Jim Crow's Defense: Anti-Negro Thought in America, 1900–1930.* Baton Rouge: Louisiana State University Press, 1965.

Nye, Russel. "The Popular Arts and the Popular Audience," in *The Popular Arts in America: A Reader,* ed. William M. Hammel. New York: Harcourt Brace Jovanovich, 1972, 7–14.

Osborne, William S. *Lydia Maria Child.* Boston: Twayne, 1980.

Owen, Mary Alicia, ed. *Voodoo Tales As Told Among the Negroes of the Southwest: Collected from Original Sources.* New York: G. P. Putnam's Sons, 1893.

Page, Thomas Nelson. *In Ole Virginia, or Marse Chan and Other Stories.* Introduction by Kimball King. Chapel Hill: University of North Carolina Press, 1969; orig. published, New York: Charles Scribner's Sons, 1887.

———. *The Negro: The Southern Problem.* New York: Charles Scribner's Sons, 1904.

———. *The Novels, Stories, Sketches, and Poems of Thomas Nelson Page.* The Plantation Edition, vol. 11. New York: Charles Scribner's Sons, 1906–1912.

———. *The Old South: Essays Social and Political.* New York: Charles Scribner's Sons, 1892.

Pease, William H., and Jane H. Pease. "Antislavery Ambivalence: Immediatism, Expediency, Race," *American Quarterly* 27:4 (Winter 1965): 682–695.

Pickering, Samuel, Jr. "A Boy's Own War," *New England Quarterly* 48 (September 1975): 362–377.

———. "The Function of Criticism in Children's Literature," *Children's Literature in Education* 13:1 (Spring 1982): 13–18.

Pieterse, Jan Nederveen. *White on Black: Images of Africa and Blacks in Western Popular Culture.* New Haven: Yale University Press, 1992.

Prather, H. Leon, Sr. *Resurgent Politics and Educational Progressivism in the New South: North Carolina, 1890–1913.* Cranbury, NJ: Fairleigh Dickinson University Press and Associated University Presses, 1979.

Quarles, Benjamin. *Black Abolitionists.* New York: Oxford University Press, 1969.

Quinlivan, Mary E. "Race Relations in the Ante-bellum Children's Literature of Jacob Abbott," *Journal of Popular Culture* 16:1 (Summer 1982): 27–36.

Remini, Robert V., ed. *The Age of Jackson.* Columbia: University of South Carolina Press, 1972.

Rhode, Robert D. *Setting in the American Short Story of Local Color.* The Hague, Netherlands: Mouton and Company, 1975.

Rice, Edwin Wilbur. *The Sunday-School Movement and the American Sunday School Union.* Philadelphia: American Sunday-School Union, 1917.

Richards, Leonard L. *"Gentlemen of Property and Standing": Anti-*

Abolition Mobs in Jacksonian America. New York: Oxford University Press, 1970.

Robinson, Roland, and John Gallagher, with Alice Denny. *Africa and the Victorians: The Climax of Imperialism in the Dark Continent.* New York: St. Martin's Press, 1961.

Rodney, Robert J., ed. *Mark Twain International: A Bibliography and Interpretation of His Worldwide Popularity.* Westport, CT: Greenwood Press, 1982.

Roller, Bert. "Early American Writers for Children (Eliza L. Follen-I)," *Elementary English Review* 8:9 (November 1931): 213–218.

————. "Early American Writers for Children (Eliza L. Follen-II)," *Elementary English Review* 8:10 (December 1931): 241–242, 250.

Roselle, Daniel. *Samuel Griswold Goodrich, Creator of Peter Parley.* Albany: State University of New York Press, 1968.

Rubin Jr., Louis D. "Uncle Remus and the Ubiquitous Rabbit," *Southern Review* n.s., 10 (October 1974): 784–804.

Saxton, Alexander. "Blackface Minstrelsy and Jacksonian Ideology," *American Quarterly* 27:1 (March 1975): 3–28.

Schirmer, Daniel B. *Republic or Empire: American Resistance to the Philippine War.* Cambridge: Schenkman Publishing Company, 1972.

Schlesinger, Elizabeth Bancroft. "Two Early Harvard Wives: Eliza Farrar and Eliza Follen," *New England Quarterly* 38:2 (June 1965): 147–167.

Scott, Donald M. "Abolition As a Sacred Vocation," in *Antislavery Reconsidered: New Perspectives on the Abolitionists,* ed. Lewis Perry and Michael Fellman. Baton Rouge: Louisiana State University Press, 1979, 51–74.

Scott, Rebecca J. "The Battle Over the Child: Child Apprenticeship and the Freedmen's Bureau in North Carolina," in *Growing Up in America: Children in Historical Perspective,* ed. N. Ray Hiner and Joseph M. Hawes. Urbana and Chicago: University of Illinois Press, 1985, 193–207.

Shenton, James P. "Imperialism and Racism," in *Essays in American Historiography: Papers Presented in Honor of Allan Nevins,* ed. Donald Sheehan and Harold C. Syrett. New York: Columbia University Press, 1960, 231–250.

Simpson, Claude M., ed. *The Local Colorists: American Short Stories, 1857–1900.* New York: Harper and Brothers, 1960.

Sinnette, Elinor Desverney. "The Brownies' Book: A Pioneer Publication for Children," *Freedomways* 5:1 (Winter 1965): 133–142.

Small, Stephen. *Racialized Barriers: The Black Experience in the United States and England in the 1980s.* London: Routledge, 1994.

Smedman, M. Sarah. "Martha Finley (Martha Farquharson)," in *Dictionary of Literary Biography,* vol. 42. *American Writers for Children Before 1900,* ed. Glenn E. Estes. Detroit: Gale Research Co., 1985, 177–185.

Soderbergh, Peter A. "The Dark Mirror: War Ethos in Juvenile Fiction, 1865–1919," *University of Dayton Review* 10:1 (Summer 1973): 13–24.

Soderlund, Jean R. *Quakers and Slavery: A Divided Spirit.* Princeton: Princeton University Press, 1985.

Stern, Philip Van Doren, ed. *The Annotated Uncle Tom's Cabin.* New York: Paul S. Ericksson, 1964.

Stone, Albert E., Jr. *The Innocent Eye: Childhood in Mark Twain's Imagination.* New Haven: Yale University Press, 1961.

Taylor, Mary-Agnes. "Edward Stratemeyer," in *Dictionary of Literary Biography,* vol. 42. *American Writers for Children Before 1900,* ed. Glenn E. Estes. Detroit: Gale Research Co., 1985, 351–362.

Thorp, Margaret Farrand. *Female Persuasion: Six Strong-Minded Women.* New Haven: Yale University Press, 1949.

Tiffin, Chris, and Alan Lawson, eds. *De-Scribing Empire: Postcolonialism and textuality.* London: Routledge, 1994.

Tourgee, Albion W. "The South As a Field for Fiction," *Forum* 6 (December 1888): 404–413.

Trowbridge, John Townsend. *My Own Story, with Recollections of Noted Persons.* Boston: Houghton, Mifflin and Co. 1903.

Turner, Darwin T. "Daddy Joel Harris and His Old-Time Darkies," *Southern Literary Journal* 1 (December 1968): 20–41; rpt. *Critical Essays on Joel Chandler Harris,* ed. R. Bruce Bickley Jr. Boston: G. K. Hall and Co., 1981.

Turner, Lorenzo Dow. *Anti-Slavery Sentiment in American Literature Prior to 1865.* Washington, DC: The Association for the Study of Negro Life and History, Inc., 1929.

Turow, Joseph. *Getting Books to Children: An Exploration of Publisher-Market Relations.* Chicago: American Library Association, 1978.

Tyack, David, and Elisabeth Hansot. *Managers of Virtue: Public School Leadership in America, 1820–1980.* New York: Basic Books, 1982.

Walker, Nancy. "Reformers and Young Maidens: Women and Virtue in *Huckleberry Finn,*" in *One Hundred Years of 'Huckleberry Finn': The Boy, His Book, and American Culture,* ed. Robert Sattelmeyer and J. Donald Crowley. Columbia: University of Missouri Press, 1985, 171–185.

Walter, Frank Keller. "A Poor but Respectable Relation—the Sunday School Library," *Library Quarterly* 12:3 (July 1942): 731–739.

Walworth, Arthur. *School Histories at War: A Study of the Treatment of Our Wars in the Secondary School History Books of the United States and in Those of Its Former Enemies.* Introduction by Arthur M. Schlesinger. Cambridge: Harvard University Press, 1938.

Warner, Oliver. *Captain Marryat: A Rediscovery.* London: Constable, 1953.

West, Cornel. "Minority Discourse and the Pitfalls of Canon Formation," *The Yale Journal of Criticism* 1:1 (Fall 1987): 193–201.

Willingham, Robert M., Jr. "Francis Robert Goulding," in *Southern Writers: A Biographical Dictionary,* ed. Robert Bain, Joseph M. Flora, and Louis D. Rubin Jr. Baton Rouge: Louisiana State University Press, 1979, 185–187.

Wise, Gene. *American Historical Explanation: A Strategy for Grounded Inquiry.* Minneapolis: University of Minnesota, 1980.

Wolfe, Bernard. "Uncle Remus and the Malevolent Rabbit: 'Takes a Limber-Toe Gemmum fer ter Jump Jim Crow,'" *Commentary* 8 (July 1949): 31–41; rpt. *Critical Essays on Joel Chandler Harris,* ed. R. Bruce Bickley Jr. Boston: G. K. Hall and Co., 1981.

Woodard, Fredrick, and Donnarae MacCann. "*Huckleberry Finn* and the Traditions of Blackface Minstrelsy" in *The Black American in Books for Children: Readings in Racism,* ed. Donnarae MacCann and Gloria Woodard. Metuchen, NJ: Scarecrow Press, 1985, 75–103.

————. "Minstrel Shackles and Nineteenth Century 'Liberality,'" in *Satire or Evasion? Black Perspectives on Huckleberry Finn*, ed. James S. Leonard, Thomas A Tenney, Thadious M. Davis. Durham: Duke University Press, 1992, 141–153.

Woodward, C. Vann. *Origins of the New South, 1877–1913*. Baton Rouge: Louisiana State University Press and The Littlefield Fund for Southern History of the University of Texas, 1951, 1971.

Wright Jr., Elizur. "Immediate Abolition," in *Slavery Attacked: The Abolitionist Crusade*, ed. John L. Thomas. Englewood Cliffs, NJ: Prentice-Hall, 1965, 11–17.

Wright, Richard. *12,000,000 Black Voices*. New York: Viking Press, 1941.

Index

Boldface indicates pages on which the primary discussion is presented for selected writers of children's literature or for their works.